A Critical Anthropology of
Childhood in Haiti

Also available from Bloomsbury

A History of Education for the Many, Curry Malott
The Making of Teachers in the Age of Migration, edited by Sabine Krause, Michelle Proyer and Gertraud Kremsner
Education, Individualization and Neoliberalism, Valerie Visanich
Capitalism, Pedagogy, and the Politics of Being, Noah De Lissovoy
International Schooling, Lucy Bailey
Teaching in Unequal Societies, John Russon, Siby K. George, P. G. Jung
Education in Radical Uncertainty, Stephen Carney and Ulla Ambrosius Madsen
A Cultural-Historical Approach Towards Pedagogical Transitions, Joanne Hardman
Anthropocene Childhoods, Emily Ashton

A Critical Anthropology of Childhood in Haiti

Emotion, Power, and White Saviors

Diane M. Hoffman

BLOOMSBURY ACADEMIC

LONDON • NEW YORK • OXFORD • NEW DELHI • SYDNEY

BLOOMSBURY ACADEMIC
Bloomsbury Publishing Plc, 50 Bedford Square, London, WC1B 3DP, UK
Bloomsbury Publishing Inc, 1359 Broadway, New York, NY 10018, USA
Bloomsbury Publishing Ireland, 29 Earlsfort Terrace, Dublin 2, D02 AY28, Ireland

BLOOMSBURY, BLOOMSBURY ACADEMIC and the Diana logo are trademarks of
Bloomsbury Publishing Plc

First published in Great Britain 2024
This paperback edition published in 2025

A catalogue record for this book is available from the British Library.

A catalog record for this book is available from the Library of Congress.

ISBN: HB: 978-1-3503-2133-5
PB: 978-1-3503-2137-3
ePDF: 978-1-3503-2134-2
eBook: 978-1-3503-2135-9

Typeset by Deanta Global Publishing Services, Chennai, India

For product safety related questions contact productsafety@bloomsbury.com.

To find out more about our authors and books visit www.bloomsbury.com and
sign up for our newsletters.

To all my teachers, near and far

Contents

Acknowledgments

This book would not have been possible without the endless kindness and forbearance of all the Haitian children, youth, and adults who have constantly watched over me and cared for me during my time in Haiti. They have taught me more than I can ever hope to acknowledge, and to them I am forever grateful.

Note on Translation

I have used the standardized McConnell-Laubach orthography for terms in Haitian Creole, and all translations are my own.

Introduction

Toward a Critical Anthropology of Childhood in Haiti

Why childhood? Why anthropology? What could possibly be interesting about an anthropological lens on childhood, especially one that focuses on Haiti? In this book, I offer a series of critical cultural reflections on a domain of Haitian contemporary life that has often been overlooked, treated superficially, or co-opted into agendas of rescue or intervention by well-meaning people both in and outside Haiti. While much scholarship exists on Haitian art, literature, history, economy, and politics, childhood in Haiti has been relatively overlooked, despite its significance as a terrain par excellence though which to explore the ways in which indigenous social and cultural belief systems, values, and practices intersect with international efforts to address children's needs and support structural change in how children live their lives. This is a landscape of both conflict and collusion, where the very nature of what counts as valuable knowledge is contested. As Northern, white, and often Christian ideologies of what is best for children become global standards undergirding change and reform in Haiti (as well as elsewhere in the world), it becomes imperative to ask a series of questions that center individual and communal cultural experience. What can be learned from looking more closely at the landscape of childhood in Haiti? How can those who hope to enact change be both more self-aware and self-critical of their efforts? What kinds of change—if any—are truly desirable and what direction should such change take? By exploring more deeply this contested terrain, I hope to show how Haiti offers a new imaginary, if we begin to see it as a place of possibility rather than as an object of well-meaning but ultimately distorting and self-defeating interventions.

A careful, anthropologically informed lens on childhood is central to this task. This is not only because much of what is being done in Haiti in the name of humanitarian and development work focuses on children, but because childhood, as Scheper-Hughes and Sargent (1998) remind us, is the primary domain in which public norms and private life merge. It is the domain in which children learn to be persons, and in which persons and society are co-constituted through cultural practices reflecting deeply held assumptions, values, and ideals. It is also an eminently political arena, indexing various forces and processes of globalization that shape both state and civil society (Stephens, 1995).

While educating and protecting childhood is often seen as key to developing the nation, in Haiti the systems that exist toward this end are often considered to be marginal or undeveloped at best. This reflects a tendency, long identified in the anthropology of childhood, in which nations of the Global South are identified as "immature," in need of discipline and guidance by the "adult North" (Valentin and Meinert, 2009) in order to develop the social norms, practices, and policies that reflect global standards for proper childhoods. In this optic, the models of what that childhood should look like are primarily shaped by Northern ideas of the "precious child" (Zelizer, 1994), childhood innocence and protection, adult-child play, parent-child attachment, and particular ideologies of schooling and its role in children's lives (among many other things). These ideas are deeply implicated in the universalizing agendas of child welfare, international social work, child rights, and educational practices that are currently being exported around the world through the work of thousands of nongovernmental and faith-based organizations. Yet the assumptions that underlie such universalizing ideas are often a mismatch with the cultural contexts and realities of children's lives. What is even more troubling—as anthropological studies in many parts of the world have shown—is that when put into practice, instead of improving children's lives, they can actually make things worse.

An anthropological lens on these issues is essential because it helps us to question what is assumed to be natural and/or universal, directing our gaze toward what is happening in a given context to shape children's lives in distinctive ways. This lens permits us to look behind appearances and refrain from making and imposing judgments and assumptions about what we *think* we know, in favor of asking the more fundamental question, "What is going on here?" A focus on the on-the-ground daily interactions and cultural practices that shape human experience allows a deeper level of cultural understanding and appreciation for the cultural logic that shapes what people value, do, and believe. This cultural logic is not, of course, some reified set of principles that can readily be articulated, even by cultural insiders. Rather, it must be inferred/interpreted, constructed from the ground up through experiences, observations, and interactions in the field. Coming to such anthropological understandings requires much time, sensitivity, and critical self-reflection.

And yet, to use the phrase "cultural logic" implies a number of assumptions that can and should be questioned. Such logic may not, in fact, be "logical" according to an outside observer's sense of what is rational in a given situation or setting. Rather, it may reflect radically different ways of thinking and living in the world that have their own distinctive order and sense. Any discourse about culture also risks essentializing persons, behaviors, or settings in ways that reduce the complexities of life into easily categorizable terms of analysis or action. Finally, as in all anthropological research, there is a question of power: Who has the power to describe, analyze, or speak? Whose voice is carried forward, against the potential objections of others? Still, as anthropologists of childhood, we ponder questions that sometimes have enormous repercussions for the ways people live their lives but that are often ignored: Who or what counts as a person, for example, and under what conditions? How do children become persons? How do people learn best? These ideas are as likely to be culturally variable as not, and they often offer an extraordinarily rich way to think about human cultural diversity. The anthropologist's task is to go deep into these fundamentals, even as they challenge us with ways of thinking and being that are profoundly different from our own.

Invisible Childhoods and Hyper-Visible Children

The anthropology of childhood has a long history rooted in comparative ethnographic research on patterns of infant care and childrearing, parental ethno-theories of development, child and youth cultures, and early learning, development, and socialization across diverse societies (Bluebond-Langner and Korbin, 2007; Montgomery, 2009; Stryker, 2015; Super and Harkness, 2002; Whiting, 1963; Whiting and Whiting, 1975). The field today is characterized by its emphasis on three basic ideas: the notion of childhood as a cultural and social construction, often as a way to contest the dominance or imposition of Western cultural and psychological assumptions about what is normal or natural in children's development; the value of children's voices and experiences in their own right (not seen through a developmental lens that positions children as immature beings on the path toward full adult status); and finally by the centrality of children as agents interacting with and shaping the world (often against representations of them as passive recipients of socialization or biological determinism). Across the growing body of research in the field, the ethnographic lens has insisted on focusing efforts toward understanding children's lived experiences in specific contexts as a way to open up dialogue on the many discourses and forms of intervention in children's lives that promote normative or desired ideals for childhood, but that often fail to account for the influences of cultural context and conditions of severe social constraint (Reynolds, Nieuwenhuys, and Hansen, 2006).

In the contemporary scholarship on Haiti, however, there has been little anthropological focus on childhood. The Haitian national institute for child welfare (Institut du Bien-être Social et de Recherches/Institute for Social Welfare and Research) itself laments the lack of anthropological attention to childhood in Haiti (IBESR, 2015: 4). While there are references to childhood in work on Haitian art and literature (e.g., Benson, 2002) and in the mid-twentieth century anthropological and sociological literature on rural family life and social organization, the only full-length ethnography of childhood experience in contemporary Haiti is Kovats-Bernat's (2006) ethnography of street children in Port-au-Prince. This work stands out as a major contribution to our understanding of how children navigate daily experiences of violence that are rooted in structural conditions that underlie social, economic, and political life in Haiti. While not wanting to minimize the violence and victimization that children do routinely experience, Kovats-Bernat also pushes back against the image of street children as passive victims: rather, he shows how they demonstrate great agency and creativity in the ways in which they establish networks of social support that enable them to survive in an environment that routinely presents enormous challenges to their health and welfare. Aside from Kovats-Bernat's study, though, with few exceptions, childhood in Haiti has simply not garnered the serious anthropological attention it deserves.[1]

At the same time, however, there is a vast literature on *children* in Haiti, consisting of medical, psychological, and social welfare studies and reports, alongside a great deal of sponsored research and advocacy material produced by nongovernmental and faith-based organizations. Indeed, across this literature, children are *hyper-visible*: children in poverty, children as slaves, trafficked children, abused children, orphaned children, stunted children, traumatized children, children out of school, street children—in sum, children with problems—who, naturally, require helping and saving interventions. Child*hood* has been neglected in favor of a focus on child*ren*, who are always seen through the lens of what they need, what they lack, how they are victimized, or how they suffer. This interventionist or needs-based approach is a function of both the extent to which nongovernmental and faith-based organizations (NGOs and FBOs) have dominated the landscape in Haiti, as well as a function of the ways Haiti itself is always constructed as the suffering Other, the place where there are always "mountains beyond mountains" ("*dèyè mòn gen mòn*"—a well-known

Haitian proverb), where suffering is a way of life, and thus inevitably a thing to be addressed and remediated, especially when it comes to children's lives.

The idea of childhood, in contrast to that of children, forces us to see the larger contours of experience, the patterns of cultural and social practice, and the terrains of value in which children lead their lives. One cannot understand individual children without understanding childhood; so too, understanding childhood gives us insight into the nature of individual children's experiences. This dynamic between the level of individual experience and that of the larger culture is important no matter where one works, but it is especially important in Haiti, for even if ignored or obscured, childhood is deeply significant in Haitian national life. This is not only because of the mere fact that it exists as a stage through which everyone must pass, or because of the youthful demographics of the Haitian population, but because it is connected to the particular visions of personhood that exist in Haiti, which are in turn connected to structural conditions as well as national ideals and aspirations. Childhood is the domain par excellence where possible futures both individual and national are envisioned and negotiated.

It is also a domain that has been greatly shaped by interventionist ideologies predicated on ideals of "best childhood" that are drawn not from Haitian sources, but from the Global North, and enacted in numerous ways through policies, practices, and research agendas of organizations, agencies, and government. Indeed, the reform of childhood along the lines of internationalized standards is part of the way in which the Haitian state itself represents its progress and legitimacy (Chin, 2003). Yet at the same time, the uncritical adoption of Northern ideals and standards can function as a force for neocolonialism, ensuring the fateful reproduction of inequitable social structures that could otherwise be uncovered and confronted. In the end, the erasure of childhood as a topic for critical inquiry in contemporary scholarship on Haiti both reflects and adds to the enduring impacts of colonial perspectives that have long contributed to what the Haitian anthropologist Gina Ulysse has identified as Haiti's "image problem" (2010).

In the chapters that follow I argue that we need to look more deeply at the cultural construction of childhood in Haiti, both to deepen and validate the experiences of children themselves as subjects in the world, and as a domain through which to explore and critique the circuits of knowledge and power that underlie contemporary processes of globalization, neoliberalism, and neocolonialism. On the one hand, a critical cultural account of Haitian childhood means taking into account the forces that structure and shape the contexts in which children live their lives: the representations of children and childhoods that circulate nationally and internationally; the politics and economies of affect that shape interactions among children and those who care for them; the dynamics of individual and communal agency, the systems of social organization and cultural meaning that shape childhood, and the broader social, political, and economic conditions that shape families and communities. On the other hand, a critical cultural account also means attending to children's narratives, voices, and performances as they unfold in ordinary space and time: the silences as well as the words, the languages of the body, the semiotics of everyday action—in sum, the totality of ways children communicate and interact with the world. All of these modalities "speak," yet their diversity and meanings are often co-opted into agendas determined by adults.

Constructing Childhood Vulnerability

Paying attention to the diversity of children's lived experiences in the Global South is exceedingly difficult when the lens used to frame inquiry is powerfully shaped by one major construct—childhood vulnerability. As a dominant lens shaping conceptualization of childhood throughout the Global South, including Haiti, childhood vulnerability is a condition of exacerbated or increased risk of negative impacts and outcomes in health, development, or welfare. While it is the situation or context that creates and sustains vulnerability, in common parlance it is children themselves who are or become vulnerable. Once individualized in this way, vulnerability as a contextual or situational condition becomes identified with vulnerability as a characteristic of the child: that is, as a collection of risk factors that supposedly inhere in individual children. This is a subtle but important distinction that has numerous ramifications, most notably in interventionist efforts that address the "needs" or deficiencies of the individual child instead of the larger situations or contexts in which children live their lives.

In recent years, a rich anthropological critique of the construct of child vulnerability has emerged, suggesting that it often positions children as passive victims in need of adult rescue, ignoring the ways children themselves make sense of their situations and act strategically to improve their chances, even under very difficult conditions (Cheney, 2010; Epstein, 2010). Oftentimes, ironically, categories of vulnerability such as "street child" or "orphan" that are assigned by aid organizations play into this process, as they offer new statuses attached to resources that can dramatically shift resource flows in communities.

Being an "orphan," for example, becomes a desirable and empowered status that is claimed because of its promise of aid, further interrupting or even damaging local social networks and excluding others who do not have the means to access the necessary identifications (Dahl, 2014; Cheney, 2017; Cheney and Ucembe, 2019).

Further, vulnerability is always locally defined and experienced; and its nuances are overlooked when criteria for vulnerability are established without close attention to the local cultural context or to the actual experiences of children (cf Bornstein, 2012). For example, while in some settings children living without biological parents may indeed face increased risk of negative outcomes, in other contexts (such as Haiti) this is a normative cultural practice and should not necessarily be seen as a risk factor for vulnerability, while other unrecognized aspects of the cultural context may be. These locally nuanced cultural understandings and practices tend to be frequently ignored or dismissed when held up against the dominant lens of Northern constructs of risk and vulnerability.

It is thus important to consider vulnerability as a set of discourses and practices that shape childhood in particular ways. While ostensibly grounded in scientific, evidence-based approaches, constructs such as vulnerability often encode a moral stance, in which cultural practices that differ from what is normalized in scientific discourses of child development become deviant.[2] Even in the United States, practices that are unobjectionable when performed by white mainstream mothers, for example, become suspect when performed by mothers who belong to minoritized groups or lower social class. A white mother, for example, can practice "free-range parenting" in which her children are given ample unsupervised opportunities; while a black mother who similarly leaves her child unsupervised may find social services at the door.[3] This effect of privilege also operates internationally, as communities within nations that have suffered from negative representation have increased likelihood of being seen as unhealthy and risky for children, by virtue of the ways their differences from norms established elsewhere leave them open to judgments of deviance. Risk and vulnerability are assigned—they are not innate.

The practical problem with vulnerability as a lens is that it tends to obscure aspects of context that are vital for adequate understanding and action. Vulnerability is produced both by structural conditions as well as agency of individuals and groups. It is shaped by both local interpretations of the situation of children as well as locally generated and relevant solutions to problems children may face. Yet, when the idea is applied by agents of development and assistance, these contextual factors tend to be overshadowed by external standards and norms. Much ethnographic research illustrates this process, as aid organizations and agents use their own definitions of children's problems as the basis for programs to assist them while ignoring the circumstances that children themselves deem as important and relevant (Nieuwenhuys, 2001). While some might object that the great emphasis in recent years on participatory research with children or on including children's voices in programs and policies designed to support them—which is now the norm across much of the humanitarian and development world—as some scholars have pointed out, these efforts in practice tend to use children's voices to legitimize adult agendas that are already in place (James, 2007). In such instances, children's voices are co-opted to serve dominant perspectives on what they need, or used as token evidence that children's perspectives have been "included." These efforts often do not go far enough to recognize the complexities and nuances of the local cultural and social settings in which children find themselves.

As I have argued elsewhere (Hoffman, 2012b), humanitarian representations that obscure the contexts of children's lives point to the need to consider how such representations facilitate cultural, moral, and political processes of neocolonialism. A number of scholars have shown how the vulnerable child represents a nexus for the working out of projects of aid that facilitate further positioning of some nations as subjects in need of guidance from the Global North (Bornstein, 2003; 2009; 2012; Dahl, 2009; Hart, 2006; Malkki, 1996; Nieuwenhuys, 2001; 2005; Scheper-Hughes and Sargent, 1998; Valentin and Meinert, 2009). Further, as a reflection of the global reach of neoliberal forms of transnational governmentality (Ferguson and Gupta, 2002), increasingly projects of aid and assistance to vulnerable children rely on partnerships between governments and Northern institutions, experts, and organizations that deliver their expertise in-country (see also Hoffman, 2021a). Rescuing vulnerable children is thus not only about individual and community benefit but also about the larger politics of childhood that informs the ideologies and practices of international aid and development.

NGOs, Orphans, and Restavèk: The Landscape of Child-Focused Intervention in Haiti

In Haiti, nongovernmental organizations (NGOs) have had a sustained and major presence in the country over the last thirty years. Often called "The

Republic of NGOs," the country is estimated to have thousands—perhaps the highest per capita concentration—of NGOs anywhere in the world (Dupuy, 2010; Kristoff and Panerelli, 2010). The sheer scale and complexity of this foreign aid, characterized by non-coordination of efforts, frequent exclusion of Haitian voices and institutions, and competition among aid organizations, has been critiqued as a major cause of the state of underdevelopment that has plagued the country (Dupuy, 2014; Fatton, 2014; Schuller, 2007; 2012). Billions of dollars of foreign aid over the past thirty years have not produced real advances in infrastructure, nor improvement in the living conditions of the vast majority of Haitians. In fact, basic indicators such as food security have not only not improved in recent years but have worsened (Buss, 2006; Fatton, 2014; Katz, 2013).[4]

FBOs and Christian churches and donors in the United States, Canada, and the United Kingdom have been major actors within this landscape of assistance, particularly in sectors targeting education and the needs of disadvantaged children and families.[5] According to some estimates, annually approximately 100 million dollars flow from Christian donors to Haitian orphanages alone (Lumos, 2017). Though quantification is unreliable, it is estimated that perhaps there are close to 300,000 children in situations of *restavèk* or domesticity (US Department of Labor, 2019); and approximately 760 orphanages housing 30,000 children (though this number is being reduced as a result of a national effort to regulate and close orphanages), and thousands of children living partly or wholly in the streets (with approximately 4,000 in Port-au-Prince alone). These numbers, though, and the categories for defining children's status, have a shifting and flexible character, as children may move from one status to another quite readily, or occupy two or more categories simultaneously, as I learned early on in my efforts to conduct research on *restavèk*.

Understanding the experiences of these children was in fact what first brought me to Haiti in 2007. I had read Jean-Robert Cadet's (1998) autobiography, in which he recounts a horrific childhood as a Haitian *restavèk* or "slave child." I was appalled at the level of emotional, psychological, and physical abuse he had to endure. Cadet's story seemed to imply that his experience was not exceptional, and I wanted to learn more so that I could potentially assist in projects to support such children. At the same time, though, as an academic, I had questions: was his story typical of the stories of other *restavèk*? What were the cultural conditions and the rationales for the practice? I needed to see the bigger picture beyond this one narrative, heart-rending as it was.

I began reading everything I could find, and my first observation was that there was, in fact, little scholarship, but a lot of media attention and organizational advocacy. The latter painted a similar picture to Cadet's—Haitian children sent away against their will by their poor parents who did not have the means to care for them (or sometimes trafficked through intermediaries) to families who promised to care for them and send them to school but who abused them horribly. As commonly reported, this abuse included frequent beating or other forms of physical punishment, denial of medical care and schooling, confinement to the home and complete separation from family and peers, sexual abuse (in the case of girls), emotional abuse, and all manner of unequal treatment such as being forced to sleep on a piece of cardboard on the floor, being fed scraps, and being denied decent clothing and participation on family outings. On top of this, the workload of the *restavèk* was enormous—he or she would take care of other children, do the washing, cooking, cleaning, animal care, and so on. The trope of "child slavery" was repeated constantly, often with a nod to the irony that the nation that had been the first to throw off the yoke of slavery in 1804 was now a global hotspot for modern-day child slavery.

This picture, I soon learned, was grossly generalized and exaggerated. In the few research studies that could be found, many facets of what was being reported in the media and advocacy sources seemed not to match up to findings generated by surveys, and, especially, by ethnographic and qualitative studies that painted a much more nuanced picture of a diversity of experiences among children in domesticity as well as the complicated conditions and circumstances that shaped children's experiences. Though research indicated that situations involving extreme abuse did exist, they did not appear to be the norm. Haitians themselves disagreed about the practice, and the more I talked to children themselves, the more complicated the picture became. Something was missing from the dominant narrative.

Not surprisingly, perhaps, my initial efforts to understand the phenomenon produced much resistance and criticism on all sides: from Haitian-Americans who assured me that since I am white, children would never tell me the truth; to Haitians in Haiti who were understandably defensive because they assumed that like most whites I was there to condemn the practice; to other Haitians who saw *restavèk* as a human rights abuse and worked (often alongside *blan* [whites, or foreigners]) in programs and organizations to eradicate the system. Then there were those who simply found it unremarkable one way or the other, and saw anti-*restavèk* activism as merely an effort to raise up the image of Haiti in international eyes or secure funds. And then there were faith-based organization staff in Haiti as well as academics in the United States who felt that doing research on the subject was ethically indefensible, for, as one put it,

"It's like doing research on someone who's about to be executed." Or, as another phrased it, "These kids don't need research, they need help!"[6]

A Perspective on Learning: The Eye/I of the Anthropologist

Anthropologists of childhood insist on seeing it principally as a social construction—a way of ordering human experience with great variability across time and place. Goals for development are shaped according to normative visions and ideals of personhood and are thus responsive to a whole range of social and structural conditions that need to be accounted for in the process of producing persons who are capable of surviving and thriving in a given environment. Learning is, of course, central to this process; both children and adults are engaged in learning about and through each other as well as through their interactions with their social and natural environments. For anthropologists, understanding the nature of such learning as a social and cultural process is a key part of understanding childhood itself.

At the same time, as learners ourselves, anthropologists recognize that whatever we come to perceive in the process of doing fieldwork is dependent on our relationships and interactions with persons and environments. Our work entwines us with those we encounter, and in these entanglements, ideally we come to recognize the contingency of our interpretations. In Haiti, as I discovered, my own learning was challenged in ways I had not experienced in all my many years of previous ethnographic work in other settings. With an undergraduate background in French language and literature, I had held teaching and research fellowships in France, Japan, and Korea, and had conducted my doctoral fieldwork among Iranians in the United States during and after the height of the Iranian revolution and hostage crisis of the late 1970s and early 1980s. Trained as an anthropologist of education at Stanford University, where I had the privilege of studying under major figures in the anthropology of education such as George Spindler and Shirley Brice Heath, my work had always taken me in directions that considered the ways culture was connected to the production of selfhood and identity as well as to inequalities in teaching and learning, often in ways undermining the very goals that had been intended. I had explored this tension within a number of domains, from studies of early childhood education to multicultural education, parenting, and efforts to support social-emotional learning in schools. Much of my fieldwork had required significant cultural immersion and language learning in settings quite distant from my white, middle-class upbringing on suburban Long Island, New York. Over the years I had gravitated toward the anthropology of childhood as a key arena for exploring the nature of informal learning as parents, teachers, and a variety of nonformal experiences shaped children's sense of self and identity. A growing interest in questions of globalization, knowledge, and power and its intersections with education and social marginality in children's experiences led me to Haiti for the first time in 2007.

Yet, subsequently, over the course of fifteen years of visits to the country for research, teaching, and volunteer work, I began to experience a shift in my own orientation to learning. I began to see that the assumptions of classical learning theory—the "acquisition theory of learning," as it has been described by Lave (1991)—were not really matching up with my own experience. This theory treats learning principally as a cognitive process, positing a flow of information from outside to inside, where it resides in individual minds; learners themselves are separate and isolated from others and from their environments. This cognitivized, individualized view of learning, I realized, was not what I was experiencing, nor was it an accurate way to describe the learning in which others around me seemed to be engaged.

Rather, something else was going on—what could best be described as a profound shift in perception, one in which the usual assumptions about the separateness of self and world, mind and environment, were challenged. The habitual logics of time and space, here and not-here, past and future, material and spiritual—all of those things that are often categorized and ordered according to a Cartesian rationalist and dualist logic—required a profound reworking if anything of value was to be learned. Furthermore, I realized that transformations in my own sense of being in Haiti were tied to what I could perceive about Haiti. This process involved an awakening of sorts: an unsettling transformation in ways of attending to things that demanded a different way to see and appreciate what was around me. The changes I experienced in my ways of perceiving led me to see others engaged in their own pathways of learning, becoming, and transformation. Over time, it seemed, these pathways converged: learning things about Haiti, learning about learning, and learning a reoriented self were all implicated in and entangled with each other.

In sum, I began to see learning as developing a capacity to respond to the worlds we encounter—in the anthropologist Tim Ingold's words, as a certain kind of "response-ability" (2018: 5). I could see it in my own responses to events and experiences in Haiti, as well as in the continuously responsive actions of children around me, as they observed, interacted, and created new ways of engaging with their surroundings. This was what one might call a deeper form of education, predicated on the development of an ability to connect with the world and to see patterns and relationships, as well as their possibilities, with new eyes/"I"s. As Ingold (2018: 5) writes, ". . . without such 'response ability,' as we might call it, education would be impossible."

Recognition of the nexus of self and other in the field has of course been a prominent trend in anthropological research for quite some time, though how this enmeshment shapes learning per se has been less of a concern. Beginning with the work of Hortense Powdermaker (1966) who famously emphasized the duality of intimacy and distance underlining all ethnographic engagements, it has undergone many different iterations in the field over time, including the reflexive movement in anthropology of the 1970s and 1980s (Crapanzano, 1985), the anthropology of self and subjectivity (Bhiel, Good, and Kleinman, 2007; Coffey, 1999), experiential anthropology (Goulet and Young, 1994), and auto-ethnography (Adams, Jones, and Ellis, 2015; Chang, 2008; Ellis, Adams, and Bochner, 2011; Reed-Danahay, 1997). While these genres are characterized by distinct intellectual traditions, and some emphasize the process of cultural interpretation, analysis, and theorization more than others, they all grapple with the ways the personal and cultural intersect in the field. My approach is perhaps closest to that of Linger (2005), who argues for bridging the gap between a focus on culture as public symbol and the personal, private realities of subjective cultural experience.

In the chapters that follow, the personal and cultural are kept in a kind of tension: neither erasing the "I" of personal observation, experience, and feeling, nor foregoing analysis, theorization, and critique, but attempting, as much as possible, to connect these domains as they emerged in the field. My approach is thus more of what might be called an experiential, auto-reflective cultural analysis than a classic ethnographic inquiry. Further, in the domain of "cultural experience" I include not only events that occurred and interactions that I witnessed or participated in while in Haiti, but also the ways whites involved in missionary and charitable work in Haiti spoke about their lives and activities on websites and social media platforms that they used to inform others about their work in Haiti. I do not separate discourse from action: rather, I see discourse as a form of action, because it shapes the possibilities and probabilities that certain forms of thought and action will occur, and because in itself it is an act in the world.[7] The chapters that follow reflect upon what I was learning as I observed and interacted with Haitian children and adults, but also with the many *blan* who worked and volunteered in Haiti, serving Haitian children and families. Indeed, a goal of focusing on childhood in Haiti could not avoid considering the roles of foreigners in the ways childhood in Haiti was represented and constructed as a field for intervention.

My status as an academic not affiliated with any church, charity, FBO, or NGO in Haiti affected this work in distinct ways. Though I am Catholic, my work in Haiti was never part of an official church-sponsored mission or partnership. Not being in Haiti with a church mission or with an NGO was a challenge in many ways. For one, it was difficult to make connections and to gain access to sites in which to conduct fieldwork; indeed, for most anthropologists working in Haiti, some sort of association with an NGO is almost necessary to gain access not only to field sites but also to other forms of support such as transportation and even housing. Second, as an academic without an organizational affiliation, I was difficult to place for both Haitians and whites. I sensed that for some of the whites involved in NGOs and FBOs, as an academic, I posed a threat to their work, since (as I was once politely reminded) they had worked hard to cultivate relationships with local people—relationships that my inquiries could potentially destabilize or undermine. While some readily agreed to interviews and assisted me with valuable contacts, others felt a need to protect their territories and interests—particularly when those intersected with specific ways of representing children that were connected to donor funding. Further, though I volunteered my time teaching courses at various Haitian universities and institutes, I was not a part of the Haitian social, intellectual, or academic elite. I had acquaintances among faculty at some Haitian institutions of higher education, but no close relationships or partnerships. Nor did I fit well within the academic community of Haitian studies specialists. I had come to an academic interest in Haiti much later in my academic career than is typical and thus was not well connected to Haitian studies scholars' networks. Finally, my work centered on childhood—a topic that almost no one in Haiti was working on. This isolated me further from the mainstream scholarship in the field of Haitian studies.

This relative isolation from the circles of belonging that frame both activism in and scholarship on Haiti has been a dual-edged sword. On the one hand, it has allowed me a kind of intellectual freedom and critical analytical distance. I have been able to focus on a topic that has been largely ignored, and I have thus had the freedom to go deep into my subject in new ways. But on the other hand, it is never a good thing to be working in isolation. One needs support, both personal and intellectual. I have struggled with my role as an academic, engaged in intellectual analysis and critique, and the tensions it has produced within my own identity as a Catholic with commitments to the active pursuit of social justice.

I would like to emphasize that the critical analyses that I offer in this book are not directed toward particular individuals, organizations, churches, or bodies of faith. They rather interrogate the larger universe of discourse that frames how faith-based actors understand their relationship to Haiti and its children. Certainly, as a Christian myself, I am not against Christians or Christianity, but against the ways culture, sentiment, knowledge, and power inform thinking and action among *some* who identify as Christian. This discourse goes beyond any one individual or group; it is an available stance, if you will, adopted by some, produced and circulated within networks of knowledge and affiliation, and it is also ever-changing. Thus the critiques I advance here must be seen as relative to both my own positioning and the always in which the world of development and intervention in Haiti is itself always moving and evolving.

Learning, Education, and Schooling: Developing a Critical Lens

The anthropology of learning in childhood stresses the diversity and multiplicity of children's learning across different settings, recognizing that especially for less advantaged children, institutionalized learning in schools often does not capture the multiple and diverse nature of learning experiences that children typically experience while living in their communities (Lancy, Bock, and Gaskins, 2010; Lima, 1998; McDermott and Pea, 2020). In many indigenous communities of the Americas, ethnographic research has shown that children are actively involved in a wide range of community activities, during which they learn through observation and participation (Silva, Correa-Chavez, and Rogoff, 2010; Rogoff, 2003). In such cultural contexts, keen observational skills are valued and cultivated, alongside what Gaskins and Paradise (2010: 99) call "open attention," in which the scope of attention is distributed across a wide field, rather than being focused narrowly and sequentially on specific elements of the environment. Learning through observation and participation is, however, difficult to study, since it is often an ". . . unmarked, fully integrated, and almost invisible part of everyday interactions" (Gaskins and Paradise, 2010: 87.)

Learning through observation and participation in daily life is sometimes considered informal learning, in contrast to the formal learning associated with schools. Contrary to representations of school learning as a superior form of learning due to its supposed transferability, Jean Lave's extensive work on socially situated learning, informed by understandings of cultural practice, has suggested that participation and observation in everyday activity is often a much more powerful source of learning than the intentional pedagogies associated with schooling (Lave, 1991: 14). Lave has also pointed out that it is a mistake to see formal and informal as two opposed forms of learning, for both are constituted in and through cultural practices that guide many domains of human activity. What does differ are cultural features of such settings and the impositions or constraints on what learners are expected to do, how they are expected to attend, and what they are expected to accomplish. In schools, an intentional pedagogy structured on verbally explicit didactic interactions, in which achievement is measured according to standards that are separate from the activities in which children are engaged (as in written tests of knowledge), presents a different sort of learning than might be encountered among children who are participating in community endeavors.

When it comes to the case of Haiti, however, education is rarely seen through the lens of ordinary activity and is instead equated primarily with *schooling*. The consequence of this narrow view of education is that whole domains of Haitian life and experience in which vital learning occurs are being erased from view. There are of course many reasons for the focus on schooling—most notably the ways in which it has long been considered as essential for national economic and civic development as well as social mobility. Schooling is expected by parents, teachers, and children alike to offer social and cultural capital that can enhance social status as well as future employment opportunities.

Yet, as the literature suggests, schooling in Haiti faces enormous challenges. Difficulties include a system that is one of the most highly privatized in the world, with an estimated 80 percent to 90 percent of schools operated by NGOs and FBOs (Edmonds, 2013), and thus out of reach financially for many. Schools suffer from a dearth of qualified teachers, a lack of basic materials, difficult access for students in rural areas, and a lack of funding for sustained reforms. There are large numbers of overage children and youth, many of whom have experienced interrupted school attendance due to economic and family constraints. Approximately 42 percent of primary school-age children are not enrolled in school and less than 50 percent of those who are enrolled manage to complete the full six years (USAID, 2021).

The language situation is a major challenge, for while Haitian Creole is the mother tongue, schooling prioritizes French, even though only 5 percent of the population actually has any true fluency in French. Because knowledge of

French is seen as the true mark of the educated person, even though Creole has been mandated in the early grades, teachers and parents often insist on teaching and learning in French. Unfortunately, it is estimated that only 20 percent of teachers have fluency in French, and thus the great majority are teaching in a language that they do not know (Guzmán et al., 2021). This situation is thought by some to contribute directly to a pedagogy that is widely characterized (and denigrated) as "rote," since teachers themselves do not know the language they are teaching and therefore must resort to copying and memorization (DeGraff, 2016; Jean-Pierre, 2016). In Haiti, language ideology and its associated practices are a direct legacy of colonial domination that persist to this day, supported and enforced via entrenched social class distinctions that impact a whole range of social processes and outcomes.

Even when students do manage to complete a high school degree (about only 16 percent are able to do so), even fewer (about 1 percent) are able to attain a university degree (USAID, 2021). High levels of unemployment mean there are few jobs available, leading to a situation where 85 percent of the 1 percent of young people who do manage to earn university degrees leave (or attempt to leave) the country in search of opportunities abroad. While schooling is highly desired for the social status it confers and for its promises of a better life, the reality is that it often fails to deliver on these promises. It simply has not served as a major motor for change and development in Haiti as it has in other places.

Certainly, one important priority for Haiti is a well-functioning system of public schooling, and there are some important efforts underway to address long-standing problems such as teacher training. New certification standards and training programs have been put in place, along with efforts to generate new models for instruction and curricula that prioritize inquiry-based pedagogy grounded in early learning in Haitian Creole (e.g., the MIT-Haiti Initiative [which promotes STEM learning in Creole], *Ansenye pou Ayiti* [a community-based approach to strengthening teacher preparation], and the *Lekòl Kominotè Matènwa* on the island of Lagonav, which promotes children's literacy in Creole alongside child-centered pedagogy and nonviolent discipline). These approaches have a valuable contribution to make toward the reform of schooling in Haiti. The Haitian Ministry of Education is involved in multiple efforts as well to introduce new curricula and to increase attainment in literacy, often working in collaboration with United States and other international agencies and organizations.

At the same time, reducing consideration of education to a discourse on schooling perpetuates the structures of colonial domination because it ignores the wealth of indigenous learning traditions and epistemologies that are rooted in the cultural practices of everyday life. Education is in fact an extraordinarily rich arena in Haiti, tied to culturally valued ways of knowing and engaging the world that are *generative.* I use this word to capture a sense of the deep value and power that is attached to becoming and growing as a person of character, spirituality, and humanity through connections to others and the natural-spiritual world. As I will show in the following chapters, it is present across multiple domains of activity and is a constant in children's experiences: from learning how to adapt to life in a household that may not be one's own, to development of talents and personal domains of expertise, to learning and teaching survival skills, to becoming highly competent observers, actors, and caretakers in social interactions with others. It is my belief that this wide and deep landscape of learning in Haiti, in which both adults and children can be teachers and learners, reflects the world view of Vodou, where teaching and learning are decentralized and depend on human connection to and communication with the natural and spiritual worlds (Michel, 1996).

Attention to indigenous Haitian cultural practices and ideologies of learning is, moreover, an important resource for thinking about reform of the educational system in Haiti. To accomplish this task, however, a more robust ethnographic literature on schooling as well as learning out of school is necessary. With a few notable exceptions (e.g., Botondo, Hensler, and Mazalon, 2019; Doucet, 2003; Jean-Pierre, 2016), schooling in Haiti has rarely been explored anthropologically, and in the work that has been done, the primary focus has been on the problems associated with the dominance of the French language. While language is a significant problem that intersects with other challenges in Haitian schooling as described earlier, there is a great need for more ethnographic work on the culture of classrooms and the sociocultural contexts of schooling beyond questions of language of instruction and sociolinguistics. The cultural and social routines of schools—especially those in a system shaped by colonial heritage—are alienating to all but the more privileged sectors of society, leaving children from lower-class backgrounds struggling to fit in and to achieve. Yet these children are not unfamiliar with learning—in fact, they have been learning all their lives, via observation and participation in a wide array of cultural activities. It is just that their particular ways of mediating such learning—their ways of observing, attending, embodying, and connecting—go unrecognized and unvalued in the formal settings of schools and classrooms. A better and deeper understanding of how learning proceeds in children's lives through ordinary engagements can be of immense value in re-thinking how institutional spaces of schools can be reformed in ways that better support them as learners.

Haiti and the Language of Deficiency

Just as childhood has been reduced to a discourse on children's needs and problems, and education has been reduced to discussions of schooling, Haiti itself has been reduced to a status of failed state and society. A profound discourse of deficiency has long shaped representations of Haitian life: failed families, failed schooling, failed economy, failed culture, failed nation. Haitian parenting and childrearing have been a particular target of criticism—captured best, perhaps, by the comments of the *New York Times* columnist David Brooks, who wrote, following the earthquake of 2010,

> Haiti, like most of the world's poorest nations, suffers from a complex web of progress-resistant cultural influences. There is the influence of the voodoo [*sic*] religion, which spreads the message that life is capricious and planning futile. There are high levels of social mistrust. Responsibility is often not internalized. Child-rearing practices often involve neglect in the early years and harsh retribution when kids hit 9 or 10.

Social media is replete with characterizations of Haitian parenting as authoritarian and violent (often by children of Haitian parents now grown up and living in the United States who have been exposed to mainstream upper-middle-class views on "good parenting"). Parenting classes are often part of FBO and NGO social assistance efforts in Haiti, most of them reflecting dominant notions of best practice in developmental psychology that stress talking to children instead of corporal discipline, social-emotional regulation, parent-child play, cognitive stimulation of the child, and so on; all of which are premised on the idea that Haitian parenting is not only deficient in meeting children's basic needs but plays a key role in the intergenerational transmission of violence and poverty (c.f. Roelen and Saha, 2021).

On the one hand, the characterization of Haitian education and childrearing as "violent" can be said to reflect an objective reality. Studies that quantify the extent of violence do show objectively higher levels of various forms of violence (e.g., Flynn-Obrien, 2016), where over two-thirds of respondents reported experiencing violence in families and in schools at the hands of parents, relatives, and, especially, teachers). What is missing, however, is an account that situates such violence within larger systems of meaning and value—that is to say, the cultural logic behind it, which also includes children's own sense-making of the phenomenon. Without accounting for such logic, the fact of violence becomes fodder for a discourse of deficit or deficiency, especially when it is seen alongside a wealth of other negative portrayals of education and childrearing that can be found nearly everywhere one looks, among Haitian commentators as often as among non-Haitians (e.g., Alcena, 2016; Merveille, 2002). This is not to confound the arguments over the moral justifiability or desirability of certain forms of childrearing over others.[8] It is, however, to place the discourse within a larger frame that helps us to see that certain representations of cultural practice are allied to forms of power and that the exercise of such power happens both at the level of representation as well as in the consequences or interventions that follow.

While there are undoubtedly many sources for this discourse of deficiency, representations of Haitian Vodou remain among the more important ones. From long-standing representations of Vodou as "devil-worship" (which it is decidedly not), to some strands of contemporary Evangelical Protestantism, both in and outside Haiti, the "problems of Haiti" have been explicitly blamed on the historical role and prominence of Vodou in Haitian life (Louis, 2019; McAlister, 2012). The earthquake of 2010 was seen as an especially telling moment, as many evangelical Christians in Haiti saw the quake as God's wrath being poured out on the nation for its continued spiritual perversion via Vodou. Though in recent years a certain revivalist reinterpretation of Vodou as a source of healing and strength, drawing on its historical role in the Haitian revolution, has shifted the balance somewhat, in the eyes of many Vodou remains deeply associated with images of backwardness, danger, and deprivation (c.f Boudreaux, 2015).

At the same time, alongside the discourse of deficiency, there is a powerful discourse of resiliency—one that has become especially prominent since the 2010 earthquake. It is fair to say that one is probably far more likely to encounter the trope of Haitian resiliency in the face of trauma and disaster than to encounter explicit depictions of Haitian deficiency. Much of the time, images of Haitian good cheer and resiliency bracket depictions of suffering and disaster—so much so that the resiliency narrative can be read as the flip side of the deficiency narrative. Neither is, in the end, productive, for just as the move from a focus on people's deficits to a focus on their strengths in education and child welfare research is touted as an advance in thinking (as it no doubt is on one level), it still does not deconstruct the basic dualism that has shaped thinking and practice. Deficits are still always already there, and strengths are always constructed in reference to them. Even more importantly, the discourse of strengths and resiliency is, like deficiency, still dependent on those who have the power and the legitimacy to make such determinations. Who decides what a strength or a deficit is? Who decides what reflects resiliency or has the power to produce narratives about resiliency?[9] The move from deficiency to resiliency still impoverishes our understanding because the overarching dualism allows both categories to retain their narrative—and prescriptive—force, reflecting the ways in which some have the power to decide what is good or bad about others. The categories and the power behind them have not shifted—only the valence has.

My goal is to offer a different perspective that does not in the end depend on the existing tropes of culture and childhood that have long shaped narratives on Haiti. I aim to accomplish this by questioning the very nature of ideas such as childhood and education and to show how developing a new way to think about these ideas is also highly dependent on the kinds of engagements and reflections that I, as a learner, experienced while in Haiti. There may well be an objective criterion or justification for saying that Haiti is plagued by deficiencies and that Haitians have shown great resiliency in facing many struggles, but when they become dominant narratives they do not permit more nuanced insight of the kind that is helpful to deconstructing the larger knowledge structures that shape global discourses on childhood and development.

Colonizing Through Deficiency: Ways of "Educating" Haiti

Academic narratives can be forms of rescue, too: and I recognize that I am engaged in this sort of project as well. It is not about restoring childhood to Haitian children, however, or restoring education to schooling; what I see rather is a re-orientation toward recognizing the critical role of learning to see, learning to perceive, and learning to know *differently*. In Haiti, this requires confronting the ongoing legacies of colonialism—especially as they shape the kinds of knowledge and discourse that are accepted and recognized as legitimate. These are often the sorts of ways of knowing valued by aid agencies, governments, funders, social welfare, and faith-based groups whose work depends on a common language of internationally agreed-upon standards of accountability and ways of defining the world through professionalized categories and constructs. While there may be efforts to render such ideas more culturally adapted or culturally sensitive, they are still used within a dominant rationalist epistemology that may be distant from the realities of local lives. The end result is that the categories and ideas that are "applied" to Haiti end up being irrelevant, at best, and destructive, at worst.

I once recall sitting in an academic conference listening to a Haitian American presenter—a very sincere, US-educated academic—describe a wonderful new program teaching children in Haiti to recycle materials. I could not bring myself to ask the question that was at the tip of my tongue, "Don't Haitians already recycle things?" Anyone who has ever spent any amount of time in Haiti would notice that people re-purpose everything, from empty plastic soda bottles for building materials to rum bottles for gasoline. Artisans recycle scrap metal to create works of art. Kids themselves recycle all the time—making inventive toys out of trash. Did they really need to be taught how to "recycle?"

My discomfort lay in the ways recycling for this presenter became a concept and category of social practice associated with Northern educated and environmentally aware sensibilities. For sure, in the context of Haiti, there is no explicit discourse on recycling, no broad social movement, no recycling *industry* to speak of, and one could argue that there is a great need for one. Yet the concept itself is not alien—it is a normal part of everyday cultural practice. Why not build on that understanding, I thought? Instead, recycling became a construct imported from elsewhere that failed to draw on the lived realities of the place. In this way it became an unintended marker of deficiency—something that Haitians needed to *learn to do*—especially if they wanted to emulate the more developed, civilized places beyond. Their deficiency was constructed through the colonizer's voice, in a way that the colonizer could remedy via "recycling education" for children.

While this is a small example, there is a whole educational industry in Haiti that is in fact built on colonizing ideas about Haitian deficiencies. This industry, sometimes labeled "capacity-building," purportedly teaches Haitians skills, world views, knowledge, and capacities they lack. There are seminars in critical thinking for Haitians who can't think critically; parenting lessons for Haitians who don't know how to raise children properly, and seminars in "financial freedom" for Haitians who don't have the skills to manage their money (wait— "financial freedom" in a country where the majority of the population earns less than $2 a day?) There are organizations dedicated to teaching Haitian women and girls to make re-usable ("sustainable") cloth menstrual pads—even though generations of women in Haiti have always used cloth, and young women today are more likely to prefer "Kotex" if they can get it. Missions groups come and teach women how to make craft jewelry—as if there weren't a wealth of local artisans who have more knowledge, more skill, and just more sheer artistry than they do. The list of educational interventions to create "capacity" is endless.[10]

So many of these lessons come from well-meaning change agents—whites and diaspora Haitians alike—convinced of Haitian needs and deficiencies. Yet these so-called needs are constructed, based on the colonizer's own values, ideals, and privileges. For Haitians, these projects are very hard to reject or resist, simply because they are allied to resources; and also because they represent an alliance, of sorts, with images and representations of a "better life" defined through Northern lenses. This is not problematic in itself, of course—except for the fact that few of these "lessons for a better life" flow in the opposite direction. While many Northern volunteers and aid workers emphasize the need to learn about Haitian culture or history (often in order to make their assistance more culturally relevant or effective), this learning does not include, for example, learning Haitian parenting beliefs and practices in order to change the way they do things back home. As Smith (2001) noted in her ethnography of rural community life, it is always the *blan* who are the experts, who come to teach Haitians about democracy, for example, even when Haitians had for centuries (and still have) a deeply democratic system of rural community organization (see also Dubuisson, 2020; Stephenson and Zanotti, 2021). Except for some *blan* committed to learning Haitian traditional arts and music or Vodou, few of the many thousands of Northern visitors to Haiti actually come to learn specific cultural practices *from* Haitians. Their purpose is, quite unapologetically, to change the ways Haitians do things. In this educational equation, Haiti is the zero-side, the infinite graveyard of lessons brought by Northern agents whose purpose is to improve Haiti by exporting their own ideals of educating toward the good life.

In the chapters that follow, I hope to change the direction of such lessons by reflecting deeply on what learning is all about in Haiti and how I myself experienced it. In fact there are many lessons that go in the opposite direction, from Haiti to her visitors, interlocutors, and change agents, but they remain unseen and unacknowledged. This is because they are often subsumed into the profound emotions that Haiti tends to generate in those who come with help agendas: how much love and gratitude they experienced from Haitians, or how much they fell in love with the children or the country, or how much they learned about themselves. Indeed, it is the self-focused lessons that are readily acknowledged—many along the lines of, "I learned what really matters in life"—a realization that is often tied to amazement that ". . . people who have so little can be so happy!" Indeed, foreign volunteers nearly always emphasize the ways their engagements with people in Haiti represent deep emotional ties—a wealth far richer than what they bring.

I once asked a Haitian man who had worked extensively with foreigners engaged in missionary and development work in Haiti what he thought explained why so many Northern whites who come to the country develop such a great love for it. He told me, "*Ayiti gen leman pou etranje yo*" (Haiti has [is] a magnet for foreigners). In the context of our discussion, my friend further expressed the sense that Haiti exerted a sort of spell (*maji*) over foreigners. At the time I thought it an interesting answer—for few if any of the whites I had talked to had explained their love for Haiti in such a manner. They had talked instead of a seed God had planted in their hearts: they felt a "burden" for Haiti. Others emphasized aspects of Haitian life and culture they loved, such as how Haiti was such a beautiful country or Haitians were such beautiful, welcoming people, or the deep relationships and friendships they had formed with local people. Few thought in terms of magnetism or spells.

This man had experienced what many from privileged backgrounds would call an "unstable" childhood. Sent at an early age to live with his grandmother (in Haiti grandmothers commonly raise the firstborn in the family), he was something of a troublemaker at school, so when he was nine he was sent back to his father so that the latter could straighten him out. Chafing under his father's control, he then escaped from home and lived on the streets for a while, before eventually getting himself back to school and managing to do well enough to join the ranks of the educated elite. Like many Haitians, however, a higher level of education had not erased his belief in spells or *maji*. *Maji* was a force to be reckoned with, a reality of living in Haiti—though one for the most part either ignored, avoided, or condemned by the vast majority of Christian *blan*. But for many Haitians, *maji* could cause trees to fall, people to die; it could cause love and heartbreak, illness, and healing. Without accepting it, whites couldn't really learn Haiti, no matter how deep their love.

Toward Personhood

The earlier discussion may suggest that I am idealizing Haiti, overlooking its very real problems with a message that Haiti does not need reform or development. That is not the case; there are many critically important things that require change—not the least of which are the highly problematic economic and political structures that continue to make daily life so challenging for so many.

A large and important critical literature on NGO involvement in Haiti and a robust scholarship on Haitian history, politics, and international affairs have contributed much to expanding knowledge of the larger context of international political economy that has led to so much that has gone wrong in Haiti over its long history.[11] Like many of these scholars, I am critical of the ways the United States and other nations have continuously undermined Haitian sovereignty through political and economic interference.

My argument supports these critiques but trends in a different direction, toward a consideration of the ways largely white, faith-based discourse and action in Haiti operate within the landscape of childhood to create new forms of white saviorism. The latter, I argue, operates on both epistemological and emotional levels, in which emotional commitments and discourses legitimize and obscure white epistemological privilege in the landscape of faith-based assistance. White emotional authority obviates the need for careful attention to and learning from the cultural context because it universalizes human subjectivities, disallowing the existence of alternative structures of feeling and belonging. In this way it supports a new form of neocolonialism in Haitian childhoods predicated on subjective identifications and privileges associated with *feeling*. The end result is largely a continuation of colonial domination through emotional and epistemological power that functions behind and often in spite of genuine efforts to advance social development.

The chapters that follow suggest opening up inquiry toward more intense scrutiny of how questions of emotion and knowledge are related to the discourse and activity of childhood assistance in Haiti. I argue that at stake are Haitian conceptualizations of personhood. Personhood is not a word one hears often in discussions of Haiti—or even within the broader scholarship on development, education, and childhood. Yet personhood, as anthropologists of education have long emphasized, is an underlying goal of all learning; and it is the sine qua non of human development. It is an essential construct that underlies culturally particular ways of learning and feeling; of social interaction, of cultural practice. It is as persons or, perhaps, as selves, that we come to know the world and the world also comes to form us and infuse itself within us. It is impossible to generate a vision for social development, or civilization even, without a vision that centers the construct of personhood.

And yet it is overlooked or rendered invisible or insignificant against internationalized Northern ideas about learning, childhood, and optimum human development. Haitians do not want to be Americans, Canadians, or French; they want to be Haitians—in a profoundly deep way that is not just about habits and attitudes, but about subjectivity: the fundamental ways the self relates to others, to the natural world, to God, and to knowledge itself. A different lens is required, one that starts by asking, what counts as knowledge and what knowledge is valuable? How can all of us with interest in and commitments to more equitable societies relearn to learn, in a sense, in a way that acknowledges local epistemologies and emotionally grounded subjectivities? Unless we do so, Haiti, so long approached as a place to be controlled, used, and owned—a status aptly reflected in the titles of some recent scholarship on Haiti—the question remains as to whether and how this domination can be reversed.[12]

In reducing education to schooling, childhood to children, and the country itself to a failed state and society, a pervasive reductionism has shaped conversations about Haiti. This reductionism reflects and contributes to the larger continuing colonial representation of poor places as being in need of saving by the more "developed" world. But it requires confrontation; it requires new avenues of inquiry that work instead to widen and broaden the terms of discourse. This is especially important in places that have been colonized and dominated for centuries not only through political and economic force but through epistemological and emotional power. In my view, part of that task is to open up discussions about how people come to know Haiti, how they come to believe and think in particular ways about Haiti, and how the divergences and diversities of knowing and being in Haiti have so often been made to conform to the passions and purposes of those who would "save" its children.

The Chapters

The chapters that follow offer critical cultural readings of childhood in Haiti as it intersects white faith-based action and discourse. Interweaving excerpts from my personal field journals, observation notes taken during my participation in a variety of research projects, commentary from interviews and organization websites and social media, and the larger scholarly literature, each chapter presents an interpretive effort to identify the ways formative and underlying ideas and assumptions take shape within white efforts to intervene and shape children's lives in Haiti. Rather than an ethnography in the classic sense, this book offers an ethnographically informed series of reflections and analyses that range across a number of issues and domains that have been important in the ways childhood has been constructed in Haiti.

There are, of course, many constraints and limitations to this project. Some of the chapters draw from research projects that I have conducted either alone or with the assistance of student teams (Haitian and American) in Haiti. Others represent analysis of trends in the wider domain of online discourse and social media. Having not had sustained opportunity to conduct participant observation research within organizations focused on child welfare in Haiti (often, I suspect, for reasons identified earlier), my views are those of an outsider and thus, of course, may not reflect the experiences of those who work inside these organizations (except as such are revealed through interviews, online comments, or organization websites and Facebook pages). However, as a white person having spent extended amounts of time in Haiti interacting with foreign volunteers as well as Haitian families and children in a variety of settings, I have had a diversity of experiences of Haitian life that have led me to reflect on many aspects of the larger contexts of childhood in Haiti. While these personal experiences are not data in the traditional sense, they have shaped the understandings and conclusions that I have drawn in this book. Finally, I cannot and do not claim that the interpretations I offer are the only possible ones; rather, they reflect *one* angle or lens that can, hopefully, expand critical thinking on issues of childhood and transform the terms of discourse and practice.

The first chapter, "Pouring Love In," sets the stage for the consideration of white saviorism as an ideology that shapes white faith-based actors' perceptions of and interventions in Haitian childhood. Situating white saviorism within the literature on FBOs in Haiti, postcolonial critiques of development, and the critical literature on humanitarian and development interventions in childhood globally, it discusses how white saviorism is grounded in a landscape of white-Haitian love. Both Christian faith and evidence-based child development psychology are used to portray Haitian children and youth as lacking love and deficient in life experiences that can then be filled with the emotional and material wealth of whites. Focusing on the dynamics of emotion in the project of white efforts to "save" Haitian children, I argue that emotion operates as a source of white representational power in Haitian childhood, wherein whites elevate their own subjectivity while erasing or obscuring the emotional lives and subjectivities of Haitians. Using examples from white actors' discourse on the deficiencies in Haitian culture and childhood, this chapter proposes that white emotion serves as an unrecognized yet powerful vector of neocolonial domination that is connected to the structural conditions of inequality that have long shaped outsider interventions in Haitian life.

In Chapter 2 ("Learning to See") I turn to consideration of my own learning in
Haiti and the ways in which it involved transformations in perception over years
of visits to the country. Many events I experienced were difficult to understand
using familiar rationalist logic based on separation between mind and material
environment and linear, temporal ordering of cause and effect. As a result, I
came to see learning as an experience of attunement or resonance between the
self and the field, where the field itself demands different modalities of perceiving
the world. Using examples from my field diaries I discuss how intuition and
spiritual sources of meaning became significant to my understanding. Linking
these experiences with questions of significance for understanding learning
and childhood in Haiti more broadly, the chapter discusses the weakness of
traditional ethnographic research methods in the Haitian context and sets the
stage for deeper consideration of Haitian epistemology and worldview and the
ways they shape knowledge, learning, and social relationships in Haiti.

In recent years relatively privileged white women from the Global North have
been very visible actors in the landscape of child welfare and education in Haiti.
Weaving selections from my field observations alongside narratives of Haiti's white
women volunteers, Chapter 3 ("These Are *My* Children") questions the meanings
of love and the ubiquity with which it presents itself within white-Haitian
relationships and narratives of child rescue. Critiquing the ways mainstream
theories of attachment have both misrepresented Haitian children's development
as emotionally deficient and obscured the more important dimensions of
belonging in Haitian life, I illustrate how white women create new identities for
themselves as Mamas, but in so doing reproduce colonialist relations of ownership
and power that have long shaped the landscape of foreign intervention in Haiti.

Chapter 4 ("Becoming Someone") focuses on the learning experiences of
marginalized children in Haiti—*restavèk* (child domestic servants) and street
children. While they are often excluded from schooling, marginalized children
nevertheless engage in what could be called self-education. As a parallel system
of cultural practice that counters and often resists the identity-undermining
nature of the formal, institutional system, self-education is a deeply egalitarian
process, achieved through cultivation of high levels of competency in ordinary
activities, acquisition of culturally valued qualities of personhood, and extremely
well-developed social relational skills. Beginning with a review of the research
literature and a discussion of the general contexts shaping childhood mobility
in Haiti, the chapter illustrates how notions of "stolen childhood" promoted
by FBOs hold Haitian childhood up against norms of Northern bourgeois
childhood and family, thus misrepresenting Haitian children's experiences.

Arguing instead that Haitian life is replete with opportunities for teaching and learning that are often unrecognized, the chapter suggests a different lens that honors and respects the cultural modalities of learning that are present, while recognizing at the same time the need for changing the larger structures that sustain poverty and social inequality.

In light of recent global debates over the dangers of institutionalized orphan care, a new model of family care premised on reuniting children in orphanages with their biological families has emerged among Haitian and US faith-based actors as the best alternative for ensuring vulnerable children's well-being. Chapter 5 ("Bringing Them Home") offers a critical cultural reading of narratives on family reunification in Haiti. It reveals a discourse about the weak and "broken" Haitian family that needs to be remade according to Northern, middle-class lines by bringing children home to their birth parents to recreate an idealized nuclear family where they can experience the stability and parental love they need in order to develop in emotionally healthy ways. These so-called "strengthened" Haitian families can then serve as the building blocks for a strengthened Haitian society. Casting traditional Haitian practices of extended, flexible households and informal child fosterage as risky because of their supposed "instability" and associations with the *restavèk* system, white discourse ignores Haitian values and traditions in which the movement of children is connected to family growth and opportunity across time and space. As a reflection of neoliberalist efforts to responsibilize parents for the care of their children, currently globalizing ideals of family reunification, when applied to the Haitian context, facilitate the nation's further positioning as a subject of transnational neoliberal governance.

In Chapter 6, "The Sensorium," I draw from recent work in the anthropology of learning to explore the important role of ecological consciousness, bodily and sensory experience in children's learning in Haiti. Video data from a research project on children's small group interactions in an afterschool literacy project, alongside the author's observations of children's household activities, formal classroom activities, and peer group interactions, reveal a powerful role for embodiment, wide attention, and distributed participation in children's learning, processes that in turn channel wider systems of meaning in Haitian society and culture, including Vodou and Christianity. Developing a notion of the sensorium as landscape of embodied, sensory human and nonhuman connections and relationships, I suggest an expanded view of childhood learning grounded in environmental and bodily experience imbued with moral significance. While children's learning within the sensorium often goes unrecognized and unvalued, it offers a rich resource for thinking more deeply about education, especially in postcolonial contexts where schools and society are shaped by social inequalities.

Much of the research and intervention on childhood in Haiti has been framed through the lens of trauma and resilience, particularly in the aftermath of the 2010 earthquake. In Chapter 7, "Beyond Trauma," drawing on sociocultural and political critiques of trauma as well as evidence from my fieldwork, I offer an alternative lens on children's experiences. I argue that the dominant framing of trauma is adult-centric and fails to embrace the ways in which vulnerable children develop and maintain valued cultural roles as care*givers*. Reversing the usual notion that it is adults who care for children, I suggest rather that children's caregiving is an important arena for enhancing connection and belonging that are key to developing and maintaining competent selfhood under conditions of extreme adversity. When seen in this way, trauma and resilience—the dominant tropes of the interventionist, Northern lens—begin to appear as an outsider discourse, barely capturing the important axes of value and meaning that animate children's ordinary experiences. Developing a critique of dominant approaches to mental health and psychosocial support in Haiti that stress emotional self-expression, the chapter illustrates how trauma/resilience and mental health narratives in general serve as another arena for whites to obscure Haitian subjectivities.

Chapter 8 ("Practicing Hope") offers a critical anthropological reflection on the dynamics of hope and aspiration among disadvantaged children and youth in Haiti. While schooling is widely considered important to hope, marginalized youth who lack schooling cultivate alternative sources of hope and personal agency through practices of movement that sustain agency, care, and social relationality in the face of structural disadvantage. Illustrating the contradictions that exist between youth's narratives on hope and the discourse of external development agents who construe Haitian children and youth as "lacking hope" (except, of course, when *they* can provide it through their programs of education and child rescue) the chapter reflects on the emerging literature on the anthropology of hope in development and illustrates the importance of understanding the larger social and cultural contexts of childhood for real change in policies and practices for youth and children.

The concluding chapter ("From Doing Good to Good Doing") returns to fundamental questions raised throughout the book on what an anthropological inquiry into childhood might contribute to social change and development. I summarize some of the implications of my analysis for reform of schooling and for practices surrounding child welfare. Contextualizing the case of Haiti more broadly, my argument considers anthropological ethics and the ways in which interventions can be problematic when they are based in ideals of "doing good." The chapter proposes an alternative lens on praxis that prioritizes instead a notion of "good doing." While "doing good" privileges the motivations, knowledge, and moral orientations of the doer (especially when that "good" is ontologically aligned with supposedly universal notions of the good life), good doing is defined contextually, according to local standards of what is valuable/ desirable, and with a narrowed, more practical and ideologically parsimonious lens (Tax, 1975). I envision a new model of praxis that prioritizes a more open agenda for dialogue between anthropologists and others engaged in social change efforts in which childhood retains its value as a space of learning, both for children and those who would shape their lives and worlds.

1. Note on research protections: except where the identity of an organization is important to the analysis, I have chosen not to identify particular organizations in this narrative, and have used pseudonyms or acronyms throughout. All quotes from online sources and social media have been anonymized to protect individual and organizational identity. All research projects upon which portions of this narrative are based were granted IRB approval from my institution.

2. Note on format: many chapters interweave excerpts from my field-notes and personal diaries within the narrative. In order to distinguish these sections from the rest of the text, I have placed them in italics.

1

Pouring Love In

Emotion, Power, and White Saviorism
in Haitian Childhood

Welcome Missionaries! Clean American Toilets Available
 —Sign spotted going south on *Route Nationale* 2, near Léogâne, 2012.

Haiti has one of the most privatized public sectors in the Americas, with about 80 percent of basic services provided by NGOs (Edmonds, 2010). Over the past thirty years, Christian faith-based organizations (FBOs) in particular have become key actors in the development and social assistance sector in the country (Carelock, 2012; Germain, 2011; Jean-Jacques, 2009; Steinke, 2020), serving as important channels for the flow of resources, knowledge, education, and "culture" (Hefferan, Adkins, and Occhipinti, 2009: 1).[1] Reflecting their growing importance as agents of neoliberal transnational governance globally, both large and small Christian organizations in Haiti have become key agents in developing civil society and partners in the Haitian government's efforts to deliver social services, especially in the child social welfare system (James, 2019; Hoffman, 2021a).

The proliferation of FBOs has been accompanied by an extraordinary expansion of participation in development and social assistance work among individual North American Christians, who engage in short and long-term missions, volunteer service trips, educational service learning, child sponsorship, organizational development, and other forms of engagement with poor communities in many parts of the world (Nagel, 2021). The emerging importance of this informal sector of development assistance reflects a shift toward a blended landscape in which a broad spectrum of faith-based actors work alongside secular actors to engage in a wide variety of projects focused on "doing good" (Ticktin, 2014; Wilkinson et al., 2022). James (2019: 220) observes that there is far less of a divide between FBOs and secular organizations than is commonly assumed, as private faith-based voluntary organizations have long served as channels for enactment of state governance and security. This is especially true in the current moment in the domains of child welfare and education in Haiti, as the Haitian government has sought to enact international standards of child welfare and care through the assistance of faith-based international organizations. While a large critical literature exists on NGOs in Haiti, less attention has been paid to faith-based efforts toward assistance and development (Jean-Jacques, 2009; Steinke, 2020). These represent an emerging frontier in which secular ideals of "doing good" intersect with morality and religion to animate a broad spectrum of activities oriented toward social and spiritual development and uplift.

The focus of this chapter is on the ways white Christian faith-based actors in Haiti narrate their work in the arenas of education and child and family welfare. According to Jean-Jacques (2009: 2), most FBOs in Haiti are not indigenous organizations but have been created by foreign missionaries, largely Protestant and North American, though they may be affiliated with and financially linked to international organizations. They reflect a continuum of faith positions and are extremely diverse in their orientations and their relationships to secular development approaches and ideologies. Some may explicitly emphasize spreading the Gospel, faith conversion, or Church-building. For others, faith informs their work but is not nearly as central to their activities. In some cases, faith-based actors position their work as a transformational alternative to mainstream secular development (Hefferan, 2009).[2]

I argue, however, despite the diversity of organizational forms and faith positions, that there is an overarching discourse among white Christian faith-based actors that reflects a shared worldview grounded in both Christian faith and the rationalist epistemologies and enlightenment value systems that have historically underlain practices of colonialism. This dispositional orientation reflects privilege (educational, financial, or class-based) as well as buy-in to particular kinds of scientific or evidence-based knowledge and perspectives that are assumed to have universal validity. In the context of childhood, this is knowledge produced by psychology and child development psychology—disciplines whose generalizations about human psychological functioning come largely from research conducted in WEIRD (White, Educated, Industrialized, Rich, and Democratic) societies.[3] This research is widely circulated globally through knowledge networks as well as faith-based and secular actors and organizations. For Christians engaged in development work, while there may be particular points of conflict between faith and evidence-based psychology, both reflect an underlying universalism that informs their work and supports convictions of its relevance to Haiti.

The faith and knowledge nexus is only part of the story behind white Christian approaches to intervention in Haitian childhood, however. There is another, deeper dimension to this work that is grounded in emotion. While often unrecognized in the critical literature on foreign intervention in Haiti, emotion represents a key domain for the exercise of white saviorism among those involved in addressing the needs of children and families. As I shall argue, emotion is a field for the construction of childhood need and for the power of whites to address that need.[4]

The White Gaze and White Saviorism

The white savior has a long history, stretching back to the notion of the "White man's burden" (Kipling, 1899), historically conceptualized as the civilizing missions of developed states of Europe through colonialism, bringing the fruits of Christianity and development to the undeveloped regions of the world. At its most basic level, white saviorism is a manifestation of structural and systemic racism, in which the primary interactional dynamic is that of server-beneficiary. It functions by holding a set of assumptions, ideals, values, and practices of white cultures and societies as the gold standard toward which people of color should strive. This is sometimes captured via the terminology of the "white gaze," which measures the political, socioeconomic, and cultural processes of Southern black, brown, and other people of color against a standard of Northern whiteness and finds them incomplete, wanting, inferior, or regressive (Pailey, 2020: 732).

A rich literature in the fields of postcolonial and post-development studies (Escobar, 1995; Feagin, 2013; Ferguson, 1994; Omni and Winant, 2015; Pailey, 2020; Said, 1979) has revealed how mainstream development discourse and practice have been shaped by the white gaze of Eurocentrism, with the result that the Global South is consistently represented as inferior and in need of external interventions. Viewing development as a discourse with deep historical roots, Escobar argues that it serves to reinforce the entanglement of knowledge and power, producing development as a technique of exercise of Western power over the rest of the world (1995). Despite these critiques of Eurocentrism and neocolonialism, however, the racial nature of the development encounter has not had nearly as much attention (Pailey, 2020; Kothari, 2006; White, 2002). As these scholars observe, most development interventions could be considered racial projects because they create and/or reproduce "structures of domination based on racial significations and identities" (Omi and Winant, 2015: 28). For Kothari (2006: 20), failure to recognize the privileges associated with race permits those who intervene in the lives of others in the name of development to avoid being held accountable for the inequalities that flow from white power and privilege. I argue that this is particularly true when the field of intervention is childhood. Because efforts to develop childhood draw from a globalized discourse of child development grounded in developmental psychology, the universalizing gaze of whiteness is less apparent, hidden behind the science of internationalized best practices and globalized ideals of child welfare and family life.[5]

In recent years, there has been much popular media criticism of the figure of the white savior. In a widely cited essay, Teju Cole (2012) wrote that white saviorism was all about whites "having a big emotional experience" in their work overseas, helping poor Africans and Asians have better lives. As the scholarly literature on volunteer tourism and global development has shown, for many who participate in both large and small development efforts, the change agent role is indeed deeply emotionally satisfying. It explains in part the ubiquity of the promises that "you can change lives" or "you can make a difference" that often accompany calls for volunteers or donations. A number of widely reported child "rescue" missions gone wrong have further encouraged popular consciousness of the dangers of white saviorism. The case of an American Christian woman in Uganda who tried to help sick children but ended up killing several after administering her own version of medical care (which led to the formation of the organization, "White Saviors No More" [www.whitesaviorsnomore .org]) is but one example of a popular cultural backlash against the figure of the white savior.[6] In Haiti, following the 2010 earthquake, there was intense media criticism of a white, Christian woman, Laura Silsby, who had attempted to round up "orphaned" children in the streets and take them to safety in the Dominican Republic without regard to the legalities of doing so.[7] These accounts exist alongside a scholarly literature that has pointed out the ways in which both secular and Christian development interventions addressing children's needs frequently exacerbate the problems they come to solve, increasing tensions over resources, and disrupting local systems of social solidarity (Bornstein, 2003; Cheney and Sinervo, 2019; Cheney and Smith-Rotabi, 2017).

Consciousness of the damage done in the name of help and development in many parts of the world has also become a focal point for debate and discussion specifically among Christians. As reflected in a number of publications such as *When Helping Hurts* (Corbett and Fikkert, 2012) and *Toxic Charity* (Lupton, 2011), a central question is how to engage responsibly in faith-based development in the face of compelling evidence that good intentions do not always lead to good outcomes. These authors argue that the transformational goals of development activity are conflicted, as the goals of spiritual and personal self-transformation exist in tension with the goals of changing other's lives for the better, raising questions as to who is the real beneficiary (Nagel, 2021: 111; see also Malkki, 2015).

Generally speaking, the dangers of white saviorism are well-recognized among faith-based actors, ideally to be countered by emphasizing partnerships between whites and local people, cultivating deep, long-term relationships, adopting an attitude of humility and respect for local knowledge and expertise, and seeing those being helped as "brothers" and "sisters" rather than objects of pity. Awareness of the dynamics of privilege and inequality in the donor/recipient relationship has been prominent in these efforts. However, in the case of Haiti, even though individuals and organizations engaged in local, faith-based grassroots development often hold visions of racial and social justice that emphasize empowerment and local cultural leadership, studies suggest that ideas about Haitian deficiencies in knowledge and skill still underlie these relationships. As Hefferan (2009) argues in her analysis of church twinning programs in Haiti, such programs explicitly frame their work as empowering Haitians to act on their own behalf by remedying shortcomings in knowledge, education, or skills at individual or community levels. She argues that in practice, despite their transformational goals and Haitian leadership, these programs reflect an alternative form *of* development, rather than an alternative *to* development. Demands for accountability, perceptions about Haitians needing to be "educated" in order to have the proper approaches to implementation, and the delicate politics of empowerment continue to act as mechanisms for the "larger worldview" (2009: 75) of American church partners to determine the course of change efforts (see also Schöneberg, 2017; Schuller, 2016).

In spite of this cautionary emphasis on aspects of culture and privilege in aid relationships, the felt sense of agency among Christian whites who feel called to go to Haiti to address children's needs remains powerful. This activity is enabled by the supposed universal relevance of professional child development knowledge as well as notions of "good childhood" as a protected space of innocence and love. The assumption is that if Haitians were educated enough and provided with enough resources, they too would see the value of this version of "enlightened childhood" and strive to emulate it. White saviorism is thus not just about rescuing suffering Haitians from their problems, but actively converting them to a white perspective on the world. Clearly this is most evident in the cases where spreading the Christian faith is the central goal, but this "conversion" takes the form more broadly in the sense of encouraging adoption of white Western/ Northern societal and cultural ideals and regimes of knowledge that are presumed to have universal relevance and to reflect universal notions of the good life.

At the same time, to assume that people in Haiti (or elsewhere) refuse such development or change (Christian or otherwise) would also be incorrect. There is much evidence that many populations desire the material and social changes that Northern development interventions bring, along with the promise of salvation through Christianity. So the issue is not really about the desirability of conversion or societal change, or the goods (or lack thereof) brought by foreigners, but about white consciousness of their privilege in this process and about the impacts (desired or not) of their activity on the freedom of others to define their own visions, values, and ideals—in sum, to lead the kind of lives they desire. When the actions of agents of development or humanitarian intervention undermine this freedom or obscure the processes of privilege and domination that portray other ways of living as fundamentally deficient, they merit critical scrutiny.

Emotions and Affect in Child-focused International Development and Humanitarianism

From work that emphasizes the emotional motivations that underlie the humanitarian "need to help" (Malkki, 2015) to the ways in which affect entwines with religious humanitarianism to create new modalities of being (James, 2019), emotions are a critical if as yet under-theorized dimension of contemporary regimes of international aid and assistance. Emotions serve as currency for development of belonging, solidarity, aid, and citizenship that often have global presence and resonance (Fassin, 2013; Hutchinson, 2014; Mitchell, 2016; Richey, 2018; Ticktin, 2014). Contemporary critical approaches to humanitarianism identify how moral sentiments motivate humanitarian responses and at the same time serve as avenues for processes of neoliberal governmentality (Fassin, 2013; James, 2019). Within this literature, emotion is not just interiorized sentiment, but an active force that creates social affinities and exerts power, aligning people and communities, supporting particular regimes of governance, and creating particular kinds of worlds (Ahmed, 2004; Lutz and Abu-Lughod, 1990).

Within the anthropology and sociology of childhood, attention to emotion has emerged as a key domain through which to critique projects of aid and assistance, as representations of childhood need among NGOs reflect the coupling of political economy and emotion (Bornstein and Redfield, 2011). Cheney and Sinervo (2019) argue that affect plays a key role in the commodification of childhood disadvantage in global humanitarianism, especially in the ways in which representations of "needy" or suffering children are used to generate sentiment among potential donors. They point out that the commodification process often misrecognizes or misrepresents children's real experiences and does harm to children themselves, while serving to reinforce "disadvantaged childhood" as a category of economic value.

This is a particularly prominent theme in the growing body of literature on child emotional labor (Boyd, 2020; Holst, 2019). Boyd shows how emotional labor on the part of child participants in Ugandan Christian Orphan Choirs generates affective bonds with audiences who are then led to provide material support. The main problem, however, is not with the existence of inequality and the fact that orphans perform emotion for reward, but that Ugandan recipients interpret this inequality in their relationship differently from donors. While the dependency it creates is problematic for donors, as is the persistence of inequality that is associated with the demand for emotional labor itself, for Ugandans the critique centers more on how Christian compassion undermines the agency of children, casting them as passive participants in the charitable relationship (Boyd, 2020: 523). Holst's (2019) work with street children working as tour guides in Delhi similarly illustrates the complicated dynamics of children's agency in the commodification of emotion narratives. Street children's narration of their lives and work is finely tuned to control the circulation of affect and capital and the compartmentalization of subject positions. He observes that the exchange of guides' emotions for tourists' capital is in the guides' interest, because it allows them to set boundaries for the emotional labor of performing their past suffering.[8]

Much of the critique around emotion in child-focused humanitarianism surrounds the ways in which compassionate activity tends to be self-serving, satisfying individual needs for love and intimacy, self-worth, or a personal sense of importance that are not fulfilled at home, (Bandyopadhyay, 2019; Bolotta, 2019; Conran, 2011; Guiney, 2018; Malkki, 2015; Mostafanezhad, 2013). Increasingly these emotional rewards are not just experienced by individuals but shared by families who travel together and experience emotional bonding as they minister to needy children in the black and brown South. In Haiti, for example, teams of mothers and daughters (or even grandmothers) have been actively involved in addressing vulnerable children's needs (see Chapter 3). Such activity is often deeply shaped by goals of parents to bring their children up with a sense of social justice and to support their urges to "do good." In other cases it is the young woman who has traveled to Haiti on a volunteer service program or church mission with "life altering" impact who then brings her mother or sisters into her organization. In the process children and their parents experience the powerful emotional rewards of helping—with the latter also often "capitalized"— that is, linked to the cultivation of emotional capital associated with the ideal global citizen, as Molz (2017) points out.

While individual emotional experiences and satisfactions, the ways emotion motivates and accomplishes social action, and the role of emotions in the political economy of childhood disadvantage are all important arenas for critique, I suggest that there is another domain in which to consider how emotion operates in projects of international aid and assistance. In the case of Haiti, and perhaps more globally, emotion works as a channel for the exercise of white privilege through its representational power. Framing their responses to Haiti as reflections of natural and inevitable human sentiment allows whites the privilege of feeling, permitting the white gaze and its assumptions about white ideals of the good life to remain the primary standard against which Haitian culture, childhood, and family life are evaluated and found deficient. I argue further that white emotion narratives are superimposed on life in Haiti, thereby maintaining white power and privilege to define Haitian experience in ways that naturalize Haitian deficiencies and the power of whites to address them. Cloaked in a surfeit of language emphasizing solidarity, mutual love, cultural respect, and caring, white saviorism evades detection because it hides behind white emotions, as whites see their work as an outpouring of Christian love that is in turn reciprocated by Haitians who love them back. In this neutralized de-racialized space of emotional exchange and solidarity across differences, the white savoir effectively goes undercover. White emotion, in sum, constitutes a key domain through which to explore the ways representational power and neocolonial saviorism continue to operate in Haitian childhood.

Pouring Love In: The Emotional Substrate of White Saviorism

Where would the Haitians be if we hadn't come in and built their schools and clinics? Who would do it? We poured concrete floors for a number of families who were living in dirt-floored huts, and they were so grateful. Now their kids don't have to sit in the dirt. (North American Missionary, 2007)

I've never known love like the love I know in Haiti. (North American Missionary, 2021)

Over the years, in my interactions with white Christians who live or who have volunteered or worked in Haiti, I have been struck by the ways in which their relationship with Haiti is described through a language of love. From ubiquitous avowals of how much they love Haiti and how much Haitians love them back, organization donors, supporters, and volunteers frame their connection to Haiti as grounded in a deep love for the country and people. For many, at the root of this discourse of love is the notion that God, the source of all love, is the source of the passion (sometimes glossed as "heart" or "burden") they feel for Haiti, as in "having a heart for Haiti" or "God has laid on my heart a burden for Haiti."[9] Those who worked with children and families in Haiti considered their work as a deeply emotional calling given by God: it was not about the individual's love so much as about divine love moving through individuals:

> I saw God move in the love they had for me, for each other. It was such a pure love. Nothing to be gained, they love you. They don't even speak my language and they love me.

> My trip to Haiti was an awesome experience that allowed me to get an inside look at the hearts of our students and how they show God's love to the children of Haiti. (RS Christian School, 2015)

> Love is one of our Village Values at [HF Project]. It influences every decision we make, and every avenue we use to fight for Haiti's vulnerable children and families. Follow along with our stories . . . as we explore what love looks like for us as we serve in Haiti! (HF Project, Facebook, 2.14.2022)

Within this larger discourse on love, one of the phrases often used is "pouring into," as in the following examples:

> Our work is about how we *pour into* the people of Haiti, physically and spiritually. (HH organization, Facebook, 8.7.21)

> Our organization is continuing to *pour into* the family, reminding them of God's love for them. (IM Project, 12.16.21)

> We are thankful for the opportunity to continue *to pour into* these young adults and help equip them for the future. (HF Project, 10.7.20)

> To create a lasting, holistic family transformation, children and their caregivers need to be intentionally *poured into*. (MHH organization, 2.7.22)

What a treat it was to *pour out love* to innocent children in the name of Jesus, and what a reward to see them smile. (TU, 2015)

Whites "pouring into" Haitian children and youth reflects a powerful image of Haitians as empty, waiting to be filled up by the missionary who, out of her spiritual and material wealth, pours love and other resources into them. Not only does it evoke an image of material lack, it conveys a notion of Haitian emotional and spiritual insufficiency, as Haitian children's own emotional lives and subjectivities are completely erased. Portrayed as spiritual and emotional blank slates or empty vessels, children appear to be waiting for whites to fill them with the love and affection they lack.

In terms of the racial dynamic, it is perhaps not by accident that the "pouring out" comes from white Christians who fill black Haitians with love. Images of Haiti as a dark, broken, and forsaken place are the background against which white love/light is fore-grounded. Numerous organizations describe their work as bringing light into the "darkness" of Haiti: for example, "HFP is a bright light in a dark place!" "We are bringing light to the broken people of Haiti!" "Our ministry at HCO is to equip and empower the future [leaders] of Haiti so that they can be the beacon in the darkness!" A first-person narrative on missions work in Haiti is entitled, *My Journey in the Darkness: Haiti Through My Eyes* (Najt, 2022). A significant part of the power of white love as it is used in this discourse comes from its racial self-innocence: the sense that pouring out God's love is simply working out God's plan to bring (white) light and love into Haitian darkness. The divine origins of this love, infused into acts of rescue and development, erases any racial consciousness. In sum, this love—and the interventions that flow from it—is racially blind and intrinsically (divinely) privileged.

"My heart hurts": Power and Emotion in White Representations of Haiti

Filling up the "empty" Haitian child or youth with love is one side of the privileged discourse of white emotional saviorism. But there is a larger arena in which emotion animates and motivates the interventions of whites in Haiti: through a more generalized discourse of *feeling*. Feelings are the protective coat of armor around white interventions in Haitian life. Their self-evident nature, their naturalness, and their incontrovertible truth prevent them from being detected as an exercise of privilege in which white emotion and its associated worldviews become the dominant frame through which Haiti is represented.

One important lens on white Christian discourse is to be found in social media such as Facebook. Long recognized as key to humanitarian and development work globally, social media are a dominant modality for individuals and organizations involved in development and humanitarian sectors to familiarize people with their missions and secure donations (Muralidharan, Rasmussen, and Patterson, 2011). After the earthquake of the summer of 2021 in the South of Haiti, for example, Facebook pages of both large and small organizations were full of posts about their relief efforts. However, instead of focusing discussion on impacts and outcomes for Haitians, for example, white North American commentators emphasized how the disaster and recovery work made them *feel*: "Seeing Haitians helping each other makes me so happy!" or "Poor Haiti . . . another disaster—this makes my heart hurt!" As I have noted elsewhere, there is a difference between saying something is terrible and saying "it hurts my heart": The latter shifts the focus onto the emotions and experience of the speaker.[10]

Organizational interventions and activities commonly evoke similar sorts of personal emotional responses among followers: for example "I feel inspired by this," or "I am encouraged" or "I am blessed to be a witness!" or "this warms my heart" or "I love to see this," or, alternatively, when a difficulty or challenging situation is described, "This just grieves my heart . . ." "My heart aches for our Haitian family!" "My heart is broken for Haiti! Lord, please send the light to this nation!" On Facebook, Christian volunteers who regularly traveled to Haiti who had not been able to visit due to security and unrest since 2019 often lamented how much they missed Haiti: "It's all so sad!" "*Our* Haiti [italics added] is not the same anymore! It's so sad." "Not being able to go to Haiti makes me so sad." "My heart is grieving . . ." "The stories of kidnappings, murders, and other atrocities from the gang-plagued neighborhoods of Port-au-Prince break our hearts! . . . Do talk to your friends about all the things you love about Haiti!" (HGN, Facebook, 8.15.22).

In 2022, while the country was being rocked with demonstrations against insecurity and the high cost of living, protestors burned a missionary plane used to transport volunteers to mission sites. In response, individuals lamented how this impacted their travel plans and prevented them from coming to help: for example, "This is heartbreaking! We were just planning our next trip! It is so sad—they don't seem to understand how much this hurts them when it keeps so many of us from helping" (Facebook, 3.29.22). Rather than acknowledge and discuss Haitian viewpoints, including the reasons for the protests (such as injustices related to gang-related insecurity preventing Haitians from traveling within their own country, while whites and wealthy Haitians could afford to take flights and bypass dangerous zones on the outskirts of Port-au-Prince), white volunteers expressed their emotions—how heartbroken they were that their travel plans were disrupted. The white emotional narrative ("We are so sad!") effectively erased Haitian viewpoints and experiences. That Haitian subjectivity is bracketed by white happiness or white dismay reveals the extent to which white emotions serve as a way to position Haiti within the dominant frame of white faith-based discourse.

It is possible that social media may exaggerate the importance of emotional responses because it is structured, for example, to encourage "liking/loving" or "disliking." However, the discourse of white feelings goes beyond social media: it can be found throughout first-person accounts of Americans who have spent time in Haiti. In Boudreaux's (2015) account of her experiences in Haiti, for example, nearly every chapter is full of references to the writer's emotional state—trepidation, fear, anger, joy; in fact the centerpiece of the narrative is about the emotional rollercoaster and eventual success of a young twenty-year-old confronting the "darkness and evil" of Haiti in an effort to rescue Haiti's *restavèk*. Haitian subjectivity is erased as Haitians either become allies in the effort against *restavèk* or enemies perpetuating the spiritual bondage of Voodoo (*sic*). The Gengels' (2013) account of their daughter's wish to open an orphanage in Haiti similarly renders events primarily through a language of their own emotional loss, struggle, and ultimate triumph. Haitians appear as supporters and facilitators of their daughter's (which becomes their own) dream, but their voices and experiences are muted in favor of a narrative that centers their own feelings and how those emotions motivated action. Petrie's (2020) account of his twenty-plus years in Haiti, though offering occasional insight into Haitian life and how Haitians experienced him, is primarily a narrative about his own emotional conditions and states as they reflected and shaped his involvement in the country. While authors' sharing of their own emotional experiences in such autobiographical accounts is certainly to be expected, when the story becomes almost exclusively about white emotions, Haitians appear as props for white feeling/action, existing only in roles supporting the figure of the white hero who wrestles with Haitian darkness.

White feeling shapes other representations as well. In an analysis of media soundscapes after the 2010 earthquake in Haiti, Elizabeth McAlister (2012) points out that the significance Haitian survivors attached to singing in response to the tragedy was largely muted; instead, it was replaced by an emphasis on

American emotions. In one telling example, she writes about a video created by American missionaries to celebrate an event where thousands of Haitians gathered to commemorate the one-month anniversary of the earthquake:

> The energetic singing of the enormous crowd was overdubbed with the slow, emotional strains of contemporary American "praise and worship" music . . . the video . . . muted Haitian voices singing Haitian songs, and like the telethon, presented American music and American voices in their place. Even as Haitians sang widely in response to disaster, these media rendered them unamplified and mute. (McAlister, 2012: 37)

As McAlister points out, the representational practices of white North American Christians rely on an "American way of knowing, divorced entirely from a Haitian perspective" (2012: 38). This way of knowing celebrates American emotions as it obscures or renders mute the emotions and experiences of Haitians, except as the latter exist in support of or solidarity with American feelings, as in "We love them and they love us back." The emotion discourse on Haiti conforms Haitians to the whitened subjectivity of those who *feel* for Haiti. It is a dominant and privileged lens in which Haitian emotional life is rendered insignificant, except in reflection of or response to white feelings.

Empowerment and the Discourse of Haitian Deficiency

One of the main ways in which nonprofits working in Haiti attempt to avoid the more egregious forms of white saviorism is through the adoption of discourses and practices of empowerment. Reflecting a global trend in international development discourse since at least the 1990s, empowerment ostensibly shifts the focus away from merely "doing for" to allowing beneficiaries to take action for themselves, promoting practices that counter dependency and ideally respect the agency of those being empowered to work for themselves and their own transformation. With their focus on listening to people and goal-setting, empowerment programs hope to avoid providing mere handouts and instead encourage self-sufficiency through jobs, education, and skills training. Empowering families to care for their children, for example, is a key element in the missions of many organizations in Haiti that seek to promote family care over orphanage care for vulnerable children (for further discussion see Chapter 5).

Yet, despite its progressive moral appeal, empowerment has not been without its critics. Kaussen (2012; 2016) discusses how the International Organization for

Migration (IOM) in post-earthquake Haiti attempted to enact new modalities of communication among Haitians that would empower them to help themselves. Along with other writers on Haiti, such as James (2010), she observes that these projects ultimately enact neoliberal values of the "ideal citizen" such as entrepreneurship, rational communication, therapeutic self-expression, and self-responsibilization that ". . . train citizens to internalize conducts and behaviors that conform to the goals of international interests" (Kaussen, 2016: 160). Similarly, Hammond (2020) observes how ethical artisanal and fashion production, while attempting to empower Haitian artisans by linking them with international markets, effectively reinforces neocolonial inequalities and undermines Haitian agency. Schuller (2016) and Schöneberg (2017) illustrate the ways ideals and discourses about equal partnership promoted by NGOs and INGOs often reinforce neocolonial relations, ultimately disempowering Haitian actors.

While it places an emphasis on self-help, the language of empowerment is predicated on deficit constructions of beneficiaries as lacking in knowledge, experience, education, and know-how—all of which need to be provided to Haitians in order to enable their empowerment. As Schöneberg (2017: 612) observes, partnerships between INGO actors and Haitians are based on assumptions that Haitians lack the knowledge to propose solutions that must be provided by foreigners. Similarly, as noted earlier, in her analysis of church twinning programs, Hefferan (2009) found that despite a discourse that strongly emphasized Haitians as "equal participants" in projects of social change, US church partners spoke of Haitians as not having the knowledge needed to be successful:

> In assuming that Haitians are people who "do not know," the "mutuality" that is supposed to characterize twinning is undermined. Instead—one group—not coincidentally, the one who controls the purse strings—imagines itself as having a "larger" worldview that permits it to take full account of the world and its operations while simultaneously framing the second group as somehow less fully aware, more partial in is knowledge and experiences. This potentially transforms Haitians into perceived "objects" of compassion rather than as . . . dynamic agents of social change. (Hefferan, 2009: 75)

Representations of Haitians as not understanding reality or lacking fundamental knowledge can be found across FBO social media. In this example, an organization describes how much their Haitian staff lack knowledge of basic medical conditions, while they themselves understand "the reality":

The reality of [the patient's] grave condition did not hit the staff, as education in and understanding of medical conditions is slim to none in common society. What they did not realize . . . was that S. has had a stroke which is no small illness that will pass after a day or two. It is not an ailment treated with a dose of antibiotics for 3 days then return to normal [*sic*]. It is not dehydration requiring an IV of serum overnight and then back to the [job] tomorrow. The comprehension of the reality was not possible for our loving [NGO] family. "His lips aren't straight" and "he doesn't want to move his left arm" and "he's too tired to talk much" . . . are descriptions that express the lack of comprehension of the gravity. (PCY, Facebook, 7.6.2022)

Assuming the superiority of Western biomedical knowledge, this comment ignores the rich perspectives on health and illness that do exist in Haiti and that reflect indigenous understandings of great importance. Instead of recognizing that Haitians may see the illness differently and through their own spiritual and knowledge systems, the writer, judging from her own biomedical perspective, simply assumes Haitians lack correct knowledge and are incapable of understanding "the reality."

Education, parenting, and childhood development represent particularly important domains for white construction of Haitian deficiencies. As can be seen in the following dialogue among US missionaries working with families and children, Haitians are said to lack knowledge of good parenting and child development:

I lived in Haiti many years and mostly worked with very low economic class or with families afflicted by severe illness. . . . These parents rarely interacted with their children the way we in the US think of good parenting.

In our experiences running a pediatric clinic parents are overall very loving . . . but they don't show affection to their kids and they almost never have played with them. Some have said playing is something kids do with each other, not something for parents to do with kids.

I agree, I do think as a general rule of thumb playing with children is not common. I think a lot of people can get the feeling parents are cold toward their children and some are, but I don't think they have had a lot of exposure to parent/child relationships outside of survival necessities.

This has been my experience as well. Much of what is taught in the US as child development is not what I observed as a cultural norm. A couple of times I got into a conversation about direct interaction, eye contact, purposeful observation and dialogue that we use with preschoolers even down to infants . . . and I was told that was not good because children need to see that adults are busy working and they will learn it at school.

(Haitian commentator) I am the founder of a school here in Haiti. In Haiti, only 10% of parents would be fine to play with their kids. From experience I know that parents believe if they play with their kids, their kids will not respect them. They think kids should play with kids, not adults. Parents don't even sit at a table with kids. . . . Most parents in Haiti think that teachers are the ones who are responsible to educate the kids while they are in school. It took me a few years to put my staff to understand that they have to read to the students. People in Haiti think that reading to kids is a waste of time.

This is a problem and stunts childhood development.

(Facebook , 3.14.18)

One organization whose mission centers on empowering a new generation of Haitian children and youth through their school emphasizes how much they are "different" from other Haitian schools. As represented in a YouTube video, the approach is modeled on US pre-k and early elementary education, with teachers sitting on the floor playing with children, plastic "activity centers," adults in constant supervision, and opportunities for pretend play (showing a boy in front of a plastic kitchen play station wiping a plastic cup):

This little guy has an opportunity to pretend at school! In addition, he will learn how to work with others. He will learn how to get what he needs in appropriate ways. He will practice problem solving. He will have the opportunity to do what he sees adults doing. He will practice skills that he will need as an adult, like cooking and cleaning. So much is learned when a child has the opportunity to PLAY! (AT, YouTube video, 3.6.2022)

I personally saw how some of these kids spent their days playing with sticks and rocks in the dusty streets before they came to school at AT. You can easily get involved in changing more lives! (AT, Facebook, 3.3.22)

Since when is playing with plastic toys so much better than sticks? In fact, children in Haiti commonly build their own toys in highly creative ways, using found objects. Since when do children in Haiti not have the "opportunity to do what they see adults doing" or "practice skills such as cooking and cleaning"? They have probably already been highly engaged in doing such work in their households for some time. The vast majority of Haitian children are having rich learning experiences as they go about their everyday lives at home and in their communities. Learning how to work with others is a profoundly important dimension of ordinary Haitian life, as children cook for their families, clean, run errands, and learn from both adults and peers around them all the time (cf. Lancy, 2010). Why would they need a plastic kitchen activity center to engage in pretend play when they can work and learn in a real kitchen?[11] A false image of deficiency in Haitian children's lives is created to sustain the image of the organization as fulfilling the supposed void in Haitian lives, all in the name of "empowerment." Further, children do not require adults to play with them in order to develop in healthy and culturally appropriate ways. Adults playing with and constantly supervising children and their activities is not the norm in Haiti; nor is it the norm in the majority of countries around the world, yet children develop perfectly adequately, as anthropologists have shown (Lancy, 2007).[12]

Another organization that describes its mission as empowering a new generation of Haitians speaks of how Haitians grow up lacking childhood experiences that enable them to learn to reason, think, plan, and use logic:

> Planning ahead is not something embedded in the Haitian culture. Imagine, in a world where you have no idea what tomorrow will bring, why would you plan for it? We are striving to help the [Haitian] staff learn to understand the importance of planning, budgeting, and being prepared for the future. . . . Planning ahead, being efficient, being prepared with an alternative idea if things don't go as planned. . . . Many of these aspects of human processing are not taught in a formal school setting, but learned from life experiences. When your life lacks experiences, it can also result in a lack of reasoning skills, logic, or efficiency. (PCY, 3.8.22)

> We have found that simple childhood games have never been experienced by most Haitian adults. They need to grow up quickly to help the family, combined with lack of child-development understanding and the value of play, results in adults who have had little chance to learn through play. . . . We aim to improve their cognitive skills and increase processing speed, develop logic and improve their critical thinking skills. . . . Seeing patterns, organizing an idea, applying knowledge, and problem solving are all aspects of the Haitian society that are lacking, and all can be learned through play. (PCY, 3.13.22)

In other posts, the organization describes its efforts to open their Haitian staff's "world view," to teach them that "there is a bigger world beyond their small cinder block home." While describing their mission as "empowering" Haitians, such empowerment is grounded on assumptions about Haitian life as fundamentally lacking in "experiences" that lead to cognitive deficiencies that whites are then positioned to remedy. Aside from its rather astounding level of condescension and ignorance, couched in a tone of concern and care, this discourse reveals the extent to which Haitian life is still being judged against a normative white and middle-class standard that is presumed to be the best. One wonders, really, who or what is being "empowered" when the lessons are so oriented toward white,

Northern, middle-class ideals of childhood that have little relevance to Haiti, and, further, paint Haitians themselves as so fundamentally incapable.

An equally important critique could be made that these educational and training approaches focus on individual behavioral change over and against broader movements for social and political change (see also Chaudry, 2019; Ferguson, 1994). Getting Haitian citizens to be "empowered communicators," for example, was expressly supported by the IOM in order to lessen potential for destructive or violent popular resistance (Kaussen, 2016). Approaches that emphasize individual-level solutions such as more training or skills development leave intact the larger political and economic contexts that create and sustain poverty and lack of access to education in the first place, and they potentially undermine the kinds of grassroots resistance efforts that would work for positive social change more broadly. As one Haitian teacher explained to me, white efforts toward sending children to school (through child sponsorship programs or giving a parent a job so that they can pay for the child to attend) really don't help in the long run because they don't produce the kind of systemic change that is needed—that is, higher quality schools (PG Interview, 1.17.22). Further, he added,

> "Once whites take responsibility for helping, while this enables the child to be sent to a school, once the child gets there the parents become negligent. It's like their responsibility is over. Then the child does what he or she wants, which often means working instead of attending the school. Why aren't there NGOs to support children working instead of going to school? Most of the kids would rather work and earn money." (PG, 1.17.22).

In largely proceeding to foster change at the individual level, empowerment relies on Western and Northern ideals of individuals as free, autonomous agents who can make improved choices leading to personal change when given coaching and material support. However, the underlying individualism that is enshrined in empowerment programs also conflicts in deep ways with the cultural and social values and meanings that shape Haitian social life. When local needs are so great, naturally some people will quite readily accept the help proffered by an outside organization. At the same time, flows of scarce resources shift the local social dynamic considerably, introducing new forms of inequality and resource competition and creating social tensions. Further, research on the so-called "paradox" of empowerment has shown that it often leaves beneficiaries with feelings of indignation and resentment, precisely because it ignores local social meanings and values and assumes that transfer of power happens in a social vacuum.[13] While some individuals may experience personal benefit through empowerment programs, these approaches refract both local needs and local responses in new directions, potentially limiting recipients' agency and undermining their social capital.

Finally, it is important to ask who controls the experience and representation of empowerment. As a construct, empowerment has an emotional valence for those who provide it: more than even material aid, empowerment discourse allows whites to feel that they can give dignity:

> [You can] help Haitian families rise from poverty to dignity. (BB website, 10.30.22)
>
> Throwing things and services at people doesn't move the needle of self-sufficiency. Giving people jobs, training, a sense of worth, dignity. . . . That is empowering. (MA Organization, Facebook, 1.4.22)
>
> Let today be the day you consider how you give, and how you can offer choices to Haitians and restore their dignity.
>
> Commentator: I am so encouraged by how you offer dignity and hope to Haitians!
>
> (HH Organization, Facebook, 3.14.22)

Dignity and self-worth are represented as qualities whites can provide to Haitians (while, of course, *feeling encouraged* in the process). However, "giving dignity" is very different from treating someone with dignity, or respecting their God-given dignity or self-worth as inalienable aspects of their very being, whether they are working or living in poverty or not. Rather, this discourse represents Haitians in poverty or without jobs as lacking dignity, which can then be provided by whites through their empowerment strategies. Fundamentally, this discourse once again reinforces white power to "fill the Haitian void" by representing even dignity as something whites can provide to Haitians.

Though ostensibly a way to work against the perceived evils of white saviorism, empowerment is still ultimately about the white power to position Haitians as beneficiaries who are now able to "help themselves" as a result of white labor on their behalf. White privilege effectively conceals the power of Northerners to define what is useful, hopeful, and good for Haitians. Haitian emotional responses and the meanings Haitians give to exchanges of resources, and even their very senses of self and self-dignity are absent, only emerging in response to white empowerment. There has been a shift in the nature of the gift, but not in the emotional privilege that underlies the provision, interpretation, and use of the giving itself.

There's a certain fetishization of suffering in the white savior mentality: both in the ways that it assumes the subjective experiences and meanings of suffering are the same everywhere (when they are not) and in the ways it exaggerates the reach of suffering. Both assumptions extend the white lens and experience to others, through an exercise of power, even when the move to compassion with the less fortunate appears genuine. This results both in making others' suffering more than it is, and also less, in that the subjectivity of the other is ignored.

I'm writing this as I sit in a cafe in Les Cayes, Haiti, on January 12, 2022, scrolling through Facebook pages of nonprofits full of messages stating that "they will never forget" the quake that 12 years ago devastated the country. They portray a whole country "suffering" and in need of prayers. They express the "deep heartache" associated with this day. "Please join us in praying for the people of Haiti today."

And all around me people are drinking, laughing, smoking, eating. A guy is flirting with a group of four women seated at the table next to mine. Nobody is "taking a moment of silence." Nobody is praying. It is 5pm, and the streets are full of people going about their business. The suffering of the Haitian people is inscribed by whites in ways that suit their own purposes. (1.12.22)

Whiteness as Intervention

As a white in Haiti, I am in many ways complicit with white saviorism. This is not because I have come with an impact agenda, but because I am perceived by Haitians as having one. Most recently, as I sat with a Haitian *"medsin fey"* ("leaf doctor" or herbalist healer), I described my interest in children's informal learning, specifically around ethno-botanical knowledge. We both agreed that such knowledge is not acquired in school and that it represents a valuable cultural heritage. But what began as a simple request to observe naturally occurring interactions among children in her family and community as children learned about plants and their uses, quickly morphed, to my surprise, into another question: "How many children do you need to participate in this project?" She said she could easily recruit them, and for a small participation fee, teach them how to make *remèd* (various "remedies" for different ailments). Perhaps I had come uncomfortably close to a domain of Haitian life that was protected because of its potential associations with Vodou (as whites in this area were known to be very strongly anti-Vodou). Or perhaps the idea of a white who simply wanted to do a lot of naturalistic observation of children was odd. Whatever the reason, my interest in simple observation and learning about children's activities was converted into an intervention project—an effort to teach children knowledge they did not have.[14]

The dominance of an image of "whites who intervene" is a product of a long history of Haitian interactions with outsiders with resources. As whites, it is a space available to us as we enter into relationships with Haiti and Haitians, and it shapes our own actions as well as the expectations Haitians have of us. It is connected to structural inequality, for without resources, I wouldn't be in Haiti—none of the whites I saw around me would be. That basic inequality permeates what we do, and we cannot escape the fact that even when we reject the idea of "saving" Haiti, our very presence is an intervention, of sorts. It is as much a fact of the history of unequal relations between Haiti and its interlocutors as it is an expression of personal intention, in which Haiti has always been a space for whites to pursue their dreams and desires to make things better.

White feelings have always been key to this process—yet almost always unacknowledged in their power to influence the narrative on assistance and their power to erase other subjectivities. Emotions are among the most readily universalized, and thus the most significant vectors of white imperialism: the sense that others feel as "we" do, that they value the same things "we" do, and want to live their lives as "we" do. Yet the habit of filtering Haiti through the lens of white emotions is one whites can work against. Recognizing the limits of white subjectivity is one way, perhaps, to avoid the insidiousness of white saviorism that reduces other subjectivities to an easily manipulated version of our own.

"Haitians love us!" In the white imagination, Haiti is full of love for whites. Anything we do for them is appreciated. And to think, what if we hadn't come? Where would they be if we hadn't built their schools? If we hadn't poured their concrete floors? We recognize the limits of our material gifts, but now, through empowerment, we can teach Haitians to take care of themselves and in so doing provide even greater gifts: hope, dignity, and self-esteem. Our hearts are encouraged, for we have poured into them, filling them with love, skills, knowledge, hope, dignity: all the things they lack in their dark, forsaken world.

For their part, Haitians had no illusions about saving or being saved, or love, for that matter. They certainly saw whites as sources of material aid, and even lovingly so, but they didn't need to project their own emotions onto whites, thinking they could fill whites up with their own emotional wealth. White saviors exert the privilege of naming the world through their own emotions, so deeply entwined with their own needs for love and power. Haitians, rather, did not confuse their own subjectivities with those of their visitors. They simply pointed out that they had clean American toilets available.

2

Learning to See

Tout sa w we se pa sa.

(Haitian proverb: "All that you see, is not that.")

One year, during the annual carnival, I went with a friend Lauren and her Haitian translator Paul to the local airport to meet someone who was arriving.[1] As we were waiting, I noticed the carnival-themed T-shirts worn by the airport staff, thinking to myself that they were nice and that I'd like to have one, but I didn't mention it to anyone. A little while later, as we left the airport, Paul handed me a bag. I opened it to find one of the T-shirts. Lauren told me Paul had to negotiate very hard for it as they only give them to airport personnel. On another field visit, I had forgotten to bring a hair clip, had been sorely desiring one. On the last day of a seminar I had been teaching, students brought me a gift—a hair clip. On another evening, I had been reflecting on the role of intuition in Haitian life. The next morning, I walked into the hotel dining room and passed a bookshelf with a single book displayed whose title was "Intuition." Once, while standing at a long dinner table wondering where to sit, I felt a very distinct crawling sensation on my back. I turned in alarm to look over my shoulder and saw a metalwork snake hanging on the wall. I cannot count the number of times a distinctive thought would enter my mind, and then hours later what I had "seen" would actually happen.

Over the years these sorts of events have occurred with great and rather astonishing regularity during my stays in Haiti. It is difficult to know whether it is having a thought or desire that causes something to happen, or whether what is going on in my mind reflects an intuitive knowledge of a reality that is going to happen. Either way, there seemed to be a kind of synergy between my thoughts, perceptions, and desires and the world of events and things.[2]

The longer I stayed in Haiti, the more I began to recognize that I was acquiring a different way to attend to the world around me. I often knew this viscerally, as I could feel the chills and tingles of what felt like flows of electric energy fill my body whenever there was some alignment between my perception and the external world. At these moments it was as if my very body resonated with energy flowing from a different, hidden, and what I subjectively experienced as a more spiritual domain. I came to realize that all of these experiences were teaching a similar lesson: that learning in Haiti was all about opening one's mind and heart to a different kind of perception, in which the usual distinctions between material and spiritual, between present, past and future, between the body and the environment, between the mind and the supposed "world outside" were suspended. Thoughts brought actions into being and vice versa. Material things spoke both to the conditions of this life and to a larger realm of being beyond the here and now.

The follow-on lesson of immediate relevance was that I needed to stop assuming that all things could be understood through the categorical, rational, linear thinking that I had acquired as a white, middle-class North American. As Tim Ingold has written,

> People do not "make sense" of things by superimposing ready-made sensory meanings "on top" of lived experience, so as to give symbolic shape to the otherwise formless material of raw sensation. They do so, rather, by weaving together, in narrative, strands of experience born of practical, perceptual activity. It is out of this interweaving that meanings emerge. (Ingold, 2000: 286)[3]

Understanding more deeply how we come to know what we do takes us to the heart of the cultures in which we work, and at the same time toward another level of both self-understanding and engagement with learning. This learning is not just about facts, or attitudes and values, or cultural practices, or patterns of cultural and social life. Though these are undoubtedly important to any ethnographic project (as are other modes of data collection such as survey research and quantitative data analysis) there is another level of learning that goes even deeper into our very being in the world, how we perceive things, how we "know" what we know, how our minds and bodies work in tandem with our environments. It is these experiences that enable us to move toward greater consciousness of how much there is to learn from others, and at the same time to be constantly aware of the need to challenge our own assumptions.

I once participated in a research project designed and led by an organization that involved Haitian and American researchers based in both Haiti and the United States. The goal was to gather information on violence in Haitian children and youth's lives, with a particular focus on the experiences of child domestic servants, or *restavèk*. As the work progressed, it seemed to me that while the design and delivery of the project met high standards for scholarship, there was something that was not quite right about it. I wrote in my field-notes:

> *I have been thinking about the survey questions and interview protocols. It seems to me that the questions about violence—indeed the entire underlying conceptual structure of the inquiry—comes from a place quite distant from the ordinary reality of the people whose perceptions it is supposed to tap into. It is, in fact, not truly grounded in that sense. One of the questions, which looks on the surface to be really open, asks, "What does* restavek *mean to you?" This question supposes, first, that people have a meaning that is already present and available to be expressed; second, that it is possible to answer such a question outside of a particular context—that is, that there is some generalizable field of meaning attached to the term that can be abstracted from context; and third, that the term itself is actually salient in the respondent's experience. None of these assumptions may be true. In that sense, the question imposes an epistemological frame without intending to. That is to say, it frames the respondent's perceptions in ways that conform to the assumptions of the researchers.* (2012)

Further, there were complications and nuances in the meaning of "violence" that the interviews and survey were not capturing. While both Haitian and American scholars were working with a mainstream social psychological typology of violence that identifies categories of physical, emotional, sexual, and psychological violence, the categories themselves were hardly adequate to capture the nuances of different experiences and meanings of violence as they were experienced in the ordinary lives of children in the context of their relationships. The idea of violence as it was framed in the study was individualist in a deep way: it assumed individual choice and control as key values framing bodily experience. The discourse of choice and control ignored the ways the body is understood and experienced in Haiti as a modality of connection to the environment and to others—something larger than the individual self (see Chapter 6), as well as the ways violence itself is a phenomenon with multiple meanings that vary across cultures. Instead, the ways violence was framed seemed to reflect a set of privileged norms commonly shared in the professional discourse among North Americans, but far from universal in their cultural salience.

While ethnographic research tends to be especially valuable in revealing local contours of cultural meaning and practice that may not be accessible by other more experience-distant inquiry methods, it is important to recognize its epistemological limitations. As a large body of scholarship on indigenous ways of knowing and learning has illustrated, how people know things, the standards they use to judge knowledge, and the value they attach to different ways of knowing can vary dramatically. How (and whether) one communicates what one knows, too, is shaped by culture. The standard interview, for example, is an unfamiliar speech genre in many communities (see Coe, 2001). In my own work, no matter how sensitive and culturally attuned I tried to be, attempts to conduct interviews with both children and adults often foundered on a formality that worked against (in my mind) any genuine and authentic sharing of individual experience or feeling. Even in focus groups, as one experienced Haitian academic who worked with parents told me, it is very difficult to get people to talk about their individual feelings and experience; they were more likely to talk about others they had known or heard about rather than themselves. Similarly, I found that efforts to question children to get them to "tell their stories" often produced standardized responses with minimal elaboration. Mostly these formal interviews ended up being treated as opportunities for performance, especially if there were other children or adults nearby—or, alternatively, treated as opportunities for sharing "trauma stories" that could lead to white support or assistance.[4] Over time, I realized, rather than conduct interviews, it was more valuable to simply spend time with children in the ordinary spaces of their lives, where it was possible to learn much more from their conversations and interactions around everyday topics and events.

Observing also had its own difficulties, and I realized that seeing or noticing itself was an art form. While I was observing, I was also being observed, drawn into a dance of perspectives, where the rules seemed diffuse: where and when do you direct your gaze? When do you avoid looking? How do you manage to observe while not looking like you are doing so? Haitian children (and adults) were keen observers, picking up on the slightest anomaly, the subtleties of action and appearance, and the ongoing flow of activity around them without even seeming to do so. It appeared to be an essential cultural skill—one that I was only gradually beginning to see and appreciate.

Of Wind and Wasps

I decided today to give the Haitian university students in my foundations of research class a group exercise. Each group was to write their research question on a large sheet of poster paper; then, their partner group was to critique the question (using ideas we had previously discussed), writing their critiques below. They were to leave space for additional comments to be added later during the second part of the activity. I gave all the instructions as clearly as possible, with ample chance to ask questions if anyone was unsure of what to do; everyone said they understood.

*But the battle had just begun! One group started writing their own question on another group's sheet. A second group ended up just writing an answer to the first group's question. They hadn't grasped the idea that they were supposed to **critique** the question. Groups came up to me again and again for re-explanation of the same thing. Some groups wanted me to tell them if their question was good or not (which would have defeated the whole purpose of the exercise which was to get them to think critically about their question!)*

I had asked the student groups to tape their poster papers to the walls when they were finished. I had 13 groups, and 13 large sheets of poster paper. The classroom was quite large and there was ample space for everyone's sheet. I taped one sheet myself to show them how to do it. But there was a lot of wind passing through the open doors and windows of the room, making it extra difficult to tape the poster paper to the bare concrete walls. I spent a few minutes in search of more tape, but when I next looked at how things were coming along, I saw that students had piled up chairs on top of desks and were climbing on top of them in order to tape the pages high up near the ceiling of the lecture room, maybe 20 feet high.

I could not understand the reasoning—why do that, after I had already specifically told them they'd have to write on the poster paper? Perhaps they thought that by doing so they could avoid the wind? But if they were that high no one could write let alone read what was written. But then again, perhaps to them, taping the paper was the more important activity, not the cognitive one I had planned. Nevertheless we did finally get the poster papers to stay put, at eye level; students themselves took over the job with extra tape once they got around to it. We now proceeded to the second part of the exercise, where groups were to circulate around the room to the other group's posters and add any additional commentary or critique. I re-explained this next part of the exercise, asking if everyone understood, to a resounding "Yes!"

*But as I wandered around the room visiting each group, students started asking me about what they were supposed to do, over and over again. I began to notice, however, that if I explained the activity to **one** of the group members individually, they would then proceed to explain to their peers, and once this happened, there were no more questions. Whether this was a kind of in-group hierarchy, a way to manage responsibility/face, or a cultural preference for horizontal, peer-to-peer knowledge exchange, it was clear that this was the way to go. I wondered if the "lack of understanding" I had perceived was due to problems of language (at this point I was transitioning from French to Kreyòl), but I also had a Kreyòl speaking teaching aide who explained everything I had said, so it was not a language problem. Something conceptual was going on.*

> *The classroom had about twenty wasp nests of varying size hanging from the walls, lights, and ceiling. One was quite large, covered with a good number of wasps. They were flying about during class; one landed on my arm and I jumped to shake it off, to everyone's amusement. Another student, though, got stung, causing a great deal of commotion for a period of time. My teaching aide pointed out the two wasps that had fallen on the ground near me. I looked and said I thought they were fighting. He said they were "making love." (2014)*

While I struggled with understanding students' habits of sense-making, I also noticed that the environment itself had intervened in our pedagogical process. Wind and wasps were both interruptions or distractions of a sort, if one chose to see them that way, but from another perspective they were intimately pedagogical: for while they might have interrupted the intended activity, at the same time they enabled other opportunities for seeing, thinking, and doing. The wind made taping difficult, but it also enabled students to think creatively about a possible solution (albeit one that prioritized the wrong thing in my mind—getting the paper to stick, versus being able to read and write on it); and it also enabled a good deal of collective energy and indeed satisfaction in finally getting multiple layers of tape to stick. The wasps were a distraction, and a painful nuisance, but also provided humor, an opportunity for collective commiseration, and, for me, another opportunity to question what I was seeing.

Another white educator with long experience in Haiti once told me that she found Haitians to have deficits in their thinking: they were unable to follow directions, for one thing. They needed everything spelled out, literally, and in detail. They lacked mechanical skill (GM, personal communication, 2009). Another educator perceived Haitians as lacking the ability to think creatively and independently; he saw a need to teach them to be "divergent thinkers." I saw these phenomena too, to some extent: any question was to be answered literally, exactly, specifically, in the correct format. I gave students a "personal reflection" essay assignment that proved nearly impossible for the great majority. Despite the fact that I had explained the assignment to the class at least ten times over a number of days, after every class inevitably someone would come up individually and ask again what they had to do. Or they would show me an example of their work and ask me to "approve" it.

An easy explanation is that students never learn to think critically, because the dominant modality of instruction in Haitian schools is rote memorization. It is certainly true that rote memorization is highly valued and in many cases it is the only pedagogical approach students are exposed to; and it is also true that instruction in French is part of this problem. According to this logic, the school and classroom context itself systematically "de-skill," demanding only a limited set of abilities to memorize or mirror information that has been transmitted by a teacher, or, more likely, a text. The reflection essay I had assigned was in this sense completely unspecified and unfamiliar, and even perhaps uncomfortable, given its emphasis on "personal" experience. There are plenty of notable examples of this deskilling process from the ethnographic literature on schooling. People who are otherwise experts in certain knowledge domains, when asked to take a paper and pencil test to demonstrate their knowledge, readily fail. It is not that they do not know, it is that they are not able to translate what they know into the demands of an academic format or exam.[5]

Yet to frame the question as one of simple differences in communication or, worse, as "deficiencies" in ability to think, fails to address the significance of the underlying epistemology that shapes Haitian life. This is the world view of Vodou, that according to scholars of Haiti, is embedded across all dimensions of Haitian culture and society, regardless of level of education, religious affiliation, or social class (Bellegarde-Smith, 2004; Courlander, 1960; McCarthy-Brown, 2006; Michel, 1996). According to Bellegarde-Smith, Vodou is a foundation for Haitian identity that resists against external, foreign imposition (2004: 22). As a coherent system of value, belief, and practice, its epistemology is centered on a notion of fusion between physical and spiritual planes of existence, in which all things are interconnected:

> The way in which Haitians achieve this fusion of the physical and metaphysical planes, rather than their dualism, which dominates Western thought, is to visualize the two planes as part of an interpenetrating continuum . . . represented by the geometric figure of the crossroads. At the crossroads stands the *lwa* Legba, who controls access from the vertical to the horizontal planes and grants permission for the other lwa to descend through the *potomitan*, the wooden post at the center of the temple (*hounfo*) . . . In this way, the substance of matter and the substance of spirit are mutually and eternally bound in a symbiotic relationship. (2004: 29–30)

In her discussion of the educational character of Haitian Vodou, Michel (1996: 286) notes the ways in which Vodou democratizes the forms of teaching and learning, as everyone and everything can be a teacher/learner. People learn and are judged only in relation to their own progress, not against external standards imposed by an outside authority. Children learn through participation in ongoing activity around them, or through modeling and observation of those more skilled, gradually acquiring a way of seeing and participating in the world that is grounded in the social reality of collective life as it connects to the invisible world. Children can be spiritual teachers for senior members of the community, and Vodou spirits (*lwa*) are powerful teachers. This is not because they teach particular lessons on morality, for example, but because they teach those who are willing a "heightened vision of the world . . . showing [us] how to see clearly" (Michel, 1996: 289).

To See What is Not Seen

I finally looked more closely at the painting hanging above my bed in the guestroom. In the foreground was a woman giving birth. She was squatting, and between her legs I could see the head of the baby crowning, with its delicate eyebrows and eyelids. In the background, up in the left corner, was a very small and finely drawn image of three white coated figures standing over a woman lying on a table, her legs pulled up and her body draped with a sheet. She was also giving birth, but she was lying down, covered, and supervised by the three white-coated figures.

The squatting woman had a traditional symbol of medicine and healing, the Caduceus, a staff with snakes entwined about it, drawn lightly on her protruding abdomen. I saw that two versions of childbirth were being represented—one indigenous, traditional, and the other a modern, medicalized version. The squatting woman had healing within her, whereas the other woman's healing was coming from without, through the white-coated doctors who attended her. (2012)

On one level, the painting represented two epistemologies, two value systems, two ways of viewing the world, and it was clear which one the painter valued. The Caduceus is a universal symbol of biomedicine and healing, but snakes are also very significant in Haitian Vodou as well.[6] In this way, the painting transcended dualism. It also seemed to have captured my own "birth" as a learner in Haiti that was calling me to transcend the dualistic character of my Western scientific/rational way of seeing the lives of the adults and children around me. The emergence of interconnected symbols and events across time and space, the reversals of the ordinary temporal modalities, the blending of the spiritual and material across domains of experience, and the unbidden sense of things hidden behind appearances—all of these were part of a transformation that drew me toward a closer relationship with a different way of perceiving and attending to the world.

Because the quintessential experience of childhood is learning, an anthropology of childhood must engage with learning and with locally significant variations in cultural understandings of learning and their supporting epistemologies. Further, a critical anthropology should allow us to see the larger structures of power that are embedded in and flow from particular understandings of learning—both our own and those of the children we work with. My learning, as an anthropologist, shapes what I can or cannot see of the learning that children and others are engaged in. To democratize the lens is essential, otherwise it is easy to dismiss other ways of learning in the world as less legitimate, or less valuable. I do not and cannot dismiss rationalist modalities of research and knowledge for they have an important role to play in expanding our knowledge of human cultural life. But when our learning begins to take shape in ways that are open to the epistemologies of the places in which we work, we can better appreciate things that would otherwise go unseen.

3

"These Are *My* Children!"
White Love and Child Rescue in Haiti

One of the more marked phenomena globally over the past twenty years has been the flow of relatively privileged young white women from the United States, Canada, and other Northern nations to countries in the Global South where they engage in projects of development and humanitarian assistance (Jackson, Payne, and Stolley, 2015; Mostafanezhad, 2013). A striking number of them start out on these paths when they are in their late teens or early twenties, taking university or church-based service trips to communities abroad where they volunteer in orphanages and encounter—often for the first time—the "shocking" realities of child lives in poor places. As a result of these experiences, these young women develop a powerful need to help poor and vulnerable children. There are a number of cases globally where twenty-year-olds, despite having little to no experience or credentials, have established NGOs to support their work. It is not uncommon for these organizations to be family affairs—often joint efforts between sisters or mothers and their daughters, reflecting in part a global trend toward family volunteerism (Molz, 2017). Media attention and humanitarian awards often follow—along with robust donor funding. Indeed, it is fair to say that the image of the new humanitarian is a white twenty-something woman who leverages her "passion" for global development by working with needy children and families in some of the poorest parts of the world.

Such is the case in Haiti, where young white women from the United States and Canada have had a marked presence in Haiti's development and humanitarian landscape. Many have in fact embarked on full-time careers serving Haiti's children and families, alongside the hundreds of churches and nongovernmental organizations that have long been involved in this landscape.[1] There are no doubt many good outcomes from this work, especially for individual children and their families whose prospects for the future are fundamentally changed for the better.

A more critical perspective, however, raises questions regarding race, gender, and the larger political and cultural consequences of white women's involvement in development and humanitarian assistance. For some, it reflects a newer, female-gendered iteration of the "White Savior Industrial Complex" (Cole, 2012; Bandyopadhyay and Patil, 2017) in which women—building on their traditional gender roles as caretakers and educators of the young—serve as the primary agents of civilizing cultural practice through their work with children. In the process, they re-enact the long-standing unequal power dynamics underlying colonialism. Further, insofar as the women are often supported by faith-based organizations, their activity also reflects the long-standing centrality of Christian ideologies to neocolonialism (Bandyopadhyay and Patil, 2017; Bornstein, 2003).

A second critique centers the nature and role of the helping impulse and its place in the construction of women's identities. According to a number of scholars, the desire to help masks deeper motivations that are about much more than providing help, but about developing a moral, relational self, that is fulfilled through the experiences of developing caring relationships with vulnerable and needy children (Heron, 2007; Malkki, 2015). In the process of helping, the larger questions of social structural inequalities are obfuscated or even erased as the individualistic rewards of the helper/beneficiary relationship take precedence. While women's own identities are expanded and enriched, the identities of those others through whom projects of self-enhancement are enacted are reduced to "grateful beneficiary."

There are also studies that have demonstrated that the model of charity that underlies such work in fact contributes to maintaining, if not exacerbating, the conditions that produce vulnerability in the first place. This happens for two main reasons: first, because help that is directed toward individuals and their particular needs does not fundamentally change the structural conditions through which need is created. Second, and perhaps more importantly, the assistance provided actually works to undermine local social relations, established resource flows, and networks of care that already exist within communities. An influx of resources often generates more "need," as people adopt the subject labels that attract charitable aid, such as "orphan" (cf. Cheney and Ucembe, 2019). Some local institutions are provided more, and others less, increasing rivalries and jealousies. External aid often upsets the delicate balance that often exists among local benefactors and those in their charge, as well as introducing new forms of inequality.[2]

As described in Chapter 1, an important and expanding body of literature in cultural studies and anthropology has illuminated the significant role of affect in international development work (Boyd, 2020; McAlister, 2008; Cheney and Sinervo, 2019). This work has underlined the "economies of affect" that shape the humanitarian work of representing and assisting vulnerable children, especially the ways in which emotional connection between the privileged and the suffering becomes a primary means for generating donor funds that support such work. From "Hug an Orphan" vacations (Guiney, 2018) to the ways attachments to vulnerable children become an individualized question of morality that overshadows important questions of structural inequality (Conran, 2011), this literature suggests that "affective labor" is central to humanitarian efforts, shaped as they are by "intensely emotional interpersonal forms of exchange" (Boyd, 2020: 534). Further, sentimental connections, empathy for the suffering, and a desire to make a difference flourish in the context of the neoliberal retreat of the state since they shift responsibility for social welfare onto the shoulders of individuals and organizations who become the primary purveyors of assistance. The "passion for making a difference" is thus intimately connected to emerging neoliberal regimes of governance and a politics of aid that centers affect as its primary currency.

At the same time, it is important not to minimize the experiential dimensions of affect in women's work with vulnerable children, especially in relation to religious faith. Among Christians in Haiti, caring for the vulnerable is often seen as a direct reflection of God's love at work in the world, and those who are inspired to work with vulnerable children see themselves as responding to a deeply spiritual call to love those who are poor or suffering. A number of books and articles illustrate the ways in which young women felt drawn to Haiti because of a spiritual call to service with vulnerable children (e.g., Boudreaux, 2015; Gengel and Gengel, 2013; Wander, 2010). At the heart of these narratives are powerful stories about love, and the ways love can both rescue children as well as act as a larger force to combat the injustices children face in Haiti (in not a few cases, leading these young women to expose corrupt orphanages supported by donors in the United States and Canada).

The role of love in the development and humanitarian work of young women is thus a deeply important and yet conflicted one: potentially lending itself to cultural and political hegemony of the White Savoir, acting as a force for the realization or fulfillment of personal needs and identities, deflecting attention away from structural inequalities, serving as a currency in global economies of affect that support neoliberalism, and motivating powerful stories of Christian faith and service directed toward "making a difference" in the world. All of these also work in and sometimes against notions of dependency and charity that have had a checkered history in international development assistance, where often local experiences and interpretations of these constructs do not match up to those of international actors (Boyd, 2020; Scherz, 2014).

Whatever its meanings and significance, love was everywhere in the narratives of women who had been drawn to working with vulnerable children in Haiti. Love was central, too, to my own experiences. I had not really thought about love until it became an unavoidable dimension of nearly every encounter, with "I love you" inevitably voiced at the most unexpected moments and in the most unusual of circumstances. As a white woman, I puzzled over the ways love was both omnipresent in my relationships with Haitians and in the ways it seemed to take on a particular valence in women's narratives about their work with children.

Passionate Attachments

The next day, when I arrived at the school, the small boy Manley immediately saw me and escorted me to his house next door, where a number of female family members were sitting in the lakou *[yard], as they usually did. Manley's mom had come to live in the area after the earthquake in 2010, when she had lost her husband. During a spirited conversation with Manley's mom, the women realized I still hadn't figured out who was who among them, so they re-explained that Lourdie and Jeanne were Manley's older sisters. Another mother there was mom to Flor, the baby; the older woman was Manley's grandmother. There was another young woman, Sara, who was sent from Port au Prince and who lived with them too, doing chores in the household. Finally there was also another middle aged woman sitting with them whose relation to the family I still didn't quite understand; she could have been another distant relative, or someone taken in after the earthquake, as so many people whose homes had been destroyed were.*

During this conversation, a Haitian man I hadn't seen before entered the lakou and immediately came up to me to ask (in English) for $2000 so that Manley's mom could pay for her rent. Trying to not look too surprised at this rather unusual (for me) shift in our discussion, I explained that I was so sorry—I didn't have that kind of money—I wasn't a missionary and didn't work for any NGO. Just as quickly as he had arrived, he simply said ok and left.

The conversation picked up again as naturally as if nothing had happened. Manley's mom clearly enjoyed correcting my halting Kreyòl. *When I asked her how she raised Manley to be such a sweet boy (he was indeed) she told me he had his father's character. Manley is loved by everyone, she added, "Even other* blan *love him." Then she said, "Map baw Manley." [I'm giving you Manley.] Manley was holding onto me for dear life as she said this and would have readily assented, I'm sure, had I agreed. I had said I loved him and he had said he loved me. But I was surprised that a mother, who obviously esteems her son and recognizes his qualities, would so readily offer to give him away. Yes, there was the material aspect—Manley would go with me to America and be educated and taken care of and have a big future ahead of him. But it was clear to me that it was more than that; it was about human relations.* (2012)

Stevenson's room was adorned with photos of white women: pictures of models torn from magazines taped to the bare concrete walls, along with birthday cards signed by good folks from America named "Cathy" and "Susan." He showed me his photo album, full of pictures of white women, many of whom appeared to be related—grandmoms, moms, and daughters posing for family photos. I asked who they were. He told me, "Sponsors." His dad had said to me earlier, as we spoke downstairs in the small parlor, "All the missionaries come and tell us how much they love Stevenson, but not all of them helped him. I think you're different . . ." (2013)

Situated on the slope of a steep hill, the orphanage was the largest and best maintained facility on the island as far as I could tell. The path up was crowded with ti machann *(women vendors) selling all sorts of candy, snacks, and drinks from ice-filled coolers. As I entered, in the company of my host family, a small boy immediately came up to me and took my hand. He did not let go the entire 40 minutes we spent there. As we were preparing to leave, the daughter of the family had her picture taken with two young girls. She asked her mom, "Can we adopt one?" Her mom said, "We already have enough kids. We can help in other ways." The little boy who had been holding my hand had been standing off to the side during the picture-taking, and I suddenly thought I'd like to have his photo too. So I went over to him, and he raised his arms to hold me, leaning his head against my body. Someone took our picture; I bent low to ask what his name was, but he did not answer. An orphanage staff member nearby said, "His name is Daniel." I felt a wave of chills come over me, that same sort of what felt like electric energy that I had come to recognize as occurring with some regularity during my time in Haiti. I exclaimed with great surprise, "My son back home in the States is named Daniel!"*

As I walked back down the hill, just one thought consumed me: that there are things I do not own or control, but that are given to me—that I am merely a recipient of God's gifts and grace. There was a Catholic Church, "Our Lady of the Sea," at the base of the hill, and the group stopped in for a look before boarding the boat. The banner hanging from the altar up front said, "It is not you who have chosen me, but I who have chosen you." And beneath that, "Suffer not the little *ones to come unto me . . ." As I stood there, the familiar tingling rush of energy like chills surged through my entire body again, and at that moment I also noticed all the white ribbons hanging everywhere on the walls. Then I remembered the single white ribbon that was taped, curiously, to the wall of the room in the guesthouse where I had been staying.*

Widner, a 13 year old I had met at the Berger School summer program for restavèk, texted me and asked if he could come meet me at the house where I was staying. I thought the request a little unusual, since we had always met at his school or his home, but said OK. He arrived promptly at 8 AM, and sat with me on the balcony outdoors. After a few preliminary greetings, he handed me a thick, neatly folded note. He asked me to open it and read it. There were three pages of passionate love poems in fine, dense handwriting—composed especially for me, he said.

I did find Manley lovable, and Daniel too—so many lovable children. Over the years I had been struck by the strong declarations of love and attachment that many white women used to describe their work with vulnerable children in Haiti: "I am extremely attached to these children!" "My heart hurts for these poor children!" "I love these [Haitian] kids!" These declarations of love and attachment, moreover, were frequently voiced alongside expressions such as, "I need help with funding some of my kids' education in Haiti" "I can't wait to get back to our children!" "These are *my* children!"—emphasis in the original—in the words of one young woman writing about the children she had rescued from the streets. She continued, "Yes, I do call them *my children* . . . because that's what I feel. They are *mine*."

The ways these white women so unselfconsciously spoke of the Haitian children they worked with as "*my* children" troubled me: since when does loving Haitian children permit one the privilege of claiming ownership over them? This was not just a shorthand way of speaking of "the kids we work with"—as a teacher might say, for instance, "my kids" when referring to her class. This was different, as these expressions emphasized powerful emotional attachment of an exclusive, parental nature. The ability to claim children as theirs seemed to be predicated on the assumption that the children in question were rescued from forsaken lives by the white women's love—almost as if they were in a way "re-born" to her as real, biological parent. The women thought of themselves as saving children through their love and in that process, children were reborn to them as genuine mothers.

The logic behind this was essentially that Haitian children are suffering and dying primarily from lack of love in their lives, and it is the motherly love of the white woman that rescues them. One young woman, Jamie, who started an organization to support vulnerable children, wrote about the saving love that her younger sister Ali had for a little Haitian girl:

> Ali was only 17, but she saved Migiline, she really did. Migiline was tiny, she was so sick, and she wouldn't attach to anyone. For two weeks, Ali just held her and played with her, even though she wasn't responding. There wasn't anger, happiness, anything," Katie says. "For a while I thought it was hopeless," Ali admits. "I wondered how I could pour so much love into her, and still get no response. I never experienced anything like it before. Finally, Migiline threw her first temper tantrum. I cried. It was great." Migiline is now reunited with her sister, living in Canada. Another happy ending. (Wander, 2010)

In this narrative and in many others like it, white women rescue Haitian children by showing love to those who supposedly have not been loved, and who suffer as a result from deficiencies in their ability to experience emotions and, especially, in their capacity for attachment.

As a prominent theme in women's discourse on Haitian childhood, attachment is mostly referenced in terms of the ways it fails to develop or develops abnormally in children who have not been loved or "properly cared for." This is a reflection of a more general trend in the research literature on orphans and vulnerable children that often identifies difficulties with attachment as an index of psychological damage due to lack of a primary caregiver in the child's life. Manifestations of attachment disorder can take the form of inability to attach (as in the earlier case), or what is called "indiscriminate friendliness"—where children who should normally be wary of strangers instead are extremely outgoing and seek to bond with anyone. Children running up to visitors in orphanages wanting to be held was one common behavior considered to be evidence of developmental abnormality.

And yet, this interpretation speaks more to developmental science than to any culturally sensitive understanding of the larger picture of cultural variation in child development. The anthropological literature on attachment has robustly demonstrated that the notion of "healthy attachment" to a single caregiver that is assumed normal in Western developmental theory is not shared in many other cultures around the world (Keller, 2013, 2018; Gottlieb, 2009; Norman and LeVine, 2008; Quinn and Mageo, 2013). In cultural and social contexts where children grow up in the care of many people (which is the case in many resource-poor settings around the world) it is adaptive and indeed psychologically healthy for children *not* to attach to a single caregiver. Too much attachment to a single caretaker is seen as inappropriate and even detrimental to the child's future as it not only goes against strong cultural beliefs in the value of sociality but works against the child's ability to manage shifting social and environmental demands. In Thailand, for example, local women explain, "It's fundamental that children don't attach themselves only to the mother. . . . They must not develop an exclusive dependence on the mother, but learn to socialize with everybody and with the environment" (Bolotta, 2017: 101). A healthy child is one who can cultivate emotional bonds with many people. While so-called stranger anxiety is considered an index of developmental normality in the United States, it is decidedly abnormal in some cultures where children are socialized to high levels of sociability toward strangers from an early age (as in the Beng case described by Gottlieb, 2009; see also Quinn and Mageo, 2013). Patterns of childrearing in Haiti reflect cultural supports for developing capacities for non-exclusive attachment as well as cultural valuation of stranger sociability.

Yet the vast majority of the white women who worked with vulnerable children failed to understand the Haitian cultural context and instead cast it as inappropriate and damaging to children. While many children do not grow up in the care of a biological parent or in a nuclear household, it is also true that children don't exist in a social vacuum; the vast majority have extended families as well as close emotional relationships with peers and other adults, some of whom serve as benefactors to them. Further, models of demonstrative family affect, with lots of parental hugs, cuddles, praise, and so on that are common in middle-class and privileged families in the United States and Canada are not the norm in Haitian families (see Hoffman, 2021a). In sum, white women's assessment of the "lack of love" in Haitian children's lives both erased the larger context of children's lives as it re-created children as emotional blank slates upon which they could pour out their love. By fulfilling the child's supposed "need for love" ("Children are dying from lack of love!"), white women could become saving mamas.[3]

From this perspective, what can one say about Manley? While acknowledging her love for him, his mother was equally interested in securing his future: How better to do that than with another (more advantaged) mother who might be able to provide an education or even, perhaps, a life in the United States? His mother's obvious attachment to him was not one of exclusivity—indeed, she wanted to give him away, and Manley, for his part, was more than willing to attach to me. Was he maladjusted? No, he was extremely well adapted to life in a place where a child does not expect to be cared for or to grow up with his biological parents. Little Daniel's efforts, too, though no doubt condemned from a Northern lens as "indiscriminate" friendliness, reflect more the ways in which capacity for attaching to others beyond one's immediate circles is a normative part of Haitian childhood. Daniel was also, perhaps, acting strategically, knowing well that the reason many foreigners visit is ultimately to adopt children. In this sense his "indiscriminate affection" was in fact entirely appropriate—intelligent, even.

As for Widner, seeing him simply as a victim of an adolescent hormone-induced crush is far too dismissive. Widner was rather cultivating a potential attachment that would stand him in good stead for his future. Though he could have had romantic and/or sexual interest, the whole thing was also about his family—creating a wider circle of belonging that would bring everyone up; it wasn't just about his own benefit or desire, nor any "lack" of affection in his life. (In fact, at Widner's suggestion, I had spent a good deal of time hanging out with his mother and other siblings, so I was no stranger to his family.) To see Widner's love as a simple adolescent crush is to reduce it to an individualistic, psychologized (read: white) frame of reference where romantic attraction is about hormones, crushes, and personal desires. Rather, it needs to be seen as part of a more complex dynamic of belonging and affection oriented not toward individual fulfillment but toward the achievement of wider, corporate, and flexible circles of belonging and attachment.

"They love us so much!"

Alongside their love for Haiti and Haitian children, the dominant trope among Northern white women in Haiti is the love Haitians have for them. As voiced by missionaries and social workers who devote their efforts to helping Haiti and its children, the appreciation and love they feel from Haitians is extraordinary: "They appreciate us so much!" "There is so much gratitude—they make us feel like part of the family!" "Every time we come, they are so happy to see us!" "Haitians truly love us!" I, too, encountered love nearly everywhere:

> Last evening I got a text message from Mario (a young man in his twenties—I had never met him, but we had had an email exchange) telling me his subconscious mind has convinced him that he loves me.
> Men are telling me right and left that they love me; women too. The kids who surrounded me while I was in the water at the beach the other day said they loved me; they knew I was a wonderful mother, because I gave them the feeling of their own mothers.

> *As I sat at the back of the classroom, a child in the back row surreptitiously showed me a piece of paper, on which he had drawn my picture, captioned with "I love you," in English.*
>
> *I told Alcinon, the 10 year old boy who had come up to talk to me in the street, that I loved him. He asked me, "Do you love me as a friend or as a child?" That he could even pose this question astounded me.*

I was surprised by the frequency with which even complete strangers—men, women, children alike—would say "I love you!" after only a few minutes' conversation. Often there wasn't even any need for a face-to-face encounter: expressions of love were equally common after a few lines of phone text or Facebook messages. I wondered if this was simply because I was white. As is well-known, whiteness evokes a whole range of associations for Haitians, including elevated social class and social status, privilege, and even aesthetics—for even when objectively relatively unattractive, a white woman's whiteness can make her beautiful. Further, could these expressions of love be seen as efforts to form attachments of a resource-beneficial kind? No doubt, as most whites in Haiti have connections and resources, and there are at least some Haitians for whom love exists at the nexus of these relationships of aid and assistance. It would be wrong to say the love is insincere: but it exists in a context structured at a higher level by the economic and political power that brings whites to Haiti in the first place.

And then, of course, there is the potentially confounding effect of language: in Haitian Creole, there is no distinction between "love" and "like": there is only *renmen*. So maybe it is not love, really, as an American would understand it. But even if the feeling were more along the lines of "liking," still, I had never encountered, either in the United States or in many other countries I had lived, such a constant stream of "I like/love yous" as I had in Haiti. So too, I had often heard other whites say, "Haitians wear their hearts on their sleeve." There is a generally recognized high level of emotional expressivity in Haitian life, which may encourage such avowals of *renmen*. In the end, though, another explanation is possible. It seems likely that love is so much a part of Haitian social discourse because it is the foundation of Haitian social life—but in ways that are unfamiliar to Northerners. Northern circles of belonging are comparatively more constrained and somewhat exclusive, bound by prior institutional relationships: work, church, clubs, marriages, families, and schools. They exist in a relatively static form, expanding only within the parameters of specific settings—a new colleague at work, for example, or new classmates at school. Haitian relationships, especially among the less economically advantaged, are structured with more fluidity and potentiality at their base: they are always predicated on the value of broadening one's circles of belonging as widely as possible. As has been observed by anthropologists (Laguerre, 1978; Nicholas and Stepick, 2008), in Haitian social relationships circles of obligation and dependency are assiduously cultivated across time and space. In this process, *renmen is* key, making it possible for even those who are strangers to be welcomed into ever widening and growing circles of belonging.

To take this argument a step further, in Haiti perhaps it is even more culturally appropriate to speak of belonging rather than attachment. Loving opens the possibility of belonging; while attachment restricts it. The whole dynamic is opposite to that of Northerners for whom individualized attachments (for a child, ideally to a biological parent, or in the family, the attachment bond of husband/ wife) are seen as key to "normal" development and family life. The Northern ideal of the nuclear family is premised on this ideal of exclusive attachment— the bond between husband and wife who "start" a family, and the exclusive attachment of biological children to an individual caretaker. In Haiti, though, families are not started by husbands and wives, and in the great majority of cases they are definitely not nuclear—they are corporate entities that husbands, wives, and children enter into. These entities extend far back through time and space— and if healthy, they are always growing and expanding, with children (and not necessarily biological ones) playing key roles in this process of growth.

White Love: Belonging and Permutations of Power

One cannot blame whites for seeing their experiences in Haiti through their own lens, especially when that lens has been shaped by their own relatively privileged upbringing, the professionalized discourses of child welfare that they have been exposed to, and Christian faith ideals of love—all of which come together that shape their efforts of child rescue in the first place. Without recognizing the underlying cultural biases that underlie the interpretations they ascribe to Haitian behavior, it is natural for white women to see their love as fulfilling Haitian children's supposed attachment needs.

At the same time, white love is not innocent, and must be seen through a larger frame of reference that acknowledges its roots in the permutations of power that have long contributed to the neocolonial dominance of Northern paradigms and regimes of truth in places such as Haiti. We have good reason to suspect the "attachments" of white rescuers for Haitian children *because of* their profound innocence, which prevents a fuller critical view of the ways in which love can corrupt, and indeed obscure, the operations of power and status that inhere in their work in Haiti. Not only does white love promote Northern views of child well-being, it confers on whites a sort of immunity to criticism; it makes them owners/masters of the narrative—a dynamic that is all too common when the objects of affection are positioned as powerless and damaged. Love that naturalizes certain forms of affect as normal or abnormal is quite capable of lending itself to ownership. The facility with which such images of damage sustain tropes of rescue speaks to the ignorance induced by the fact that a good part of the larger cultural meaning system surrounding childhood in Haiti is absent. The individual child abstracted from his or her social world and seen only through his or her vulnerability and neediness easily becomes the empty container into which the emotions of rescuers can be poured. Filling the supposed empty emotional spaces of children's lives, white love takes over the very being of the child, as children of Haiti become the white woman's own children—"*my* children*.*" Their otherness is dissolved—and the coloniality of the relationship is hidden behind the innocence and goodness of love for the suffering child.

The perception of being loved by Haitians is inevitably filtered through white identity and its needs, shaping the way Haitian expressions of affection are understood. In this way, the sense of being loved by Haitians may reflect a particular perversion of white perception—as white needs for self-validation, self-extension, self-recreation, and even procreation cover over Haitian experience, shifting its direction in self-validating and affirming ways. So hospitality and generosity—virtues commonly practiced in Haiti—when directed toward whites, become for whites clear evidence of love, even when for Haitians they are simply normal ways to treat a guest. It is the white lens that turns them into "love." It is not that Haitians don't love, but that whites perceive love in ways that refract Haitian meanings to satisfy white longing for validation and meaning.

This also means that white conviction of "being loved" erases the possibility that there is, behind the scenes, resentment and dislike. Those who are left out of circuits of white support, or those who have seen the ways white aid has done little to change the status quo in Haiti, do not love:

Our team—including Haitian-American Pastor Albert and his white wife and the rest of the visiting missionary personnel—were returning from an afternoon spent at the beach, riding in Pastor Albert's open truck. I had never had much experience of "hanging out" with missionaries before. All I knew was that Pastor Albert had a great following locally and that, as our team members had told me, he was doing

"good work" in the local community. As we climbed the hill up to the guesthouse, I
saw a man by the side of the road look directly at us and lift his hand to his nose to
pinch it shut. I am not sure if anyone else noticed the dramatic gesture, but even if
they did, no one said anything.

White narratives of Haitian love are self-sustaining by the very fact of the absence of any deep attention to the Haitian side of the experience. When there is so much ostensible appreciation, hospitality, and concern for their welfare shown by Haitians, what is going on beneath the surface doesn't even register in white consciousness. Indeed, the power of white love is that it erases anything that doesn't fit within its own self-narrative.

In this, it replicates the age-old colonialist dynamic that positions those on the receiving end as grateful servants who "love" their oppressors. Love for one's oppressor is a well-known condition, and it is one that positions the Haitian in relation to the benevolent white in a de-facto parent-child role. White mamas aren't wrong, in that sense, in that they build on this deeply colonialist relation to construct a modern savior role, enacted through those most vulnerable to being re-made in the savior's image—children.

In evoking pseudo-parenthood ("*my* children"), the reframing of the savior-rescued child as a parent-child relationship expresses love for the child, of course, but also a troubling sense of "using" the vulnerable child as a platform for an emotional economy that is an extension of the rescuers' own identity and needs. One might even read this process as a form of white guilt being worked out in Haiti, as whites "rescue" those they have historically oppressed, while proclaiming the innocence of God's love and the ways it "lays a burden" on the white heart.

So I must ask myself, through what lens was I seeing the "love" that was so abundant and seductive? I wanted to believe it, yet often I could not. I have even found myself angered by it on occasion—the sheer persistence of it, the often disarming sincerity of its expression. I have never attached myself formally to any of the organizations intent on saving children in Haiti, though I too have stepped in to help on occasions when it was asked for, and sometimes when it wasn't. Yet the love has always troubled me: Could I trust it? Did the Haitians who so freely announced "I love you" draw from some deeper wellspring of the heart—a genuine sense of connection that cannot be explained on any rational level? Or was such "love" tangled up in the dynamics of aid, or in whatever aesthetics of whiteness and sexuality one chooses to imagine? In the end, I think it was all of these.

I am not against love; nor am I, for that matter, against acts of individual charity, for these are part of what it takes to live as human being in places such as Haiti. I am against the ways love is used and transformed into a discourse of ownership and self-making for many of Haiti's white mamas, as it also imposes its own visions of what is good and right. Such visions are institutionalized and linked to white narratives about the deficiencies of Haitian lives when judged through a white lens. It is a rigid kind of passion that wants to conform others to its own ideals of well-being. In that there is no love, only power.

4

Becoming Someone

Personhood and Education among
Haiti's Marginalized Children

*The captive was educated and protected within the cocoon of private
life. Her personhood was her only property. It was something neither the
colonist nor the state could seize. . . . She necessarily had to combine a
knowledge of the rules of the plantation with the development of a parallel
system of knowledge that enabled her to take care of herself. This system
had to oppose, and might substitute for, that of the modern, colonial
state. . . . This parallel system became the foundation for the world she
built. Its primary function was to delay or even potentially prevent her
absorption into the plantation society. . . . Her intimate world was born
through a daily, relentless struggle against the public life organized for her
by the state. . . . The masters didn't understand how important these worlds
were. . . . Through their self-education, the captives eluded the vision of the
authorities.*

From *The Haitians: A Decolonial History* by Jean Casimir. pp. 328-330.
Translation copyright © 2020 by the University of North Carolina Press. Used
by permission of the publisher. www.uncpress.org

This chapter defines a vision of education that underlies the worlds of the
"captives" of the modern Haitian state: those children and youth who are being
failed by the formal educational system. This includes a vast number of those
who occupy the low-status fringes of society—street children and children in
domesticity (*restavèk*) who may never go to school, as well as the many with
limited or interrupted formal education who are consigned to schools of poor
quality. However, against the ways dominant discourse portrays such children as
"lacking childhood," I advance a different narrative that is grounded in a more

thorough understanding of a process of self-education that infuses and animates their lives. This self-education constitutes a parallel system of cultural practice that counters and often resists the identity-undermining nature of the formal, institutional system—whether delivered by the state or in the multitude of private schools run by foreign entities that constitute approximately 85 percent of the schools in the country. Practices of self-education exist in fugitive spaces of ordinary life and derive their strength and indeed flourishing from wellsprings of cultural practice, value, and meaning grounded in Haitian history and culture— resources that are often ignored and obscured by the overwhelming emphasis on schooling in accounts of contemporary Haitian society.[1]

As I use the term, self-education has a dual meaning: it captures both the agency of persons as well as the intended goal or purpose—the development of the self or person. In this account, the notion of "self" does not assume an isolated, autonomous individual; rather, it draws from notions of personhood that extend beyond individuals into the collective social relational and natural worlds. I do not intend to paint self-education as an alternative to schooling, nor do I suppose that the failures of schooling do not matter, especially given the clear connection between schooling and the possibility of social attainment. Rather, my goal is to offer a different narrative that provides insight into the ways in which persons can generate alternative pathways to an identity that matters, especially in contexts marked by extreme constraints imposed by poverty, social inequality, and neocolonialism.

Victimized and Vulnerable: Stolen Childhoods, *restavèk*, and Street Children

Often, during the course of a greeting (which, in Haiti, normally consists of a number of back-and-forth confirmations of well-being of self and family), one is asked, "*Epi koman aktivitew?*" (And how are your activities?) This question refers to the things you are engaged in that reflect your work, interests, contributions, or roles in your community. It does not necessarily imply or reference a salaried job or occupation (though it may) but it does suppose that you have an arena or domain in which you exert your abilities and energies. Unless one is a *vakabon*—a "vagabond"—a socially useless person evoking an image of borderline criminality, everyone has "activities," though they may not have jobs or much formal education.

This question has always impressed me, for it brings to mind a vision of persons who are socially engaged and who are developing themselves and contributing to society even without much schooling or salaried work. It is a vision of personhood that is egalitarian in that it assumes all people have a domain of their own in which they exert their energies and talents regardless of the often severe constraints—including poverty, lack of access to schooling, and unemployment—that characterize the lives of so many in Haiti. It is a question that supposes, in sum, a kind of personhood.

This vision of personhood extends as well to those for whom the question might potentially be the most problematic—those children and youth who are often absent from school and marginalized from the public sphere and the status structure that governs Haitian life: in sum, street children and *restavèk*. The dominant image of these children is one of vulnerability and victimization, captured most poignantly in the trope of the child without childhood—the "child slave" and the abandoned orphan or street child (for further discussion see Hoffman, 2012a; 2012b).[2] As represented in the discourse of the many NGOs and FBOs engaged in *restavèk* advocacy, these are children who are sent away to lives of servitude by parents who lack the resources to care for them; they are abused, treated as less than human, and kept from school to labor tirelessly. The dominant narrative is that *restavèk* and street children have had their childhood stolen from them (see also McCalla, 2002):

> Economic deprivation, violence, abuse, underage domestic labor, absence of state services, family separation—the odds are stacked against young people in Haiti. They are effectively having their childhood stolen from them. (McConville, 2019)

> The physical chains may have been removed, one resident missionary explained, but the mental chains remain. The people have never had the opportunity to see what a family unit looks like. . . . Children, from the time they are able to walk, have to do so much work—especially girls—and so much of a child's learning before being able to read and write is stolen from children in Haiti. (Missionary interview, cited in Montcreiff, 2006: 35)

The idea of stolen childhood appears frequently in reference to vulnerable children within the global agendas of international policy and social welfare (cf. Balagopalan, 2008). This discourse derives its moral and ethical force from a certain bourgeois ideal of childhood in which children remain at home with their birth parents, are sent to school and kept away from work outside the home, and are given ample opportunities for play. By contrast, the world outside the protective cocoon of the birth family is constructed as one of deviance, abuse, and risk. In the words of one Christian organization active in anti-*restavèk* advocacy,

Haitian parents are no different from parents elsewhere. They love their children and want them to grow up at home. Still, each year tens of thousands of rural Haitian parents send their children away to live with families in distant cities. They do so in the hope that their children will be sent to school. In reality, many end up in homes where they are subjected to exploitation, abuse, and neglect and are never sent to school. Today in Haiti, one in eight children are trapped in slavery. (BB website, 2022)

This lens assumes that all else being equal, Haitians too would want their children to "grow up at home"—an assumption that reflects a vision of family life common to educated, relatively privileged social classes in the Global North. This is not an ideal aligned with deeply held cultural notions of family as well as the economic constraints that shape family life in many nations of the Global South, including Haiti, where child fosterage is a widely accepted social practice with important cultural as well as economic rationales (Archambault, 2010; Chin, 2003; Penn, 2009; Leinaweaver, 2008; Schwartz, 2003; see additional discussion in Chapter 5.) This literature demonstrates that circulation of children to other families is not simply a response to poverty but reflects a complex system of cultural ideals around child rearing, development, and education, as well as culturally shaped ideas of family life that do not conform to northern assumptions about the primacy of parental caretaking.[3]

For other Christians in Haiti, *restavèk* represents the powers of evil that afflict Haitian society:

When I look at the word restavek, I don't think about a definition or a statistic. I don't even associate it with particular individuals. I look at this word and I think, Darkness, Evil . . . In our school most of the children who are restaveks live with individuals who openly and religiously practice voodoo [*sic*] . . . Oftentimes those who practice voodoo [*sic*] allow the darkness to completely take over the lives. . . . I have to pray against my flesh not to think of people who have restavek as monsters. I want to curse and spit and yell at them for the way they treat these children. (Boudreaux, 2015: 146, 148)

The widespread representation of the *restavèk* system as slavery is largely fueled by international media and advocacy organizations, Christian missionaries (both Haitian and white), and some members of the educated Haitian middle-class and elite (including the Haitian diaspora) who have long played key roles in promoting internationalized standards for child protection in Haiti. As noted earlier, while not all Haitians condemn the practice, the negative representation of *restavèk* reflects a generalized sense of Haitian society and culture as, at best, deficient in its protection of children, and, at worst, as actively allied with the "powers of evil" that are commonly associated with Vodou, especially among Protestant and evangelical Christians (see Louis, 2019 for further discussion).

It is important to contextualize narratives of slavery and stolen childhood against a larger picture of high levels of mobility and in-country migration for children in Haiti. Significant numbers of children do not grow up in the care of biological parents. According to one study, 32 percent of the children surveyed were not living in a household headed by a biological parent (Pierre, Smucker, and Tardieu, 2009: 17). Using data from the first Living Conditions Survey of Haiti, Justesen and Verner found that only one in three children (aged 0–14) lives with both biological parents (2007: 3). Another survey of youth conditions in Haiti (Lunde, 2010), shows that in a sample of randomly selected youth age 10–24, 64 percent reported having moved away from their birth household, with more than half having moved *before* age ten. Among those who moved, 56 percent had moved two or more times, with as many as seven moves recorded (Lunde, 2010: 116–17). Lunde (2010) and Justesen and Verner (2007) also suggest that there are strong positive motivating factors for domestic migration among Haitian youth, since such migration increases the probability of being employed. While migration to urban centers appears to be most common and offers increased educational and employment opportunities, migration patterns in Haiti also include urban-to-rural movement as well as rural-to-rural movement. Couples who are separated, for example, will send children to one another; some parents will send children to the countryside from an urban area so that the parent can work (Brand, 2004: 41). High levels of unemployment, along with family stressors such as death, separation or divorce ultimately lead to high mobility among parents as well who migrate in search of better opportunities for work or improved living situations. To a great degree, adult conjugal and economic mobility co-exists with and conditions child mobility (Berggren et al., 1995: 2). This picture is complimented by cultural preferences for extended households and *lakou* (family residential compounds) which promote shared resources and childcare, and by the perceived economic value of children. Especially in rural areas, children are regarded as an important labor resource and will often be sent to live with other families both because they can perform important work in the household and because the move is regarded as potentially advantageous to the child's future opportunity (Schwartz, 2003). The conditions that shape child mobility are indeed complex yet too often simplified or reduced to immediate parental economic need.

Against the narratives of slavery common among anti-*restavèk* advocates, scholarly research paints a different picture in which situations of extreme abuse, though they exist, are not the norm; rather there is a high degree of variability in treatment as well as ambiguity in the status, as some children may perform basically the same work as *restavèk* and yet they are not referred to as such (Cooper, Diego-Rosell, and Gogue, 2012). The main difference appears to be the type and extent of work the child engages in, with the *restavèk* performing significantly more labor than other children (Pierre, Smucker, and Tardieu, 2009). However, as far as physical treatment and access to basic resources such as food are concerned, some research finds that *restavèk* children are in fact significantly better off than non-*restavèk* in the same household (Haydocy, Yotebieng, and Norris, 2015).

While parental death and resource constraints play a key role in precipitating a child's move to a new household, multiple studies of the phenomenon suggest that there are other perceived benefits, mainly in the extent to which moving away from the natal household represents increased future possibilities and opportunities. While the possibility of obtaining schooling is an important immediate "pull" factor, both parents and children themselves see the move through a lens emphasizing its equally important informal educational value— that is, it is seen as a way to "become someone" through informal learning or apprenticeship in the new household (Sommerfelt, 2002: 92). This informal learning, known as *fomasyon* (training or guidance), involves a complex set of ideas that reflect learning oriented toward cultivating qualities of personhood, including self-discipline, ability to adapt oneself to others' needs and living conditions, deference and respect, persistence, and endurance in the face of hardship. It also entails mastery of diverse competencies and skills, sometimes within apprenticeship-type relationships. In sum, the experience of *fomasyon* is considered necessary for creating "capable individuals" (Sommerfelt, 2002: 60; Sommerfelt, 2015; Schwartz, 2009; Smucker and Murray, 2004).

Further, contrary to the idea commonly promulgated among FBOs that children are passive victims of adults, trafficked into or otherwise confined to households against their will, existing research shows that children see moving to another household as an opportunity to improve their life chances and they may actively seek out such opportunities. This may involve moving away from birth parents or caretakers who cannot or will not actively meet the child's needs, or in which they experience excessive physical mistreatment. Not only do they welcome the initial move as a potential step up or improvement in their living situation, but they may also leave subsequent placements that prove to be unsatisfactory, either searching out other relatives to live with, finding other placements, or moving into the street (Hoffman, 2010; Smucker and Murray, 2004; Cooper, Diego-Rosell, and Gogue, 2012; Pierre, Smucker, and Tardieu, 2009). In sum, despite this complex terrain of aspiration, mobility, and education that shapes the lives of disadvantaged children, the dominant narrative remains that of the child whose childhood has been stolen, forced out of the love and care of their natal family into situations of exploitation and abuse.

Contesting Stolen Childhood: Spaces and Places of Learning and Becoming

But who or what has stolen childhood from Haitian children? Has childhood in fact not been stolen, but rendered invisible when seen through the globalized norms of proper childhood? To assume that children have no childhood is a consequence of seeing poor children's lives primarily through the lens of vulnerability and victimhood. This lens prevents us from understanding the ways children navigate their lives across multiple domains outside and beyond the confines of the support of state, civil society, and school (cf Balagopalan, 2014: 11; Patel, 2019). Especially, it prevents us from acknowledging and understanding the ways learning and education are ongoing processes of cultural and personal significance across the many places that children inhabit, including extended households, streets, peer groups, natural environments, as well as the ways in which children participate in ordinary activities of labor, production, and creation that animate the spectrum of community life. This education constitutes a parallel system of learning and self-development through cultural practice across multiple domains and settings. It is, as Casimir reminds us, a system of education that is "invisible" because it occurs not in the formal institutional environment of schools but in the domains of everyday life. For those children who are largely excluded from schooling and from its promises of future opportunity, self-education is an alternative domain for "becoming someone."[4]

Pascal

I had been walking the path that traverses the village and runs up over a steep hill, hoping to visit another community on the other side. On the way I met Pascal, a friendly and engaging 15 year-old. He greeted me and accompanied me as I walked, his bare feet seemingly impervious to the stones, sticks, and roots that littered the path. Later, he led me in a different direction up the hill to the house where he was raised by his matant *("aunt"—no blood relation—a common term of reference among restavèk for their primary caretaker). A pile of dried ears of corn lay in the yard; and I could also see the field nearby where they had recently been harvested. The aunt greeted me and directed him to bring a chair, freshly painted and solidly made, for me to sit on. Pascal also brought out a fresh coconut, which he sliced open with a machete and offered to me.*

There were a number of other children there who were observing my visit; they appeared to range in age from three or four to perhaps 13. As we sat, I noticed that it was not his aunt who disciplined the other children, it was Pascal, and he was an expert at exerting control. He reprimanded the older one who was about to try to cut a second coconut with the machete, holding it against a palm tree and within inches of a young girl sitting there. He also corrected the behavior of the other children continuously, telling them to stop their dezòd *(misbehavior; literally, "disorder"). I wasn't sure exactly what they had been doing wrong, as they all seemed well-behaved to me, so at one point I asked Pascal what was wrong with their behavior, and he replied that one of them had been making pebbles roll down the dirt slope.*

As we visited a beach a while later, he shared more details about his upbringing. He came at the age of three to live here, upon the death of his parents (or so he was told); he remembered nothing of them. He explained that he did everything— carrying water, cooking, cleaning, running errands, purchasing necessities, taking care of other children—basically helping with any kind of task. He was also attending a part-time trade school where he was learning tailoring. When I asked about the harsh treatments restavèk *generally received, he said it wasn't just* restavèk, *any child can be punished for pretty much anything, because it is seen as* fomasyon *(training)—a necessary part of bringing up children well. In his case, though, his behavior was so good that he hardly needed to be punished. Our conversation was interrupted by a phone call from his aunt, asking him to do something for her.*

His status as a restavèk *clearly did not dampen his self-esteem, energy or ambition. I could see that he took his household work seriously and was proud of it; he told me he had become an expert cook and even offered to cook for me if I wanted him to. He had plans for a future as a tailor; all that he needed at the moment was a sewing machine.*

Another day, we went to purchase some local white rum [klerin] and a street child came up to us and asked for some money. I wanted to give but had no change. So Pascal asked the vendor to make some small change with a bill I had; he took it and distributed it to a couple of different kids who were hanging around. I was glad he was doing this, and not me, for I was wary of the image of the blan *giving*

handouts. But he was something of a "boss" among the kids in the area, he said—
someone who by virtue of effort and ambition was making something of his life.
He was creating an identity as someone whom others could look up to as a patron,
upon whose generosity and good will they could depend. The fact that Pascal was
a restavèk *did not seem to create in him any sense of victimhood—if anything,*
it seemed to motivate him even more strongly toward a socially competent and
relevant identity. (2014)

Later, I saw that Pascal's relationship with the street children was not unique; it was part of a system of patronage where those who have relatively more means establish relationships with those who have less. It was a complex system of sharing and redistribution where even objectively small differences in available resources were significant. That Pascal himself had little money was not important; what mattered was his willingness to give to those who had even less. I noticed a similar sort of patronage in the relationship of a friend, David, with street boys. One day David shared the remains of his food with a street boy who came up to us as we were sharing a meal. I asked David if he took care of the boy, and he told me yes, he had relationships with a number of the street boys whom he supported with food, small gifts of cash, and odd jobs, such as washing his motorcycle. Like Pascal, he also said the street kids called him "boss."

These relationships were interesting for a number of reasons, but most of all in the ways they contributed to the construction of meaningful personhood, that is, "becoming someone" of value through acts of generosity that reflected capacity to care for others. This process involved not only personal ambition but the maintenance of relationships of giving that solidified social bonds. One achieved personhood through a combination of moral integrity, self-discipline, personal ambition, mastery of skills or competencies, and cultivation of social relationships in which one demonstrated generosity. Despite his relative poverty and social marginalization as a *restavèk*, Pascal had carved out an alternative, highly competent self—one that if not resistant to the social stigma associated with his status, at least afforded him an alternative identity of value.

Over time I observed a pattern in how other *restavèk* and street children—all considered on one level to be stigmatized and socially worthless—nevertheless cultivated particular talents or abilities that were recognized among those who knew them. According to David, the ragged-looking street boy who had come up to us was in fact an "expert swimmer and diver." Mr. Pierre, a school headmaster, told me about an orphaned *restavèk* boy in his school who could imitate any signature and had developed a whole side business in false papers. I encountered many street children with great talents and learned expertise: One was an expert dancer, another recited poetry, another created and worked with puppets; another constructed elaborate moving replicas of things like a backhoe out of scrap wood and metal. This was in addition to their obvious skills in more common activities such as washing vehicles, vending, running errands, and unloading delivery trucks. While living in a family that had a number of *restavèk*, I asked one of them about her work; she proudly told me she knew how to do laundry very well. Another was proud of her cooking skills. Rather than being ashamed of their work or lacking self-esteem because of their status, the children had developed domains of expertise that they felt proud of and that gave them a strong sense of personal value.

Kervens

Kervens was 10. His father died in the 2010 earthquake and his mother brought him out to Les Cayes afterwards, leaving him with an "aunt" while she returned to Port-au-Prince. He has had no contact with her in the five years since then. There are also a lot of other kids living at the house where he is staying. He has never been to school. I asked what kind of work he did, and he said "everything"—he washed dishes, swept, did laundry, helped prepare food—whatever anyone asked him to do. He actually worked not just at the house where he was staying but at a number of other houses as well; they called him to do things for them in the mornings. They "paid" him with coffee and sometimes by giving him some food. Most days at noon he went swimming. He spent afternoons begging from customers at the beach bars, where he usually found people who gave him some food and/or money. When asked why he begs, he said that he does it so that he can buy things, like sandals. As far as his general treatment was concerned, he felt he was treated well at the house, though sometimes he was beaten by people on the street or the beach. He liked dogs and had one at home. He had a lot of friends and they usually hung out together.
I: What do you like to do?
K: I like to work.
I: What would you like to be?
K: I'd like to be a mechanic.
I: What thing would you like to change?
K: The thing that needs to change is for [us] to go to school.
I: Do you go to church?
K: Yes, I go to the Catholic church with people at my house. I pray a lot and I ask
   God to change my life.
   I decided to teach him to write his name. I asked him to sit at my table, and wrote out his name on a piece of paper. I then gave him a pencil and asked him to copy. With great care he tried to copy each letter as best he could. I did the

same for my name, then for a few other common nouns such as "plaj" (beach) and "kokoye"(coconut palm). One of the adult waiters nearby had noticed all this, and, probably trying to be helpful, came over to write "plaj" in English, Creole (again), and French. As soon as he did, however, Kervens dove under the table and hid. After the waiter left, he emerged and took a small stick and tried to copy his name and the words in the sand. He kept practicing; then a friend of his came over and joined him. Another boy joined them too, and they all practiced writing the words I had taught them in the sand. The next day, Kervens came and told me, with great pride, "I can write by myself!" (2015)

Though Kervens lacked schooling (and keenly desired it, like most of his peers), he was a capable and ambitious learner and had developed many capacities as a *restavèk*/street child. What struck me so powerfully was his love of work and relentless desire to prove himself of value through becoming expert in his everyday activities, as well as his eagerness to learn a schooled skill such as writing. Perhaps equally important was his ability to form and maintain relationships with multiple households where he worked. He was working and learning and creating an identity of value despite the circumstances of his life, though undoubtedly it was not an identity recognized or legitimated by society. It was held and nurtured within the domain of his private life.

Sophia

Sophia was a nine-year old restavèk *living at Mme Yveline's. Much of the time she was constantly being ordered or called to do something. She worked tirelessly taking care of all the household tasks. When I asked her (somewhat hesitatingly as I had feared she might feel ashamed), she was proud to show me where she slept—her "house" ("lakay mwen") as she called it. She took me to a tent out back behind the main house, with a piece of cardboard on the ground where she slept, along with another girl, little three year old Kenya, for whom she appeared to be the primary caretaker.*

Yet in the evenings, when the workday was done, she sat on Mme Yveline's lap and they shared some affectionate moments. I asked her why she came to Mme Yveline's and she told me simply that Mme "wanted" her. There was another older girl of 19 living and working there too, who was originally from Boucan, which she said was quite far. She came from a large family, she said, and was schooled only up to the fifth grade. I asked her if life was difficult for her here and she said, "No, I wanted to move here." So there were three non-biological children all living here who worked in the household. The three year old Kenya, I learned, was actually a neighbor's child, but she was living at Mme Yveline's. Even she worked— I often saw her sweeping the floors and fetching items that were needed.

> *I did not sense that the children were suffering or held against their will; in fact, they displayed great motivation and energy in their activities. Like Kervens, the girls were proud of their work in the household. It also seemed that working well could lead to a kind of informal membership in the family. I remembered that I had earlier met a young man of 20 who had been a restavèk for most of his life. He had told me it was not uncommon for the restavèk to stay with the host family even beyond the teen years, as bonds of affection had taken root through shared experiences of living together.*
>
> *M. Pierre told me his family had restavèk when he was growing up; they were sent to school. He shared a story about one boy who wrote his mother a long letter telling her he wasn't happy and that he wanted her to come and take him home. His parents discovered the letter and contacted the boy's mother and told her to come. She did come, but when she arrived she was angry and punished her son for wanting to come home instead of being thankful for the opportunities he had as a restavèk.*
>
> *I shared with M. Pierre a bit about Sophia, who, despite her relentless work load, would climb into her aunt's lap affectionately in the evenings. This was not so surprising, Pierre said. He told me that there was a very affectionate orphaned boy in his community who had adopted him. The boy, whose father had died, came up to him one day and said, "You are my father." (2013)*

Though learning to work well was clearly connected to becoming someone, just as important, if not more, was a kind of apprenticeship in social bonding, or emotional attachment, that emerged through the experiences of living and working in a host family. This appeared to be a kind of development of capacities to give and receive affection that transcended the circumstances of death or other loss of connection to biological family. A wide capacity for sociality, for bonding with others, related or not, seemed to lie at the heart of this learning. This bonding could be seen as an essential aspect of personhood that emerged in and through experiences of loss but that transcended them, leading children to a sense of themselves as capable not only in labor but in the emotional core of social life as it is lived in Haiti. One man, now grown and successful with a career as a teacher, told me of his experiences as a *restavèk* growing up. His father had had many women but had left him and his mother without support. His mother tried to earn money by having sex with other men, but she got pregnant again. So at that point she arranged for him to live as a *restavèk* in another household, but they didn't send him to school. So he left that family and found another to live with. He told me that while it was hard, he learned how to do a lot of things while living in these families. Of the things he had learned, I asked what was most important to him, and he said, "The experiences made me able to understand other people, how to treat them and relate to them" (RY Interview, 2012).

Walking with children

The children led me along footpaths that meandered among the homes in the area.
When we finally arrived at Widner's house he was proud to show me his garden of
plantings in front. He also took me around back and showed me the cooking fire,
with a chunk of wood that still held an ember—he blew on it to show me it was still
lit. In the yard there was a rock face, with many cracks in it, filled with what seemed
to be trash. But it turned out this was storage for useful items. Widner pulled out a
piece of bicycle tire inner tube, half of soda bottle that contained some sort of green
solution to clean shoes, and scraps of fabric. He also showed me his hoe.

Then, without skipping a beat, he showed me the electrical cords that were
used to beat him and the other children—draped over a bush, alongside drying
laundry. He and the other kids showed me their wounds. Widner had a freshly
bandaged leg wound, caused by the electrical cord. Lahens showed me the scars
on his arm and lifted up his shirt to show me a huge one across his belly—also
the result of being whipped with the electrical cord. Sometimes adults threw rocks
at them. They explained that the violence is a generational thing: their parents
experienced it from their parents. It was simply normal. (I was surprised to learn,
later, that Widner was a "timoun lakay" [a child of the house—not a restavèk].
It was clear that extremely harsh discipline was not something that only restavèk
might experience.)

As we walked through the area, I noticed that the kids were extremely attuned to
the trees, plants, and animals in the environment. They enjoyed naming them all for
me. When I asked about the medicinal uses of some of the plants, one immediately
pointed to a plant by the side of the path that was used for "la grippe" (flu/cold).
One of the young girls was quite explicit about how to prepare and use it; besides
boiling (to make tea) one could crush the leaves and make a kind of poultice to place
under the nose. The kids all contributed to the discussion. I told them I knew about
asosi (a medicinal plant often used to flavor klerin and to treat fever), and later
on our walk, one of the boys handed me a bunch that he'd collected along the way.

One objective of our walk was to show me a Mapou *[cottonwood tree]. They all*
knew its location. When we got there I was impressed with the girth and size of the
tree; the huge gnarled limbs were covered with aerophytes. I asked if we could leave
the path and go down to the tree but they said no; it had "bad spirits."[5]

When we returned to Widner's house, his mother was there, along with a friend
of his, looking very unhappy. Widner explained to me that the friend had been
severely beaten. Though Widner and the other kids were sympathetic, at the same
time it did not seem to be a big deal to them. I asked the reason for the beating: it
turned out his friend had overslept.

Afterwards, we all took another walk to visit the local spring, and on the way,
the kids asked me what I thought about the beating. I said I didn't like it; Widner

and the others agreed, and the mother agreed too, though she said she beat anyway,
even though she knows it's not good to do so. I asked her if she was beaten as a child
and she said yes, it's a habit; it's because she was beaten as a child, she beats. "But,"
she added, "it's important for the child to grow up well."

During an interview with Jude, now a relatively successful young man (who
had not been a restavèk), he shared that he was harshly beaten as a child at home
and at school. It is necessary, he said, to create "respect" for others in the child. At
school he was beaten for "dezòd" (talking about something not related to class);
a child could also be beaten for playing marbles (or other kinds of games) during
the school year (since these activities are reserved for summers only). According to
him, female teachers were the worst in terms of harsh discipline. Beating children
for misbehavior is a very common perspective in Haiti, he said, and it would be
difficult to change unless the "politics of childhood" were also to change—meaning
the government would need to undergo a sea change in its approach to childhood.
(2013)

Contrary to some of the advocacy and research literature that claimed *restavèk*
experienced significantly more physical abuse than other children, Widner told
me that biological kids were beaten as much as if not more than *restavèk*; I had
heard this from other children as well.[6] At first it was hard for me to reconcile
the violence that nearly all children experienced with their wonderful sociality
and affectionate manner. Combined with their extreme workloads—wouldn't
all that work and extremely harsh discipline result in kids who hated work, who
lacked motivation or aspiration, who complied with authority merely because if
they did not they would be punished? Would it not produce children who were
somehow emotionally compromised, with poor self-esteem, and unable to relate
well to others? Indeed, the dominant narrative was that these were slave children
whose childhood had been "stolen" from them: They were not growing up with
their birth parents, they were not being cared for in stable families; they were
harshly disciplined; they were often not going to school. They did not have adult-
child playtime; they did not have toys, they did not have the consistency needed
to develop so-called "healthy" attachments to caregivers.

And yet, here were children who displayed great affection, who had
enormous capacity for social bonding, and who were both capable and proud
of their abilities. They were keenly attuned to their environments, and displayed
extensive knowledge and learning about them. They grew up with the capacity
to navigate spaces far larger than their own households—households that
were almost never nuclear. They were always observing and always developing
competencies, whether in street-side vehicle repairs, making and selling food,

or performing small services for patrons in bars, restaurants, and markets. They were often primary caretakers for younger children. Eight- or nine-year-olds could shop and prepare full meals for their households. Adults sent even three-year-olds on errands alone to purchase things at markets, expecting proper change. Why do we see this as "stolen childhood," when the children themselves have approached these spaces as important learning opportunities, with evident agency, enthusiasm, and pride?

Becoming Someone: Teaching and Learning in Everyday Spaces

If one looks closely at the lives of youth and children in Haiti, one finds a rich tapestry of experience that belies the dominant narratives of children as "lacking childhood" or as growing up damaged and in need of rescue.[7] While going to school reflects a keen and often unfulfilled dream for disadvantaged children, and it is often considered the best route to becoming someone in society, in the absence of school, learning and goals for self-development do not simply disappear. Rather, learning is integrated into the experiences of everyday life, as children participate in ordinary activities alongside others. Events such as fixing a broken bicycle in the street become opportunities for learning, as children crowd around to observe a more skilled peer engage in the repair process. Children and youth will observe skilled adults at work, too. For example, at an outdoor car repair business by the side of the road near where I lived, there were always a few neighborhood boys who would regularly hang around and observe the car mechanics at work.[8] I frequently saw a toddler who lived down the street but whose mom dropped him off at the house during the day while she worked keenly engaged in observing the vehicle repairs. Observational learning is ongoing and constant as children move in and out of any number of activities and spaces during the day. It could be said that children are, in fact, exposed to a far more diverse set of opportunities for learning than the typical student confined to a classroom with a diet of rote memorization for a good part of the day.

In some cases, skilled adults may take on a child or youth as an apprentice to learn a particular trade or art. This appears to be the case for various arts such as traditional drumming (Wilcken, 2021, personal communication). In everyday life, one can also witness many occasions of coaching, where someone engaged in an activity will be given advice, help, or direction by an observer who is more knowledgeable or more experienced. This happened at the beach with Kervens, who coached his friends as they learned to write their names, and I saw many other instances that involved an older child helping a younger one to perform a skill, without adults hovering over or encouraging them. At one house where I stayed, a *restavèk* girl of about thirteen who went to school part-time would teach another four-year-old girl who lived in the house (and who also worked) how to write in the evenings, when both were done with their work for the day. I also observed younger children assisting those who were older: in one case, a boy of about ten offered advice to a slightly older youth with a long stick who was working with the electric power lines to a house, apparently in an effort to tap into the power grid. In another house where I stayed, a slightly older girl would help a younger one with schoolwork, both of them lying together on the floor in the afternoons. What was most significant was that except in cases of formal apprenticeship, these situations of mutual aid and peer coaching were not instigated, directed, or supervised by adults—they reflected children's autonomous self-motivation and caring engagement with others.[9]

A diffuse, socially egalitarian learning environment appears to characterize learning in everyday spaces—a relational environment that is quite different from the hierarchical environment that exists in formal schooling.[10] Beyond its importance in Vodou, this view of social egalitarianism in teaching and learning is in many ways at the core of social life in Haiti, as people learn and teach others through relationships and shared participation in everyday life activities, all within a context shaped by a profound consciousness of the ways the spiritual world intersects with and is ever-present in the natural and social environments.

Another socially significant setting for learning and teaching in Haiti are traditional forms of collective social organization, such as *konbit* (work groups), a variety of church groups (such as the *brigade*—youth groups in Protestant churches), branches of national/international organizations such as the Boy Scouts, and arts *atelier* (workshops). While their educational function is not often obvious, these settings serve as important arenas for skill development, mutual teaching and learning, and for achieving goals of personhood and social relational status.

A Haitian youth who was an active participant in the Haitian branch of the international world Scouting Association emphasized the educational role of the Scouts, describing them in this way:

> *Scouts are an auto-educational movement. Scouts are different from the "Brigades" that are the youth groups in Protestant churches; Scouts are inclusive of all religious orientations and they don't discriminate as to formal*

educational level. Scouts help youth learn to become better citizens to create a better society for tomorrow. They have numerous civic action projects, working in homes for aged, reforestation, and other environmental issues. They organize many activities and camps too for the street kids, some of which have spiritual focus. Many people ignore them [the street kids]. But we organize "kan de fomasyon ak animasyon"—training camps that include singing, dancing, crafts. We even had a project that was helping street kids learn skilled trades such as plumbing, masonry, electrical work. It was supported by a French organization. Participation was completely voluntary and we had many street kids involved.
(GR interview, 2016)

Some studies have suggested an important role for self-education among disadvantaged students who nevertheless persist in schooling. Botondo, Hensler, and Mazalon (2019) found that students independently self-organized into learning groups after school or on weekends that allowed them to do homework and study together, and that these groups reflected strong cultural values such as self-discipline, autonomy, cooperation, and solidarity with others.[11]

Far from being learned only in school or in the birth family, these values are cultivated through a rich landscape of childhood experience based on participation in community life, living and working in different households, and many forms of voluntary collective self-organization that can be said to reflect the diffused and culturally rich understanding of teaching and learning with deep roots in Haitian understandings of human development and spiritual life. Children's experiences must be seen against these larger forces and sources of value; when we do so, we find that the landscape of learning is rich, infused with multiple perspectives and diverse resources that contribute to the emergence of strong and capable identities. As Bolotta (2017) argues in the case of street children in Thailand, and as the children in Haiti showed me, there are multiple possibilities for self-formation beyond the natal family or the school.

The following account, cited here at length, captures many of the themes discussed earlier, as the Haitian author describes the talents and abilities of a *restavèk* who lived with his family:

Angelia, one of Auntie's (my great aunt) god-daughters . . . came to live with us as a restavek when she was 16 and I was seven.

A fascinating aspect of Angelia was that she could make things. She often acted on a whim: like the day she decided to reduce a mixture of milk, sugar, and an assortment of spices into my idea of heaven, or the spring she planted a vegetable garden, gave me my own pigeon peas, and awakened in me the idea that I could grow things. To my young mind, it seemed that everything Angelia needed, she made. She was a seamstress and master embroiderer who, in a few days, could turn a plain square of linen into a summer dress hemmed with a flower garden. When she needed oil for her hair, she simply collected some seeds and pressed them.

What to do? To make way for neo-liberalism, the Haitian family itself would have to be destroyed. The opportunity for an onslaught came in 1998, when a book by Jean-Robert Cadet recounted a harrowing life as a restavek. Mr. Cadet's experience is *entirely atypical* of the restavek system. He describes being transferred as a very young child to an abusive family. . . . What he describes is, at best, a perversion of this system of partial adoption, and at worst, rings untrue. His story, echoed by many, led to great outrage . . . and a declaration of the restavek system as being a form of child slavery. (Chery, 2014)

A Shift in Perspective: From Categories of Children to Experiences of Childhood

The spaces and experiences of learning and the personal capabilities and identities that animate marginalized children's lives are almost never accounted for in the popular media and advocacy literature. I myself had been greatly influenced by Cadet's narrative and, as I mentioned earlier, it was that book, more than anything, that had drawn me to Haiti initially with the goal of learning more about the lives of *restavèk* so that I could assist in projects to combat the practice. As I immersed myself in the field, however, I realized that the category was a kind of artifice: useful for NGOs or FBOs to identify a category of child who could attract donor funding, but one that hardly captured the larger context of children's experiences. Further, it was rarely used in Haiti among Haitians themselves (except when the word was used as an insult). I had heard it said that Haitians avoided talking about *restavèk*—the so-called "dirty little secret"— to avoid the shame associated with having one, or the shame associated on a general level with the practice when seen against the enlightened visions of childhood and children's rights shared by foreign and elite advocates of child protection. While possibly true, this reasoning did not seem to capture the way that "*restavèk*" was not really a category with great salience in people's everyday experience, in spite of the fact that it had taken on an outsize significance in the accounts of its detractors, both Haitian and white. All children work, and all suffer harsh physical punishment; many children move to live with other families when facing difficult circumstances, and even when they do not, because such movement is associated with perceptions of improved opportunity. Except when it was used to actively stigmatize someone, it wasn't something people worried about or even clearly agreed on as social category in their everyday experience—except among whites or those who worked with them, where it ironically became an index of stolen or lost childhood.

When the lens was broadened, one could see that children's experiences of marginality were in fact extremely diverse and constantly in flux—a fact often ignored in the ways *restavèk* had been characterized by whites as a clearly defined issue of slavery that required intervention. In my work I discovered many street children were former *restavèk* who had left because they were not treated well (cf Kovats-Bernat, 2006). Other children were for all intents and purposes living as *restavèk* but were not categorized or recognized as such (as noted by Pierre, Smucker, and Tardieu, 2009). In fact, I spent weeks living in and visiting households where children were clearly doing the great majority of labor within the household and who were subject to harsh discipline, did not go to school, and did not have any other sleeping arrangements other than cardboard on the floor. But the guardians did not consider (or, at least, did not label) the child a *restavèk*, even though the treatment the child experienced was no different from the standard portrayal of *restavèk* situations. There were "orphans" who were former *restavèk* and street kids who managed to get themselves into orphanages (seen as a better option); and some who also left orphanages to join other families. There was a constant circulation through a variety of living situations and it was not unheard of for kids to occupy all three of the statuses at different times or even sometimes some of them simultaneously.

To complicate this even further, among *restavèk* whether or not a child was in or out of school was also difficult to determine. While there were clearly cases where children never went to school, many had some schooling. Some went to part-time schools (often afternoon schools) and some had gone to regular schools. Some were in and out of school based on the resources they could summon. There were also cases where the child was considered to be "in school" even when they were not attending regularly, or at all.[12] Thinking in terms of clear categories, statuses, or types of victimization was thus impossible if one wanted to understand the landscape of childhood. I gradually realized that categories such as "*restavèk*" and "street child" that might be useful for research or advocacy imposed an analytical distance on children's experiences that interfered with grasping their meaning and significance. They were misleading in the sense that they distracted from the constantly shifting realities of children's lives as well as from the broader social and cultural contexts of childhood that shaped Haitian life.

It was only when I began to know children better that I was able to keep the categories or statuses from dominating my lens and begin to look at their experiences—especially, the experiences that shaped their learning and engagement with the world, and the ways in which these were strongly formed in relation to desire, will, and aspiration (see Chapters 7 and 8 for more discussion). Difficult situations and hard lives with birth parents—parents separating, dying, and lacking resources to support or "help"—seem to lead children to see any place other than the family of origin as a potentially better option for a future. Schooling was often an expressed desire, for it was the surest path toward socially recognized status or value; but even in the absence of schooling, neither the learning nor the aspirations for becoming persons disappeared, and youth built on their experiences in alternative spaces to learn for themselves and educate themselves toward personhood and hoped-for futures.

It is ironic that these desires and capacities have gone unrecognized and unvalued, invisiblized by white agents of rescue and development who would give children back their childhoods. Because they have internalized images and ideals of a privileged, protected middle-class childhood, where play and schooling represent the only proper experiences for children, they fail to see the learning that happens outside of such spaces. Instead, children's experiences outside the domains of the nuclear family and school are represented as deficient and damaging. Certainly this process of negative representation is not only the product of white discourse imposed on Haitian childhood but also a reflection of the neocolonial epistemological heritage that continues to undergird Haitian society. This is a lens that validates models of elite, formal schooling that are inaccessible for the vast majority, yet still highly valued as pathways to status. White saviors are complicit in this project, however, because they, too, reduce education to schooling, casting shadows over the alternative spaces of self-development that are claimed by the most marginalized, and that can also, in some cases, represent spaces of resistance[13].

What the aforementioned narratives illustrate is, on the contrary, the abiding importance of ways of learning that connect oneself to others and that prioritize learning in private domains and in social settings of ordinary life. In this sense they illustrate the struggles of fugitivity, a condition that arises when a dominant institution, society, or epistemology indexes or marks others and their practices as inferior or unworthy. One's sense of selfhood necessarily moves underground, to alternative spaces, where it can better thrive away from the foreigners' gaze and apart from the damning visions of proper education, proper family, and proper childhood imposed from without. The latter inevitably refract Haitian experience and render it "less than." Fugitivity is thus a way to protect one's ways of being from the efforts of others to dominate and control.

In the neocolonial space of stolen childhood and white saviorism in Haiti, then, the captive is also the fugitive: educating, learning, and becoming occur in unrecognized spaces, away from the gaze of white saviors and others. Education in fugitivity is always an education toward personhood, especially when it occurs in the shadows of colonialist domination that is bent on conforming the identities of those it marginalizes to its own visions of selfhood. As Leigh Patel writes, "Learning is both maintained and protected, even when it has been forbidden, foreclosed, and seemingly withered through colonialism . . . educators have much to learn about learning itself and that much of that learning must come from beyond brick and mortar schools." (Patel, 2019: 256).

If children have had their childhood stolen from them, they could not be learning or educating themselves; they would not be engaged in and with their social and natural environments, becoming full persons of great capacity, agency, sociability, and fortitude. To see marginalized children and youth in Haiti as victims of poverty, society, or improper parenting and family life is to deny the salience and value of Haitian childhood, as it exists, to Haitian constructions of personhood. And it is also, once again, to impose a neocolonial view of what knowledge is valuable, that supports the existing social class inequalities that afflict the delivery of education in the formal system.

This is not, of course, to dismiss the significance of the latter, nor to claim that childhood is full of rosy, self-affirming experiences. It is not; children struggle with social exclusion, lack of access to school, and with caretakers who do not meet their needs. These are persistent structural conditions that have had undeniable effects on children as individuals and on their communities. But this is not the same as "not having a childhood." Indeed, denying children "childhood" is not the fault of Haitian parents, society, or global poverty; it is the work of those whose limited vision imposes erasure on the lives of those whom they purportedly seek to rescue. Arguably, if they had listened to and learned from the children and youth around them, those who claim childhood is "stolen" would look back at themselves and recognize their own role in the construction of its disappearance.

My last evening in Haiti, Natalie and I decided to go to an outdoor music cafe. After a while, Natalie had to leave and the two young men who had befriended us sat down at my table. Along with most of the other patrons they sang along with the Haitian rap music, every note, pause and word in perfect cadence. As the music and the singing continued, one of the youths asked me to teach him some Italian—I had no idea why. After some time, we moved into an English lesson with me writing down the English translations of expressions he gave me in French. Soon an elderly man with a shock of long, white hair came up and wordlessly leaned against the balustrade next to my table. We nodded in greeting. He remained there, immobile and silent, watching closely as I continued to write down English translations of the French words provided by the young man at my table.

As this activity continued, I noticed a boy dancing in the street. He was extremely talented; he picked up every nuance of the music and change in rhythm perfectly, performing a great variety of steps and original movements. According to one of the young men with me, the boy was a street kid who was something of a friend whom he looked out for; the kid had left his parents in some village to seek his own fortune.

As the music boomed, the boy danced, the motorcyles idled, and the smoke from the street-side barbeque vendors rose to fill the air, I sat teaching Italian and English in a bar, to a youth who wanted to learn and had found himself a teacher, and to an old man, who was looking on and learning in his own way.

5

Bringing Them "Home"
Children and the Remaking of Family in Haiti

The youngest of the children spent their days in metal cribs, lined up in large rooms. They were fed and changed. If visitors came, they were held. The older ones, and perhaps the healthier ones, played freely in a yard outdoors, and they did so vigorously. But then there was an older girl, kept in a crib with the toddlers. Smiling beautifully, she stood and held out her arms to me as I passed by, once, twice, three times. I couldn't leave without holding her. I picked her up and she melted into me; I could feel her ribs beneath her shirt. After some time I put her down, but as I did so, her sobs began, so I stood her on her feet in the crib and held her against me again for many minutes. I saw her glance out at the other children in the yard—the children her own age. Perhaps there was hope. Malachy, the boy who had been accompanying me on my visit (and whose role there was unclear—he seemed to be hanging around so that he could practice English with foreign visitors though he might have had other responsibilities), told me she was six, but that she was placed here with the toddlers because she "refused to play." By this time, my eyes were teary. At this point, Malachy left us, saying he knew I would send him the dictionary he had requested. The girl leaned into me and held on even more tightly. A Sister arrived with cups of milk on a tray; as she gave one to the girl, I noticed that around her other hand there was a tightly wound black leather belt. (2008)

I had visited the orphanage, run by the Sisters of Charity, with parishioners traveling as part of a twinning missions trip organized by my church.[1] Along with the other volunteers, I played with some of the older kids and held infants in the nursery. We foreigners were major playthings for the kids. They swarmed over me, hugging me, playing with my hair and the buttons on my sweater. At one point I had four kids in my lap while a group of others stood behind me, waiting for their turn. There was laughter and much horseplay. The children were clearly enjoying this occasion to interact with the visiting *blan*. The event felt something like a show—a performance with which the children were quite familiar.

According to child development psychologists, kids running up to foreigners in orphanages is a sign of disordered attachment. As one missionary wrote of her own experience:

> A child ran up to me and jumped in my arms, clinging tightly to my neck. This ostensibly loving gesture was a clear sign of attachment disorder, which leads some kids to display excessive familiarity and affection with strangers. . . . Desperation parading as affection. Severe neglect made manifest in clutching arms and legs that wouldn't let go. There were no adults present. The oldest child, likely around 14, was left in charge of the children. I came to learn that the children were locked in their rooms at night. Also, that most of the children were not actually orphans, but remembered their parents and where they came from. I was sick with grief and anger. (Thompson, 2017)

Despite the ostensible similarities in our experiences, I did not sense that the kids who ran up to me and hugged me at the orphanage had "attachment disorders." In fact, quite the opposite—they were full of cheerful enthusiasm, and seemed to take much fun in hanging on to me and the other *blan*. Even the older girl in the crib who so desperately clung to me could have been expressing a longing for attention and affection—quite normal needs, given the circumstances. Like many of the children in orphanages in Haiti, which have long served as channels for overseas adoptions, she was no doubt quite aware that whites came to orphanages to adopt children, and so why shouldn't she attempt to express affection? Why couldn't her behavior be seen as strategic rather than disordered?[2] Indeed, if anything, the children seemed more than capable of expressing emotions and relating to others as they interacted with energy and cheer on the playground and organized themselves in "taking turns" with the *blan*. This is not to say that this orphanage, or many others like it, was well run or provided optimal care. The belt wound around the nun's hand was a clear sign that harsh physical discipline was used when deemed necessary. Confinement of young children to cribs for long hours of the day, without opportunities for social engagement, was certainly not optimal, and could be considered abusive.

In Haiti, as in many other resource-poor settings around the world, it is estimated that 80 percent of the children in orphanages have living parents; that is, they are "poverty orphans," placed there by a parent or relative lacking the means to support them. A study conducted by the Haitian national child protection and welfare institute (Insitit du Bien-être Social et de Recherches [IBESR], as reported in Lumos, 2015; 2017) revealed extremely poor conditions in many of the approximately 760 orphanages in the country (only 35 of

760 were given a rating of acceptable) and widespread misuse of donor funds. In response to a perceived dramatic rise in the number of orphans following the 2010 earthquake, many orphanages had been established that were little more than businesses, often set up to participate in lucrative foreign adoptions. At the same time, despite the often horrendous conditions in these institutions, North American Christian donors regularly provided millions of dollars of support.

In response to this situation, and reflecting a growing global consensus on the dangers of institutionalized orphan care, in 2014 the Government of Haiti enacted new policies to prohibit the construction of new orphanages, restrict the number of foreign agencies allowed to operate in Haiti, and restrict numbers of international adoptions, with the aim of complete de-institutionalization of children by 2030. Working with a few major international organizations such as the Lumos Foundation (UK), Bethany Christian Services, Terre des Hommes (Switzerland), and other Canadian and US faith-based organizations, IBESR's goal has been to revamp Haiti's child welfare system, using these organizations alongside their connections to local donor-supported churches to promote a new family care model for children in Haiti. The primary goal is reunification of children with birth parents whenever possible. If that is not possible, the goal is to place the child with extended family, or, finally, in family foster care. Adoption and orphanage care are recognized as necessary in some cases but strongly de-emphasized. The goal is to support birth families with healthy models of functioning where children feel safe and are protected.[3] Parental training and coaching for reunification and foster care as well as ongoing supervisory visits by social workers are considered critical. IBESR's goal is one standardized family care/foster care system, in which it works alongside the international FBOs in selection and training of foster families as well as providing regulatory oversight.

This shift toward family reunification over support for orphanage care has begun to have a significant impact in Haiti, as many faith-based organizations have shifted their missions toward this newer model, reflecting an emergent global consensus on the value of family for children's well-being. Yet it is important to ask what "family reunification" actually means across different contexts where family has historically and culturally been understood through multiple lenses and with different meanings and significance. What model of family and family relationships are being assumed in "family reunification"? How do these understandings relate to and frame Haitian lives and experiences? A critical cultural perspective is important because this discourse and the interventions associated with it have practical as well as representational power, and they refract Haitian culture and cultural experiences in certain ways that may not, as many assume, be relevant or beneficial to either children or the society as a whole.

This chapter offers a critical cultural reading of narratives on family reunification in Haiti, revealing how this approach privileges Northern assumptions about proper parenting and family life. While child well-being is the ostensible (and laudable) goal, it is inevitably bound up with questions of representational privilege, political aims, and global discourses. Not only are these norms a mismatch with realities in Haiti, they construct Haitian families and childhood as deficient in comparison with Northern norms. The argument, in this case, is not about whether family care is better for children than orphanage care; it may well be. Rather, it is about what model of family is at stake. This critique hinges on how formulations of biological parenthood are being imposed unthinkingly on Haitian lives in an effort to remedy them by conforming them to Northern, socially privileged constructions of proper family life and child development. One might say that saving orphans has begun to shift toward what is perceived as a more impactful agenda: saving the family. Efforts to operationalize this idea in Haiti both encourage deficit constructions of Haitian culture and reposition Haiti as a place to be governed by enlightened transnational actors.

Projections: Mainstream Psychology and the Genesis of Haitian Childhood Deficit

The easy jump to labeling Haitian children in orphanages as suffering from attachment disorders is but one instance of the power of white outsiders, armed with knowledge of mainstream child development psychology, to characterize the development of poor, black children as pathological (and thereby, of course, to generate a role for themselves as "saviors" of those children). Generated largely through research on and in WEIRD (Western, Educated, Industrialized, Rich, and Democratic) populations, mainstream psychology and its sub-field, child development psychology, privilege models of human mental and emotional functioning that assume that the ways white, middle-class people's minds work are representative of those of the rest of the world. However, as previously mentioned, Henrich, Heine, and Norenzayan (2010) pointed out that mainstream psychology is based almost entirely on research with subjects from WEIRD societies. Not only are WEIRD subjects unrepresentative of the rest of humanity, they are often outliers. Arnett (2008) argued that while American psychology produces research findings that are supposedly applicable to the whole of the human species, its research is based on only 5 percent of the world's population—those living in the United States. In the light of these critiques, in 2017 the American Psychological Association itself adopted a policy resolution toward promoting more "global perspectives" in psychological research, pointing out that its assessment methods and samples have been widely used around the world but without consideration of cultural differences that affect validity (APA, 2017).

In the field of child development, specifically, consciousness of cultural bias in many of the claims that are regarded as universals of child development has been expanding in recent years. Attachment theory is one of a number of these child development orthodoxies that have been challenged.[4] While widely taken as universally relevant (see Keller, 2018), attachment theory has been subject to a number of critiques that illustrate how cultural contextual factors, including parental cultural goals for learning and development, as well as economic circumstances and other important aspects of local ecology, shape children's experiences and cultural goals for development in important ways, leading to results that challenge the universal relevance of these theories. For example, Norman and LeVine (2008) have shown, using evidence from Germany, that standardized measures of attachment reveal that two-third of German babies are "insecurely attached." According to the theory, this would mean that two-third of German children are at risk of personality disorders. Rejecting this interpretation, they point out that German mothers are guided by a cultural model of development that stresses child self-reliance and avoidance of giving excessive parental attention; what the assessments instead reveal is a cultural process that is producing children with the dispositions appropriate to the German context, that when seen through the lens of the theory, appear problematic. They conclude that the basic concepts of attachment research (secure vs. insecure attachment and maternal sensitivity vs. insensitivity) are moral judgments that reflect an American cultural ideology that when applied to other cultural contexts result in inappropriate characterizations of other cultures as pathological.

Numerous studies and reviews of attachment literature demonstrate that attachment theory represents a Western, middle-class orientation to personhood that is inappropriately applied in other cultural contexts where the goals for child development and the social-ecological settings in which children develop are quite different (Bolotta, 2017; Keller, 2013, 2018; Otto and Keller,2014; Quinn and Mageo, 2013; Schmidt, Keller, and Rosabal Coto, 2021). This research has shown how the assumptions of necessary emotional bonding and demonstrative affection between caretakers and children are not universally practiced; and, further, strong emotional attachment to a single (ideally, biological) caretaker is neither expected nor culturally supported (Alber, 2003; Gottlieb, 2009; Keller, 2013; see also Norman and LeVine, 2008; Penn, 2009).[5] In fact, children may be socialized to avoid attachment to primary caretakers such as mothers, and mothers to avoid expressing emotion to children; children may be socialized to be very friendly to strangers and thus display no stranger anxiety, and parental responsiveness can be defined quite differently according to cultural context. In sum, normative expectations for children's socio-emotional development are highly culturally variable and they often do not look like the norms and ideals promoted by mainstream developmental psychology. Yet, children in such societies grow up well-adjusted and with normal social-emotional competencies valued by their communities.

In the case of Haiti, then, given the lack of both anthropological and culturally adapted psychological research on children and childhood, we cannot know whether large numbers of children who spend time in orphanages are suffering from attachment disorders. Ethnographic research on street children in Haiti and elsewhere, who are also growing up largely outside family care, suggests on the contrary that despite the recognized dangers of street life, such children possess high levels of resilience, that they develop strong social-emotional relationships with peers, and that their mental health is often no worse than that of children living with families (Aptekar, 1991; Gebretsadik, 2017; Hecht, 1998; Kovats-Bernat, 2006; Offit, 2008). Cenat et al. (2018) showed that while street children experience multiple traumas such as neglect, maltreatment, and abuse, similar to the kinds of things that children might experience in orphanages, the vast majority showed self-efficacy in responding to traumatic experience, presenting a level of resilience between moderate and very high. When research on children in orphanages takes careful account of the socioeconomic and cultural context, findings reveal levels of resilience and overall mental health that are no worse than those of children living in family care (Whetten et al., 2009). A possible explanation is that in Haiti, where children are often raised apart from their biological parents, their capacities for social and emotional bonds are cultivated across a wide and diverse social field rather than focusing on a single dyadic relationship with one parent or caretaker (see also Clermont-Mathieu and Nicholas, 2015). This points to a great need for social and cultural contextualization of research on vulnerable children and specifically for more qualitative and ethnographic work on questions of children's health and development that considers the important mediating factors of cultural and social context on developmental outcomes.

What is not in question, however, is the ready availability of "attachment disorder" as a popular diagnostic among white actors in Haiti to frame Haitian children's development. It is readily applied by many whites in Haiti with good intentions to "help." The problem is that the application of mainstream psychology and its privileging of white middle-class norms of functioning in contexts where they are not relevant is almost guaranteed to result in mischaracterizations of Haitian children's behavior and development.

Reunification: Toward Nuclearizing "Broken" Haitian Families

Pathologies of attachment in the development of Haitian children in orphanages are deeply connected to broader representations of Haitian families as "weak" or "broken." The broken Haitian family discourse runs throughout reunification advocacy (see Hoffman, 2021a), and it characterizes weak families in Haiti as the root of Haiti's social problems. While poverty is often recognized as the reason parents separate from children and thus parents are not blamed for placing their children in an orphanage, the broken family is identified as the proximate target of external interventions. The assumption is that bringing children back to their biological parents builds stronger, healthy families, where children feel safe and loved and can experience healthy attachments. It is a discourse that has circulated widely among major global child protection organizations.[6] While de-institutionalization advocacy explicitly recognizes a "continuum of care" that includes extended family care and foster homes, it prioritizes the nuclear family as the ideal family type (Brown, Cohon, and Wheeler, 2002; Faith to Action Initiative, 2022; Save the Children, 2012). Reflecting this view, the Haitian national strategy for child protection clearly affirms the child's right to the knowledge, affection, and material support of biological parents (IBESR, 2015: 2), while also noting that the biological family appears to be in crisis due to poverty and other social problems. These factors are considered to have led to an abandonment of parental responsibility on the part of birth parents who are "not invested in their role" (Gallie and Marcellus, 2013: 35), resulting in high rates of parent-child separation (Ashley et al., 2019; Udy, 2014: 67).

Reuniting children with birth parents is thus the first priority of the child protection strategy since this is where the child is assumed to be best protected, despite the irony that in Haiti birth parents are the most common perpetrators of physical violence against children (Flynn-O'Brien et al., 2016). Indeed, in my own work with children separated from their birth families, whether currently in the streets or living with another family, a persistent theme was that the child had left the birth family to escape parental beatings or parents who failed to provide for the child's basic needs (see also Chapter 8). The great majority of children expressed the idea that when parents do not support or "help" the child, the child should leave and find a better situation, whether that be an orphanage, the streets, or another domestic situation (Hoffman, 2010a; 2012a; 2012b). Other research in resource-poor settings has demonstrated that "Living with one's family can be one of the riskiest locations for a child . . . where abuse is more abundant than food" (Kenny, 1999: 384, quoted in Lancy, 2010: 449). The fact that the birth family in Haiti is the setting in which children are most likely to experience violence clearly goes against the reunification discourse that represents the birth family as the safest and most "protected" environment for children.

As partners with the Haitian government, organizations working in the field of child protection emphasize a logic of stabilization: bringing the child home stabilizes the family, and stable, intact families can create a strong community and society, as can be readily seen in mission statements of organizations involved in family reunification efforts:

> Focusing on the whole child leads to healthy, stable adults able to care for their own families. Thus increasing overall community stability for generations. . . . Maintaining children in their families and communities must be the first step towards social balance in Haiti.(Gleason, Cox, and Pop, 2016: 10–11)

> We work to . . . restore broken family systems. . . . Our services empower each client to meet their own individualized goals for sustaining themselves and their families. (HM, 2020)

> Through our family hope program, we strive to build healthy relationships between children and their families . . . empowering them toward the independent care of their children. . . . It is great to see families reconciled, strengthened, and reunified! (CHI, 2020)

> At MLS, we believe in keeping families together. Our goal is to encourage mothers and fathers to feel empowered and equipped to raise their children in their home as a family. (MLS, 2020)

> What if we could allow [a mother's] children to live in her loving care, understanding that they belong to a family? [Our] family strengthening program can help not just one but several generations. (IM, 2020)

The explicit goal of family reunification is to transform Haitian society by fixing broken, unstable, and unhealthy families to produce a stable and autonomously functioning family unit. These reunited families are then able to serve as the building blocks for a transformed Haitian society.

One of the major ideas behind white iterations of the "broken family" is its supposed lack of love: the idea is that children need to be brought home not just to any family but to "loving families" and "loving homes." Drawing directly on ideas of Haitian child and family emotional deficits as described earlier, the supposed lack of love in children's lives is attributed to broken and unstable family relationships that can be remedied by whites working toward remaking the Haitian family as a space of love and affection:

> *We help families to bring their children home . . . so children can be raised in loving families. . . . The most important thing . . . is to keep that family unity in place. . . . Every child rescued from an orphanage in Haiti and brought home to a loving family is creating a future for this county.* [Photo showing child writing on a blackboard, "I love my family."] (Lumos Foundation, 2020)

> *Our first priority in Haiti is keeping children stable and safe with their family of origin. When that's not possible, we find local foster families who can provide a loving home . . . so that children can thrive.* (Bethany Christian Services, 2020)

> *Our vision . . . is centered around keeping Haitian families together. . . our goal is to protect children who have been orphaned by pursuing a loving family for each one.* (CoP, 2020)

Photos of smiling mothers and fathers embracing their children often accompany these statements. A promotional video for family-based foster care posted on a website for one large organization working in partnership with IBESR (Bethany Global, 2020) captures this ideal of the stabilized, reunified, loving family: one sees a Haitian family where both mother and father are present and at home; parents are shown sitting at the table talking with kids; parents are portrayed as children's partners, sharing activities with the child such as supervising homework. Both mother and father are shown playing with the child (with balloons, no less!). A "family dinner" shows parents sitting down to eat with their children. The video places the child at the physical as well as emotional center of the family, symbolized most powerfully in the final scene of a family hug, with the child squeezed between the parents in a loving embrace.

This representation of family life reflects an ideal of the nuclear, upper-middle-class two-parent family, characterized by notions of the "precious" child who is at the emotional center of family life (Zelizer, 1994), where parents believe in the value of play with children and have the leisure and resources to do so (Lancy, 2007), and parents serve as pedagogical coaches, reflecting an upper-middle-class ideology of family life centered on "concerted cultivation" (Lareau, 2003). Yet this model of family life is not common in resource-poor settings in many parts of the world, and it is even uncommon among many poor and working-class communities in North America. In Haiti, typically fathers are often absent from the household; parents do not play with their children, nor do they relate to children as pedagogical coaches or "homework supervisors"; parents and children do not regularly sit down at the dining table to eat together and share "family time." As can be expected, given the central role of Northern faith-based and international child welfare organizations in enacting family foster care in Haiti, the video reflects Northern ideals of the healthy family that are circulated as best practices in international child protection/welfare and held up to Haitians as the ideal toward which they should strive. Significantly, it is the *child-at-home* who is positioned at the center of this process: it is the child brought home who has the capacity to stabilize the "broken" Haitian family and re-establish the stability/health of the community.

The idea that the nuclear family is best for children has long been present in international discourse on vulnerable childhoods, and it has deep roots in the globalization of norms regarding childhood and child welfare (Archambault, 2010; Chin, 2003; Penn, 2009) and state building (McEwen, 2017). However, as Chin (2003: 310) argues, the nuclear family ideal is not universally valued or practiced; indeed, it is unattainable in resource-poor societies despite the desire of governments to promote it as evidence of their democratic progress and legitimacy. As McEwen (2017) argues in the case of pro-family politics in Africa, the nuclear family ideal exerts a hegemonic force on local governments and communities that must be confronted in the resistance against neocolonial practices and policies.

The Haitian Reality: A Different Lens

In great contrast to the earlier images, Haitian family life has for the most part never prioritized the ideal of two biological parents raising their offspring in a nuclear household. Haiti's social landscape is deeply marked by social class inequalities and urban-rural divides, as well as high levels of economic constraint that shape families and households in powerful ways. Fluid household composition, child circulation/fosterage, and traditions of distributed/shared childrearing are long-standing patterns in Haiti, reflecting both cultural traditions such as the *lakou* (shared household residential compound, with spiritual and psychological significance), as well as responses to a variety of stressors, including food insecurity, loss of income, parental death, and divorce or separation. As described earlier, internal migration of both adults and children due to economic or educational needs or perceived opportunities is exceedingly common.

Further, in Haiti the family is not reducible to the household, as Fjellman and Gladwin (1985) note. Biological family members do not always live together even when their relationships are intact; and an extensive anthropological literature on Caribbean family systems, including Haiti, identifies practices of child circulation and fosterage as an important adaptation to difficult and demanding environments (Smucker and Murray, 2004: 15). In this context, family is understood as an inclusive, corporate concept that in real terms functions as an extensive network of people not necessarily connected through blood; kinship ties can be created by sharing resources, residence, help, or labor (Sommerfelt, 2002: 24). Except perhaps among the educated and socially privileged classes, and often enough even within them, childrearing follows an allo-parenting model that relies on shared childrearing (sometimes in the context of the *lakou,* [Edmond, Randolph, and Richard, 2007; Nicholas, 2014]), as well as the intergenerational obligations and relationships (such as god-parentage) that are highly significant to Haitian ideals of family. Children may be raised preferentially by a grandmother or god-parent rather than by the birth mother, and as discussed earlier, they are regularly sent to live for periods of time in other households, serving as companions or as helpers. Demonstrative emotional interactions between parents and children are not expected and children are trained from an early age to contribute to the family through chores and other forms of household labor, including preparation of meals, cleaning, and marketing, or, in rural areas, animal husbandry. Children spend most of their time when not working or in school in peer groups, away from adult supervision. These patterns of childrearing are unexceptional and can be found among many societies around the world. Yet, in the discourse of family reunification, these patterns reflect the "broken" family that lacks love and stability and needs remaking along Northern middle-class lines.

Informal Fosterage in Haiti: Another View

In faith-based discourse the idea that Haitian families are broken and inappropriate environments for children's emotional development stems in part from the perception that Haitian practices of informal fosterage that involve sending children away from birth parents are risky for children, due to the presence of the *restavèk* system. As described earlier, *restavèk* is often considered to be a form of modern slavery (Terre des Hommes, 2013). This is a key reason why Haiti is thought to need a "professionalized" system of fosterage that can work against current Haitian practices of informal fosterage. Organizations are clear about the need to develop "firm distinctions" between Haitian traditions of informal fosterage and the new professionalized and "internationally recognized practice of foster care" (Gleason, Cox, and Pop, 2016: 25).

Yet by casting traditional systems of informal fosterage as unhealthy or risky for children, or more generally as a reflection of weak or broken family system, family reunification advocacy fails to consider the locally conceptualized advantages of such placements: opportunity for children's upward social mobility through increased opportunities for formal schooling, as well as the equally significant cultural value attached to informal learning of skills, competencies, personal dispositions, and habits of character that connect to aspirations for full personhood in Haitian society (as described in Chapter 4). As mentioned earlier, studies suggest that families and children themselves consider living with another family as an *opportunity* for the child to advance in life rather than a step downward into servitude (Schwartz, 2003; Sommerfelt, 2002; 2015; Smucker and Murray, 2004).

Most importantly, the circulation of children to other families is strongly connected to ideals of family growth and solidarity across time and place (see Nicholas, 2014). In contrast to the ideal of the autonomous, child-centered nuclear family widely promoted in the Global North, the ideal Haitian family is not nuclear, inward-facing, or child-centered; it is rather realized through obligations and cultivation of relationships across a wide terrain of social and geographic space—goals that are integrally related to and achieved through the practice of child movement away from birth parents. The wide and shifting terrain of the non-nuclear, non-biological family and household can be read as an important avenue for achievement both in terms of social status as well as in a practical sense of maximizing opportunity for both adults and children.[7]

In Haiti, then, beyond their affective value, families are expected to serve as networks of possibility and opportunity for both adults and children as they attempt to make lives for themselves in difficult circumstances. In opposition to the image of Haitian families as "weak" or broken when children grow up apart from birth parents, the strong family in Haiti is the one where children are raised in and exposed to an ever-widening sphere of relationships and opportunities beyond those provided by birth parents. As Billy and Klein (2019) argue, parental voluntary separation from children in Haiti is not an index of disinvested or irresponsible parenting; it is instead an index of the opposite: a sense that the child sent elsewhere will be the family's golden child, the child who will in fact save the family through his or her capacity to extend the family outward in new spaces that promise new resources for the future. This rationale supports both placement of children into *restavèk* situations as well as sending them into orphanages where the hope often is that they will be adopted. While this looks to whites like a severing of the parental bond, for Haitians it is not conceptualized in this manner; it is rather considered an expression of confidence in the continuation of a family that does not depend on parents and children living together for its survival. This vision of family is in great contrast to the individualization and spatial localization that is tacit in the empowered "parent"/nuclear family model reflected in reunification discourse.

In sum, the "broken" Haitian family discourse is built on an amalgam of inaccurate and deficit representations concerning Haitian culture, childhood, and parenting, fueled by the science of mainstream developmental psychology, that fails to account for the powerful role of cultural and social context in human development and thereby imposes tacit moral judgments on societies that pursue alternative views of what constitutes childhood and family. In the guise of building a stronger society in Haiti, one can read a transnational effort, led by NGOs and FBOs with the support of the Haitian government, to reform the most basic arenas of Haitian life, childhood, and family, and to impose a more Western, Northern ideal of social functioning. This process ultimately solidifies the position of Haiti as a society in need of white rescue.

Concepts and Theory: Disadvantaged Childhoods and Neoliberal Governance

How does the case of Haiti speak to the larger paradoxes of neoliberalism as it intersects with global ideologies and practices of development? Recent trends in thinking about disadvantaged childhoods point to the role of neoliberalism and its impact on impact on framing globalization of ideas about child protection and child welfare (Burman, 2012; Cheney and Ucembe, 2019; Cooper, 2017; Mahon, 2010; Stooke, 2014). Family and childhood—and especially those families and children deemed vulnerable—are key arenas for the enactment of neoliberal policies via responsibilization, standardization, surveillance, monitoring for compliance, and positioning children as human capital/investments for national economic development (Balagopalan, 2008; Sims, 2017). As Keddell (2018: 94) writes: "The vulnerable child discourse and its related concepts are refracted through a neoliberal responsibilization agenda aimed at their parents. . . . In this way, vulnerability is deployed as a mechanism of governance that impacts differentially on different groups of children and their families in contact with the child protection system." In this process of parental responsibilization, the nuclear family model assumes a valuable role, since it can be more easily subjected to an increase in surveillance, accountability, and other mechanisms of internal and external social control.

Further, despite the apparent "retreat of the state" in contemporary forms of neoliberalism, as Ferguson and Gupta (2002: 989) point out, the state as a governing force does not really disappear; rather, its functions are transferred to transnational actors and organizations:

> [New] modes of government are being set up on a global scale. These include not only new strategies of discipline and regulation . . . but also transnational alliances forged by activists and grassroots organizations and the proliferation of voluntary organizations supported by complex networks of international and transnational funding and personnel. The outsourcing of the functions of the state to NGOs and other non-state agencies . . . is a key feature, not only of the operation of national states, but of an emerging system of transnational governmentality.

This argument is of particular salience in Haiti, where the outsourcing of the state's role to NGOs and FBOs has been well documented (e.g., Edmonds, 2013; Schuller, 2007; 2012; Kristoff and Panerelli, 2010). I argue that the new model of family-based care in Haiti, supported by international organizations and FBOs in alliance with the Haitian state, represents a further development of this transnational governmentality, as families are reformed along state-sanctioned internationalized norms. The social and regulatory operations are no fewer; but now they are managed differently, flowing from transnational sources through local actor assemblages.

Faith-based actors play an important role in this process. The vast majority of actors in the family care movement are affiliated with Christian faith-based missions and churches. This is no accident, of course, not only because of the dominance of Christian organizations in the aid and assistance landscape in Haiti but also because in Haiti Christianity has long been positioned as key to societal development and uplift by evangelical Protestants, including both whites and Haitians, who see the all the ills of the nation as originating in its historical connection to and continued overshadowing by Vodou, as Louis (2019) and

McAlister (2012) have pointed out. The consequences of Haiti's "pact with the devil" (Louis, 2019) during the formation of the Haitian nation are, in this view, being played out continually in Haiti's supposed inability to develop; childhood and family are key grounds for the enactment of spiritual warfare (McAlister, 2012) against forces of evil that afflict contemporary society.

From the perspective of those active in the family preservation movement, the logic is that the broken family is the root of the broken society and state (not the reverse); thus if you reconstruct families you can virtually reconstruct the society and, ultimately, the state. The principal domain of action is the family, to be remodeled along the lines of the Northern nuclear ideal predicated on love and stability. Further, the stable family depends on stabilized individual selves: children's lives are stabilized once they are "brought home" to families headed by fathers, and fathers themselves come home to assume roles as "protectors" (echoing the important role of the father as leader/protector in the Christian family): "Bethany strongly believes in the role of men in family preservation and family based care. Fathers play a crucial role in the protection of families in Haiti . . ." (Gleason et al., 2016: 27).

In this way, the Haitian cultural practices of solidarity across generations and spaces are reformulated toward ideals of affective bonding and solidarity within the nuclear family. It is ironic that the cultural and economic pressures to provide greater opportunity that underlie parental and child mobility in the first place are now reinforced, and perhaps worsened, as all responsibility now falls on the reunited or re-constituted nuclear family to provide that opportunity. This is especially the case for families that have given children to orphanages or other families in the first place with the objective of growing and strengthening their future resources, who are now expected (often with marginal livelihood support) to now take such children back, albeit with "improved" parenting skills and supervision.

Fundamentally, this neoliberal-Christian model produces family as a key domain for societal transformation, in which moving children (and moving parents) are fixed "at home," through a process of social-spatializing: replacing local norms of distributed family, flexible households, and circulating children with norms of fixed, stable, cemented nuclear families. These reconstructed families are supposed to function as autonomous units, separated from the larger social network of kin and relations across time and space, while also brought under the guidance of transnational assemblages of faith-based organizations, local churches, and local governments, all of whom enact a widely circulating global discourse of child welfare and family focused on particular

Northern accounts of advantaged childhood. This sedimentation of the family, of course, produces selves that are far more amenable to the key processes of monitoring/surveillance that underlie the professionalized family care model. In a deeper sense, they are compliant with the larger neoliberal project of rescue, in which the Haitian "failed" state and its culture and religion are brought into line with international standards and values.

Toward the Future?

This critical analysis has specifically avoided the question of the benefits of de-institutionalization for orphans and vulnerable children to look at the ideas that currently underlie narratives concerning family in reunification and preservation efforts. There is no doubt that much needs to be done to reform the institutional care system in Haiti (as elsewhere) to better serve the needs of children and families. At the same time, despite its often positive tone of empowerment and validation of Haitian "strengths," the family reunification discourse in Haiti is implicitly biased, drawing upon long-standing negative images of weak and unstable families that need to be stabilized/nuclearized according to Northern ideas of "best practice" in order to advance child protection. These deficit portrayals, while carefully avoiding mention of Haitian culture per se as being at fault—still evoke what Paul Farmer (1994: 349, quoted in Sommerfelt and Pederson, 2009: 428) calls ". . . myths about what is wrong with Haiti and Haitians . . . that appear with surprising regularity . . ." As Sommerfelt and Pederson (2015: 428) argue, ". . . analysis too often merely conforms to these myths rather than undertaking serious efforts to understand the complex social, economic, and political structures of which child relocation practices are a part." In that sense the negative representations of parenting and childhood in Haiti commonly held among Christian missionaries and other faith-based actors involved in family reunification reflect a continuation of and contribution to the ongoing "symbolic violence" (Joseph, 2016; Louis, 2019) that Haiti has long been subject to by well-meaning white saviors.

More effort is needed to explore how the current narratives on child welfare and family in Haiti conjoin neoliberalism, neocolonialism, and global flows of Christian ideology. The role of the IBESR as a partner with churches in both the United States and Haiti in the enactment of new child protection approaches merits more inquiry, for despite assurances that the movement is Haitian-driven, its ideologies reflect Northern trends in thinking about children's needs and well-being, rather than the valuation of Haiti's own long-standing practices. The movement for family-based care could, in my view, be much enhanced in practice if it worked to support Haitian models of extended family care as they exist, instead of promoting children's return to birth parents—a process that reflects a misguided idealization of biological parenthood as a necessary space of love, bonding, and attachment. The latter simply reflects the imposition of white emotional priorities over Haitian ones. Haitian cultural traditions and economic exigencies suggest that "bringing children home" to birth parents is unlikely to be sustainable in the long term without drastic changes in the Haitian economy and political life.

There is a need for more dialogue between anthropologists and those engaged in changing and developing social policy, particularly around the question of who gets to define "what is best" in the realm of child welfare and global development interventions. The power of Northern ideas to influence and shape global social policy around child well-being remains a problem in need of confrontation. It is not simply a question of having "local leadership" and "partnership" between international and local agents, because often enough local agents are just as likely to buy into Northern norms of best practice as a reflection of a more progressive, internationally minded modernity. Yet developing a more culturally relevant approach cannot happen under conditions in which local social and cultural conditions and practices are ignored, portrayed as deficient, or otherwise erased from official consideration in the search for alternatives. Indeed, the latter processes, for long operating in Haiti with the support of both Haitians and others, have opened up avenues for intervention and control in Haiti that have produced little but intensification of long-standing injustices and continued positioning of Haiti as a nation in need of rescue.

The Sensorium

Embodied Being and Learning in Children's Everyday Experience

In Haiti, as a white person raised and educated in the United States, one is pressed to assume a rather different understanding of the body than that which is familiar. Beyond the confines of Cartesian dualisms of mind and body, spiritual and material, self and other, human and nonhuman, a rich lens opens up, where one can read an ecological framework for being and learning in which these dichotomous understandings slip away, replaced by a profound sense of connection, enmeshment, or entangling. Within this worldview, human and nonhuman agents are always present and interacting in processes of learning that extend far beyond the confines of institutional arrangements such as schools. In its rough contours, it is a worldview quite familiar to people from many indigenous communities, but it is also one that has often been obscured or lost in many modern contemporary societies. It has been a particular casualty in communities ravaged by centuries of colonialism and neocolonialism—forces that have underlain an extractive view of being and learning, built on a philosophy of divided existence privileging human superiority and control over natural places, resources, and forces. As Taylor, Pacinini-Ketchabaw, and Blaise (2012: 81) write, describing an emergent "post-human" view of education, this view of learning ". . . involves a shift from learning-as-cognition to a focus on connections between humans and non-human others; a move from the primacy of the written and spoken word to the re-emergence of the embodied self; and a recognition that other-than-human agents are always present in processes of learning."

Understanding how this lens shapes childhood is essential because it underlies several domains of childhood experience that are significant arenas for rethinking assumptions commonly held about childhood and education, in

Haiti as elsewhere. Recent rethinking of learning across a number of disciplines has pointed to the ways in which much learning in indigenous communities occurs through processes of observation and participation in everyday life. As elaborated across a rich body of scholarship, Learning Through Observation and Pitching In [LOPI] (Gaskins and Paradise, 2010; Paradise and Rogoff, 2009; Rogoff, Najafi, and Mejía-Arauz, 2014; Rogoff, Mejía-Arauz, and Correa-Chávez, 2015); is a key theoretical lens shaping research on children's learning across many indigenous communities in the Americas. LOPI draws attention to how children grow up learning many skills and competencies through everyday activity. Motivated by the desire to contribute to their families and communities, and exerting their own agency and initiative, children learn largely without any explicit adult "teaching" going on (cf. Lancy, 2010). This learning involves the cultivation of culturally shaped forms of attention and participation that stress children's intrinsic motivation and capacities as autonomous learners.

While much of the work on LOPI focuses on learning in the context of community social relationships and activities, other scholars have advocated for more attention to the role of natural ecologies in this process (Bang et al., 2015; Zarger, 2011). Focusing on such "relational epistemologies" with the natural environment permits an exploration of the ways in which the "more-than-human . . . is a routine, though deeply unexplored, part of human learning that impacts both what is learned and how learning happens." (Bang et al., 2015: 304). Zarger (2011: 377) points out that children's learning is intimately connected to their participation in the environment, often understood as "working" in the environment.

In conjunction with this literature, across the learning sciences, research on embodied cognition has also illustrated the profound role of the body in the processes of learning and thinking, pointing out two facts: one, that thinking and learning are processes that go beyond the individual mind or brain to include the environment; and, second, the brain is not the sole resource for performance, problem-solving, or critical thinking (Paul, 2021). An emerging body of research provides extensive evidence that we think through our bodies, using the social and material elements present in our cultural settings (Ingold, 2000; McDermott and Pea, 2020; Paul, 2021). This understanding of learning moves far beyond the notion of transmission to focus how learning involves the development of capacities for sensory perception that are acquired via participation in both human and nonhuman environments (Ingold, 2000).

Building on this scholarship, in this chapter, I focus on the centrality of the body and the senses in children's learning through their participation in social and natural worlds. A focus on the sensual ecology of learning reveals a dynamic space in which the physical and spiritual, corporeal and moral, social and individual, human and nonhuman, are all experienced as interconnected domains for learning. This is a space mediated by agents of all kinds that together form a wide and complex sensorium[1] that underlies children's learning, development, and attainment within the contours of Haitian society.

A group of kids were out in the neighborhood at dusk, as they usually were, carrying the ubiquitous big yellow water containers. I asked where they were getting their water. They led me to the front yard of a nearby house, partially obscured by a huge wad of barbed wire, where there was a well. One of the boys, Jalen, 13, pulled away the cover, dropped the plastic bucket that was attached to a long length of rope, and proceeded to haul it up, pulling alternately with each arm, smoothly, gracefully, and yet energetically. The others—a few girls and boys of varied ages— one just a toddler—stood nearby, watching and giggling. Jalen took the bucket of water and proceeded to pour it carefully into the small opening of the big yellow container. Despite the near darkness, he did so expertly, not spilling even a drop. I tried lifting the container—it was only about half full at this point—and found it extremely heavy. He showed me how he lifted it with ease. Then one of the younger girls (perhaps 6 or 7) put on a similar performance. She dropped the bucket and hauled it up, then proceeded to pour the water into her own container, though she was less expert with the pouring and Jalen stepped in to help her. They smiled at me throughout this activity, clearly enjoying showing me—the ignorant blan—*how they drew water. I asked if they were related or just friends; Jalen said they were friends—they lived up on the very steep hill nearby. That is where they had to carry the water, both morning and evening.* (2022)*

This afternoon, Jalen, Dikenson, the girl who had drawn water the other evening, and a few of the others in their group were with an older youth, Makenzy, in his "Philo" year of secondary school. I had mentioned earlier that I'd wanted to climb the hill, and they offered to take me. Makenzy asked someone in a house nearby if he could go with us, and we set off. They suggested that the way I had thought to go (that I'd seen many times from the road below) was too steep, so we took another route that hadn't been visible. It threaded among small homes that clung to the side of the hill, out of sight of the main road. This route was very steep, too, as well as narrow and rocky, and Makenzy held my hand to steady me as we walked.*

As seen from below, the hill looked barren and empty—covered with rocks and grass. But at the top, to my surprise, there were a lot of people—many more, in fact, than I had ever seen in the neighborhood below. Some had evidently been watching us from above, as we made our way up. There was a church, with a congregation gathered outside, singing. In an open area nearby there was a large backhoe, with a number of kids clambering over it. There were many small homes and tents with people about—lodging for some whose homes had collapsed during last summer's earthquake. The hilltop was evidently a vibrant center of community life. We walked around a bit and in another area I noticed clumps of what looked like tall grass; Jalen told me it was vetiver. When I said I couldn't smell it he further explained that it's the roots that have the perfume, and that these plants were too young to harvest. He added that when grown they even get to be as tall as a person! Makenzy said that its oil is used in airplane fuel.[2] As we turned to go down following another route, they pointed out the names of other plants, and we passed a second church, from which came the greatly amplified sounds of singing and clapping. One of the children added, "There are lots of churches here." We passed a goat tied to a small tree, its rope twisted. I suggested untwisting it, but they said, "Se pa pou nou li ye non" (It's not ours). Finally, back in the neighborhood below, Jalen stopped to touch a plant by the side of the road; when I looked, he opened up a pod to show me cotton. We arrived at the rusting hulk of truck cab, abandoned by the side of the road. The boys gleefully climbed in and pretended to drive it, spinning the steering wheel wildly and providing loud "horn" sound effects.

The Body and the Senses in Haitian Culture

The hill was a fascinating place: when seen from the road below, it appeared to be a barren stretch of rocks and grass, with nothing to suggest the number of people and the wealth of activity that could be found there. I recalled the way my experience mirrored that of Melville Herskovitz, as he encountered the Haitian village of Mirbalais for the first time:

> The first glimpse of the country gives no hint of a numerous population. It is as though this valley, like so many other things in Haiti, had set out to belie its own reality and, in this impression, at the very outset to point to the lesson that the observer must seek well beneath the surface if he is to attain any understanding of the country and its people. (1937: 3)

As outsiders, we both initially perceived the emptiness of places that were, in fact, quite full of people and activity. We had not realized the partiality of our perspective: partial in the sense of being incomplete, and partial also in the sense that it reflected our privileged way of knowing the world—one that equates what one can see with what is true.[3] In the spiritual tradition of Haitian Vodou, tall hills and mountains (along with waterfalls, caves, freshwater springs, and especially springs that flow into saltwater) often embody deep spiritual meaning and are considered privileged sites for churches and Vodou religious ceremonies. As features of a landscape that embodies spiritual significance, they are considered points of connection that enable a meeting of the earthly world with the spiritual world. Such points of connection are the domain of *Legba*, the spirit (*lwa*) who serves as the guardian of the crossroads. All ceremonies begin with seeking his permission to open the pathway between the spiritual and material worlds.

At the very beginning of my work in Haiti children themselves had taught me this lesson, though it was one I did not recognize until much later. I had concluded a discussion with a group of *restavèk* children and youth and had brought pencils to hand out afterward, telling them that they could each have two. As I did so, I noticed that the children had spontaneously begun to form crosses with the two pencils, raising them up for me to see. I took some photos in order to remember the children. It was only a few years later, when reviewing the photos in preparation for a talk, that it suddenly dawned on me that the crosses were meaningful: the children were offering a blessing of the crossroads, opening up the pathway between the material and spiritual worlds, preparing me in a sense for my future work in Haiti. I hadn't been able to see this until much later, when I had developed greater awareness of Haitian epistemology and worldview.[4] The crosses reflected children's collective connection to an indigenous spirituality and meaning system that infused everyday life. They were dwelling in a landscape rich with embodied, spiritual meaning in ways I had yet to appreciate.

In the worldview of Haitian Vodou, the body is considered the primary locus of learning and knowledge (McAlister, 2004; Michel, 1996). Landry (2008: 56) writes of how central this realization was during his experience of conducting ethnographic fieldwork in Haiti: "I have come to understand learning in Haitian Vodou as an embodied, sensuous, and active phenomenon. . . . I realized how important the body was, both in Vodou and more generally, with the process of learning in Haiti . . ."[5] Building on Paul Stoller's (2010) idea of "sensuous scholarship," which argues that people in different cultures have entirely different ways of knowing the world shaped by their understandings of the senses and the body,[6] Landry recognized that these sensorial and embodied experiences are intimately involved in knowledge and learning; it was not enough to observe, one had to experience another kind of knowledge through "dynamic embodiment" (57).

When seen through this lens, then, the entire episode on the hill began to look different: it was in fact an embodied experience of teaching and learning. Our bodies, senses, and the environment were central to our perceptual activity and social engagement, as the children drew attention to various features of the landscape we moved through and imbued them with meaning. The children were in fact teaching me the entire time, from showing me how they drew water, to the moment they led me on the right path, to the knowledge they shared with me about plants and churches. Our walk was an embodied classroom, as they expertly moved over the rocks, steadying me, our bodies linked, while they shared their knowledge of *things I could not see, both figurative and literal:* the correct path, the hidden roots of vetiver, the moral lesson about not intervening with something that doesn't belong to us (the goat); the cotton hidden inside the pod. And then there was the "dead" truck brought to life through sheer exuberance; the stalled backhoe made into a huge jungle gym; the energetic performances of drawing of water at the well that were such clear displays of skill and pride: "This is how we do it!" All of these things were part of a vast embodied sensorium of teaching and learning.

> When we returned to the area below the hill, near the house where I was staying, we sat together on a low stone wall that ran beside the road. Another boy joined us, Emmanuel, 8. He had a toy—a long stick with a plastic wheel attached to the front that he "drove" with fantastic speed down the rock and gravel road. I asked him if he had made it and what it was: "Yes, it's a motocyclette." And then he took off with it again. I watched as over the next few minutes he ran back and forth with it. Then, putting it aside, he scaled the tall cinder block wall of a house, and after that climbed onto small lorry parked nearby, and finally wrapped up his performance by doing cartwheels in the road. By now the sun had set, and Jalen asked me if I was cold. I said no, but he said "li fe frèt." (It's cold.) An older adult, perhaps in his early 30s, walked by and motioned to one of the boys, who got up and went to him. They walked together, the man putting his arm around the boy's shoulders. Seeing the intimate gesture, I asked Jalen if the man was his elder brother, cousin, or father. "No," he replied, "that's his friend."
>
> We sat for a few more minutes, and then another man came and started up the lorry. The boys asked me if I didn't want to go home. I realized that they had been sitting with me to keep me company—they hadn't wanted to leave me alone. They had tried to give me a hint earlier when they mentioned it was getting cold. Now I understood. As I got up and said good night, they jumped into the back of the lorry and took off. (2022)

Again, here was a lesson—a few, in fact—about Haitian ways of relating and being. The first lesson was about care: they had cared for me by not leaving me sitting alone. Beyond that, they had tried to teach me that feeling cold meant night was coming and it was time to go home: they did not say "we need to go home," but they taught me how to convey meaning through references to what the body could sense. They had taught me, too, another lesson: that friendship is wide, and that age can be insignificant in relationships. I realized how limited my lens was when I had assumed that the older man, with his display of physical affection toward the young boy, had to be related to him in some way. Emmanuel, with his amazing creativity and energy, taught me to see how closely the body was enmeshed in its environment and how it even seemed to draw energy from it. From his creative use of discarded things (a stick and a plastic wheel) to the intimate engagements of his body with the walls, roads, and empty vehicles, Emmanuel's very being connected them all in ways that were both entirely normal and yet in another sense completely extraordinary.

The Sensorium of Teaching and Learning: Mediating Meaning through the Body

The role of the body and senses as a locus of meaning-making is in turn directly related to the ways personhood is conceptualized in Haiti. As Strongman (2008) observes, in contrast to the Western idea of a unitary self that is fixed within the body, in the Afro-diasporic philosophical and religious tradition,

> The location of the self vis-à-vis the body can be and is culturally constructed through the senses. The body and its self need not be coterminous. The self need not reside inside the body, but may be imagined or placed externally. In different ways, current scientific discourse coincides with Afro-Diasporic philosophy in its exposure of subjective inwardness as an illusion. (8)

For Strongman this Afro-diasporic model of personhood allows for a wider range of subjectivities than the Western model of the self as contained and fixed within the body. Indeed, in the Haitian worldview, bodies can readily shift form; there is no necessary division between human bodies and those of animals and other spirits.[7] Material objects can be imbued with power and exert power over others (*pwen*); they can be receptacles for spirits (e.g., jars [*govi*] that hold the spirits of the dead in Vodou altars); trees such as the *mapou* (cottonwood) can be dwelling places for spirits. It is commonly believed that photos can embody of the spirit of the person represented.[8] Thus in Haitian epistemology there is a certain interpenetrating and coterminous idea of body, self, and environment.

The implications of this worldview are important for a deeper understanding of learning in Haiti. Children grow up in a sensorium—a richly embodied and sensory world in which the boundaries, borders, and categories so familiar to Western philosophies of the self are dissolved. As I use the term, the sensorium is more than the sensory apparatus located in the brain; it is, in fact, an extended brain, reflecting an enmeshment of cognition with the senses and the environment.[9] The body-environment nexus is one part of this sensorium and it plays an important part in acquisition of knowledge and learning. It is key to the kinds of learning and being that children experience across a range of settings.

> *Entering into the tree-shaded schoolyard, where, since the quake, many of the lower-grade classrooms are still being conducted under tents and tarps, one is struck immediately by the noise level: from every direction children are engaged in some form of energetic oral recitation, often musical, that alternates with the equally energetic voices of the teachers, who lead the students in these oral exercises. Not only are the students actively engaged in reciting, they are physically engaged as well: they sway or lean into each other as they sit on crowded benches; they stand and use their bodies, jutting hips and arms left, right, front, back as they recite together. Teachers moved up and down the rows of benches; sometimes they sat on the benches, too, next to the students, and they often moved among the students to give one on one assistance with solving problems or correcting writing. Students would be called to come stand at the front of the class, directly facing the teacher, to give their recitations. (2011)*

As I described earlier, criticisms of schooling in Haiti often focus on the rote nature of instruction, the lack of emphasis on critical thinking, and the use of harsh discipline. One readily observes teachers simply quoting material from textbooks and having children copy it down, choral recitation, or recitation of memorized materials. Teaching may simply consist of having students copy a text written on a blackboard. Question-answer forms of engagement between teachers and students rely on what Jean-Pierre (2016: 226) calls "ventriloquism," merely the recitation of facts or information from another source. Yet what is not often noted is the embodied nature of these activities. As in the illustration earlier, "rote" learning—which that most certainly was when judged from a mainstream North American lens—was extensively corporeal: choral responses and recitations were full of sound, movement, and gesture, suggesting both a different cultural understanding of learning as well as a more embodied, sensory one.[10]

Indeed, as I explored the ways children were engaged in learning in an informal, afterschool literacy project (for further discussion, see Hoffman, 2021b), I began to see that their learning involved extensive engagement with the body, senses, and the environment in ways that referenced larger meaning systems in Haitian culture.[11] Analysis of an extensive corpus of video data recorded while students interacted in small peer tutoring groups revealed that students used their bodies and other material elements of the environment (such as erasers) in surprising ways as channels for creating meaning and learning.[12] Further, children consistently demonstrated patterns of wide attention to the surrounding environment as they engaged in their interactions and activities, rather than focusing narrowly on specific tasks at hand—a pattern, as Gaskins and Paradise note, that is common in indigenous American communities but not valued in North American settings as it is seen to reflect inattention (Gaskins and Paradise, 2010: 99–100).[13] They also illustrated a great deal of cooperative initiative toward helping others, along with a pattern of socially distributed learning and participation (in which one student would "perform" while others observed) reflecting the cultural importance of observation and performance to learning.[14]

> *Fabienne was an eight year-old girl who worked in the household of an elderly grand aunt. I was sitting in the lakou (courtyard) one day with Fabienne's grand aunt and another elderly woman visitor from the Catholic church they attended. Sitting with a rosary and a religious booklet in her lap that contained prayers, scripture readings, and pictures, the aunt was flipping through the booklet and having some difficulty finding the pages she was looking for. Fabienne, who was working in the open kitchen nearby, noticed this. She quickly came and intervened, finding the page that had an illustration of the Sacred Heart of Jesus. Her aunt then took two small photos of two children, along with one of Pope Francis, and carefully placed them face down on the illustration of the Heart of Jesus, closing the booklet. (2014)*

This event reveals many of the themes mentioned in the earlier discussion. Though Fabienne was occupied in the kitchen, she was also simultaneously closely attuned to what was happening around her (attending widely), so much so that she could readily intervene to find the pages of the prayer book that the adult could not. Further (as in distributed participation), she did not hesitate to come over to offer her help. Finally, this event also illustrates a local understanding of embodiment— how the material and spiritual flow together, as mentioned earlier. Placing the children's and Pope Francis' photos on top of the sacred illustration would allow the blessings of the Sacred Heart to flow to them, reflecting the ways material and spiritual domains are not separate in the Haitian world view, but interdependent.

Toward a Critical Understanding of Culture and Learning

In her study of how childhood is represented in Haitian art, LeGrace Benson wrote, "Most children in Haiti live only partly in the secular world. Out in the mountain villages, children live their earthly lives in a pervading spiritual environment." (2002: 202). Benson claims that while some Haitian artists have spoken of being aware of this pervasive spirituality, most academically trained Haitian adults have so well adapted to the secular world that they fail to see the embodied spirituality that shapes Haitian childhood.

Across the settings described earlier, from the hilltop climb to the elementary classrooms to the afterschool literacy program, it is clear that learning is mediated through the senses and the body, both of which are experienced on social as well as spiritual planes. While one might expect to see such an integration more readily as children participate in the natural environment, it appears to be present even in the relatively more formal environments of the school and tutoring program, even though it typically goes unnoticed and unvalued in those more formal settings. Indeed, it is sometimes actively *de*valued, as can be seen in the responses of the American research assistants who considered children's capacities for wide attention to be a form of inattention. As Bang et al. write, "The idea that everything has a role to play [in learning] may cultivate a wider and keener scope of observation and motivate a deeper analysis of how the more-than-human and humans might build a sense of belonging." (2015: 307). In Haiti, this sense of belonging to worlds more than human is both the foundation for and the central lesson of the sensorium in which children live and learn.

In social systems where colonial legacies continue to shape formal schooling, as in Haiti, indigenous psychologies of learning are often suppressed in favor of outsider, colonial ideals as to what learning is or should look like. The de-legitimization of indigenous approaches to and capacities for learning produces a constrained view of children's personhood and subjectivity, attempting to conform it to institutional expectations and demands. The latter imposes a false fragmentation on children's lives and are often at odds with the ways children are continuously engaged in learning in and across diverse environments outside of the school.

Present reform efforts emphasize the need for Haitian schooling to become more "child-centered" and for classrooms to promote more critical thinking, which would appear to be a positive move against the heritage of the colonialist "banking model" (Freire, 1970). Yet without attention to the particular affordances of culture, these too can become an avenue for continued neocolonial dominance, as they impose outside sensibilities and foreign notions of the "individual learner" within social contexts that are quite different and shaped by different notions of attention, participation, and personhood. These affordances are grounded in the embodied agency of children to make meaning through relations with others and their natural worlds. Though these capacities have for the most part remained unrecognized and undervalued, they are ever-present and remain a vital part of children's lives. In fact, they thrive in the ordinary spaces that children inhabit. A critical cultural lens on children's learning demands embracing the embodied, spiritual, and more-than-human world. The latter is essential to a genuine transformation of schooling, as well as to the broader transformation of society.

At the bal (dance) *Sunday afternoon, there was a woman, otherwise dressed to go out, with a full head of tightly wound curlers in multicolors—yellow, red, orange, purple, turquoise. Her head bristled like some kind of tropical cactus flower. An old man with very black skin and a head full of long white hair was there, too, hanging around in the open area near the dance floor. He kept telling me, in English, "We are both* blan, *and* blan *are the best." He repeated this statement about 20 times during the hour and a half I remained there. On the dance floor, someone passed me a turquoise fan, edged in white lace, with a picture of the Virgin Mary on it. I fanned myself briefly and passed it back. The strains of Auld Lang Syne, played to a* kompa *beat, let us know the* bal *was over.* (2015)

The *bal* presented a wealth of sensation: colors, sounds, smells, voices, music, movement; but more than the sensations themselves were the ways they were interwoven and connected in ways I could never have imagined: curlers as adornment, white hair as index of racial belonging, Auld Lang Syne as *kompa*, the Virgin Mary as cooling solace for sweating bodies. As a white in Haiti, I ask myself, how can we whites ever hope to understand—let alone improve on— children's lives when we fail to see the wealth of the more-than-human environment in which they are living and learning? We have seen them suffering, but have we seen them learning? The powerful thing is that the sensorium gives us hope of improving on our own ability to see and learn.

Beyond Trauma

Caring, Relating and Belonging in Children's Lives

Since the 1970s, trauma has become increasingly recognized as a global public health issue, framing much research and intervention in the fields of child and youth development, welfare, and education around the world (Magruder, McLaughlin, and Borbon, 2017). As a lens for framing children's experiences across a range of behavioral settings, trauma draws attention to the ways adverse experiences of many different kinds may profoundly impact child health and well-being into adulthood. At the same time, it is well recognized that not everyone responds similarly to adversity; some demonstrate resilience—the capacity to respond to adverse experiences in ways that support and promote well-being—or "successful adaptation"—despite high-risk status and threat (Masten, Best, and Garmezy, 1990: 426). Concern that trauma underlies many instances of childhood failure to thrive has led to a global growth of education and early childhood programs based on "trauma-responsive" or "trauma-informed" care, approaches that aim to recognize when and where trauma exists and to build children's (and caregivers') capacities to respond to adverse circumstances in healthy ways. These approaches extend into mental health and education efforts that seek to offer psychosocial support to children facing violence, war, forced displacement, natural disasters, and other difficult life conditions.

Given the frequent and powerful impact of natural disasters in Haiti, including earthquakes and hurricanes—on top of high levels of economic stress, violence, political unrest, and insecurity, it is often claimed that Haitians suffer from a high rate of trauma-related disorders, even as the country lacks significant capacity to address such mental health issues (Auguste and Rasmussen, 2019; Pierre et al., 2010). Since the 2010 earthquake, however, NGOs have been instrumental in raising awareness of mental health through educational campaigns and psychosocial support to victims, helping to popularize notions of trauma and post-traumatic stress (Kaussen, 2012; Obert, 2020). In their exploration of local idioms of distress in Arcahaie, Haiti, Lichtenberg et al (2022) observed that participants' familiarity with biomedical categories of clinical psychology and psychotherapy such as trauma was likely due to the efforts of NGOs and an influx of mental health professionals in the post-earthquake period. These organizations and individuals often took as their mandate training and education that would enable people to talk about or express their emotions as an important aspect of dealing with stress and trauma (Wall and Gerald, 2012, quoted in Kaussen, 2016).[1] Perhaps as a reflection of the increasing popularity of trauma as a construct in Haiti, in the months following the August 2021 earthquake in the South of Haiti, for example, Haitian teachers told me that every aftershock made kids panic and run out of school buildings: "*Yo twomatize*" ["they are traumatized"] they said. (Teacher focus group interview, January 2022).

In media and faith-based advocacy on Haitian childhood, trauma is a major theme, often discussed in the context of children's responses to natural disasters, societal violence, institutionalization, and family breakdown. *Restavèk,* orphans, and street children are considered to be particularly at risk of having been traumatized due to the violence, abuse, and lack of appropriate care, emotional socialization, and support they are assumed to have experienced.[2] Yet, even as Haitians are assumed to experience high levels of trauma and children's experience is often framed through the lens of trauma, Haitians are at the same time frequently portrayed in the popular as well as academic literature as endlessly resilient in dealing with adversities. Indeed, as Derivois et al. (2018) argue, research studies have consistently shown that the most vulnerable populations in Haiti have the highest resilience scores.[3] They consider a number of different explanations for this, including difficulties with defining and measuring resilience and trauma, "paradoxical coping strategies" that may reflect "pathological resilience" (such as when residents of Port-au-Prince took to the streets to dance in the rain even after a major natural disaster, Hurricane Matthew, left entire portions of the country cut off and thousands feared dead), and Haitian marronage—an effort to resist the methodological and conceptual tools of the international humanitarian and scientific community that "claims to understand them or help them grow." Here I argue that the "paradox" of Haitian trauma/resilience suggests that the normative Western/Northern psychological discourse on trauma and resilience is not only inadequate to understand the dynamics of Haitian childhood experience; it may even represent yet another imposition of Western and Northern subjectivities on Haitian lives. A new line of inquiry is necessary that can reach deeper into the less often recognized modalities of children's relationships within their social and natural worlds.

Toward a Critical Sociocultural Lens on Trauma

Despite the current global popularity of trauma as a lens on human experience, according to Fassin and Rechtman (2009: 7), the "trauma narrative" demands a critical lens that rejects its naturalization. They write, "The simple fact that within the last two decades it has become standard practice to send psychiatrists and psychologists to places where people have been involved in or witnessed dramatic events should invite reflection."(8) Arguing that trauma is as much a moral category of consciousness as a psychological one, it is imperative to consider how the idea of trauma functions within a larger discourse of political and social boundaries and inequalities. Such a lens reveals the extent to which trauma facilitates processes of international humanitarianism, state-building, and international governance (Fassin, 2007; James, 2010; Kaussen, 2012).

In the Haitian case, a number of scholars have offered critiques of the ways trauma narratives have commodity value, as those identified as traumatized victims may strategically narrate and perform mental, emotional, or physical suffering in order to achieve particular ends such as material support or recompense (James, 2010; Stodulka, 2015). James (2010) argues that these often falsified or exaggerated stories of trauma or injury are not only used strategically to secure access to material support on the part of the *viktim* but also on the part of organizations themselves, as reflections of "the power of the trauma portfolio in cultures of humanitarian and development aid . . . both institutions and individuals authenticate and circulate portfolios of suffering to demonstrate their competence in promoting rights, justice, and reparations" (112). Kaussen (2012) showed how psychosocial support initiatives for earthquake *viktim* that emphasized emotional self-expression enabled the "traumatized" to become better subjects for neoliberal projects of governmentality. Further, educational and psychosocial support initiatives can promote an individualistic lens on suffering that obscures its social contextual dimensions. As Bolotta (2019) writes,

> The widespread use of psychological notions within humanitarian and social intervention identifies the causes of social suffering in the individual rather than in the political and economic processes that produce social inequalities. Through clinical categories such as trauma, and practices of therapeutic listening, marginalized groups' [suffering] is "psychologized" and individualized, that is to say, depoliticized. (2019: 6)

A second body of critical literature focuses on the over-extension of trauma globally as a category for framing personal experience. This work points to the fact that cultural responses to adversity display wide variation and may not fit into Western biomedical diagnoses (Gilmoor, Adithy and Regeer, 2019; Kaiser and Jo Weaver, 2019; Patel and Hall, 2021; Theisen-Womersley, 2021). In arguing for a cultural approach to trauma, these authors suggest careful attention to idioms of distress that do not fit the Western diagnostic criteria, as well as local narratives and explanations for suffering that are not captured by standard criteria.[4] Considering cross-cultural differences, Kidron and Kirmayer (2019) write:

> What is noteworthy is the multitude of differences being noted across all layers of processing, from the meaning attributed to the event to the symptomatic responses to the meaning. Furthermore, ethnographic research suggests that such idioms of distress take on their communicative meaning in specific social contexts, and therefore require a broad understanding of complex and fluid cultural conceptions of wellness and distress and a detailed exploration of their actual use in a particular instance. (Kidron and Kirmayer, 2019: 3)

A significant literature already exists concerning the ways Haitian understandings of health and mental health differ from biomedical approaches to these questions. (Galvin, 2022; Kaiser and Fils-Aimé, 2019; Méance, 2014; Sterlin, 2006). Such differences are believed to have led Haitians to a marked preference for the use of faith-based healing over Western mental health approaches and services (Auguste and Rasmussen, 2019). As Lictenberg et al. (2022) point out, in Haiti there is a great deal of heterogeneity in the ways people understand and respond to distress. Differences in geographical location, alongside complexities of local interpretations of Christianity and Vodou, varied exposure to biomedical discourse, and pressures to conform to white expectations in discussing mental health all contribute to a very complex field in which a biomedical lens often conflicts with Haitian experiences. James et al. (2012: 111) write:

> A core objection concerns whether foreign, often Western, professionals with embedded assumptions about what constitutes trauma, what pathologies are likely to result, and how best to treat them have any role at all in post-disaster mental health work with people of another culture. Practitioners importing their own culture's explanatory and treatment models have been accused of disrespecting, and perhaps disrupting, the very real effects of local modes of resiliency and healing.

While some research recognizes the need to take into account the nuances of culture and religious belief systems in addressing the experiences of Haitian children in particular (e.g., Cenat et al, 2018; Karray et al., 2017; Roysircar and

O'Grady, 2021; Roysircar, Thomson, and Geisinger, 2019) the relevance of the trauma and resilience framework itself for exploring children's experiences of suffering has rarely been questioned. As a result, there is much less room for understanding features of childhood experience that do not conform to the expected dualism.[5] This is not to say that cultural relevance has been neglected in efforts to address children's mental health, but that it is often enacted on levels that rarely challenge the deepest assumptions about personhood, emotion, and social relations that characterize a given culture and that may diverge in significant ways from the norms in Euro-American cultures. These deeper dimensions of culture, such as those that shape individualism and collective relational dimensions of personhood are not easily captured, even by "culturally relevant" adaptations of frameworks and approaches (Kim, 2010).[6]

Arguably, the issues of governance and power that underlie dominant discourses around adult experiences of trauma are intensified when the focus is on childhood, given the latter's key positioning as an arena par excellence for state-building and transnational governance. When "healthy childhood" is at stake, particularly in the black and brown South, the imperative to address supposed pathologies of mental health is intensified, furthering the moral legitimacy of international actors to intervene and protect ostensibly traumatized and fragile childhoods that are considered to be the basis for healthy societies. While constructs such as trauma/resilience are certainly valuable in some situations, especially when they are used with close attention to the cultural context, the lack of attention to alternative frameworks beyond trauma/resilience in exploring childhood experiences of adversity is problematic. Reflecting on his own turn away from psychology through experiences working with street children in Bangkok, for example, Bolotta (2019) came to realize that supposed universal psychological constructs such as "trauma" and "attachment" that he had been trained in and initially tried to use to make sense of the children's experiences were inadequate.[7] Efforts to characterize children's experiences of adversity within the framework of trauma/resilience may indeed miss locally significant dimensions of cultural and psychological functioning, further obscuring effective ways to address their needs under difficult conditions.

Thus it is important to consider a broader set of questions regarding personhood and culture that are often not broached in children's experiences of adversity: What cultural meanings do children give to their experiences? What locally salient cultural practices do children use to navigate their lives? How do cultural understandings of the self and its relations to others and the natural world mediate children's experiences?

Culture, Trauma, and Entanglement

On occasion, when meeting *restavèk* children in the South of Haiti, I would ask them to draw their house. Inevitably, in addition to a dwelling, the drawings almost universally featured flowers, trees, and/or plants, as children's drawings often do. Yet there was something quite different about them: often the flowers and trees were not placed alongside or around the house, as might be expected, but were instead attached to or growing directly out of the house, as if they were extensions of the house itself. I always found this curious and wondered if the children had somehow learned to draw their homes in this way. Most of them had spent very little time in school, and few had much experience with drawing. I also wondered if drawing trees or plants coming out of houses was something kids all over the world would do, when asked to draw their homes.[8] The Haitian children's drawings seemed to represent the house itself as if it were alive and growing, a part of its natural environment.[9]

Once when working with another group of children, I followed the house drawing activity up with another exercise: I asked them to draw the members of the family living in their homes. I gave them a diagram to fill out, with a circle in the center for "Me" with lines to bubbles around the outside for them to name family members. Remarkably, the same thing happened—even these drawings were handed back to me with pictures of trees, plants, and flowers attached to either the "me" bubble or the other bubbles. There are many possible interpretations, but to me the drawings reflected a strong sense of human-environment interdependency or intermingling, and/or a sense of the family as itself alive—as if it too were growing. Even if the plants or flowers were a way to beautify the house or person, the same underlying connection to nature was present. What this revealed to me is that children were *dwelling in nature*, not just homes or families, and this nature was represented positively in intimate connection with their representations of home and self. To me, this was important, because these were children commonly considered by whites as traumatized due to the fact that they were *restavèk*, and yet the drawings seemed to reveal a sense of spirituality, life, and growth.

Years later, I learned that "House Tree Person" tests are a common form of psychological assessment often administered to children to evaluate their mental health. A number of studies have in fact employed the HTP test with Haitian children in order to assess their levels of trauma and resilience (e.g., Afolayan, 2015; Roysircar et al., 2017; Roysircar, Thompson, and Geisinger 2019). In the classic HTP test, children are asked to draw the house, tree, and person separately.

However, even when attention is given to cultural dimensions in interpretation, the fact that children are asked to draw these things separately automatically imposes an external frame on the child's lens: most importantly, the possibility that, as I found earlier, these are all meaningfully related and experienced together in children's worlds. In sum the very structure of the assessment reflects assumptions that obscure a more culturally relevant understanding of the child's experience.

Tim Ingold's work on environmental perception conveys this idea of interrelations between the human and the nonhuman worlds in children's experiences. Ingold's central concern is to understand how people perceive the world around them, and how and why these perceptions differ. Drawing on the work of Gibson, Ingold argues that "perception of the environment"

> is not the achievement of a mind in a body, but of the organism as a whole in its environment, and is tantamount to the organism's own exploratory movement through the world. If the mind is anywhere, it is not 'inside the head' rather than 'out there' in the world; . . . it is immanent in the network of sensory pathways that are set up by virtue of the perceiver's immersion in his or her environment." (2000: 3)

Thus, in Ingold's view, mind is immanent in the natural environment: they are enmeshed, or entangled: constructed reciprocally through sensory and practical activity in the world. If perception is not the achievement of a mind in a body but of the organism as a whole in its environment, then psychological assessments that enforce dualistic distinctions or artificial categorizations may miss deeper understandings of human experience.

Ingold's ideas appear to recall the concept of human-environment relations that is so important to Haitian Voudou, where the person is conceptualized as part of a much larger universe of spirits, ancestors, and the natural world all of which are connected and must be in harmony, and in which persons and the world co-create each other (Sterlin, 2006; Pierre et al., 2010; Michel, 1996). While this enmeshed understanding of the mind, body, and environment is often highlighted in the religious and medical anthropological literature on Haiti,[10] it has rarely been recognized within the dominant psychological frameworks that shape white interventions in education and child welfare—most of which reflect globally circulating mainstream understandings of psychological functioning. Yet in Haiti, children's growth and development might be more accurately understood as a reflection of their environmental enmeshment, in which perception, action, and understanding are moving pathways through various relations with human and more-than-human worlds. This helps us to understand the meaning of the children's drawings I discussed earlier. They are windows onto an entangled conceptualization of the environment in which houses and even people themselves are enmeshed and made alive through their relations with the natural world.

Developing a Different Lens on Trauma/ Resilience: Focus on Care

What are the implications for understanding trauma and resilience? There are many possibilities. Given the importance of the mind-body-environment connection in children's experiences, it seems important to contextualize trauma and resilience not as purely individual mental or emotional responses, but as relational processes of a self-in-the-world. When seen in this way, a different yet very salient domain of childhood experience emerges centered on the dynamics of care. Most of the time, conceptualization of care in the context of childhood trauma is on the ways a child can benefit from having a caring adult to lean on who can help them process the difficult emotions trauma creates; relationships with caring adults are often seen as a primary protective factor in children's capacities to respond to adverse experiences. However, while relationships with supportive adults may be helpful in some cultural and social contexts, they may not be as important in contexts where human relationships are understood differently, and where adults play less important roles in children's lives than they do in more economically advantaged societies. This is especially true in cultural communities where children spend most of their time in the company of peers and siblings, free from adult supervision. In these contexts, as a good deal of research has shown, peers and siblings are often more important sources of socialization and care than adults (Keller, 2018; Lancy, 2015; Mosier and Rogoff, 2003; Rogoff, 1981).

This suggests that the emphasis on adult care for children through supportive, caring relationships may in some cultural contexts be somewhat irrelevant to children's abilities to manage adverse experiences, even those involving chronic distress. As noted earlier, many disadvantaged children who are subject to high levels of risk to their health and safety live their lives largely apart from parents or other adult caregivers, and yet, they display high levels of resilience and overall mental health. Indeed, such has also been observed in research on street children in a number of countries, including Haiti (e.g., Cenat et al., 2018;

Hecht, 1998; Kovats-Bernat, 2006; Theron and Malindi, 2010; Offit, 2008; Panter-Brick, 2002). If so, this can be taken as evidence that in some cultural contexts relationships with supportive adults are not necessarily the most important or most salient features of children's abilities to manage adversity.

Even more radically—as some ethnographic evidence suggests—Northern understandings of trauma and resilience may privilege a culturally biased view of care itself, in that they overemphasize adults as caregivers for children, when in fact it is often children themselves who are the caregivers for others—including adults—within their social networks. While children as agents of care for adults might be criticized as an unhealthy "adultification" when seen through the lens of mainstream psychology, what if it were understood differently, as a proper and indeed valued role for children, essential to the development of local models of social relational personhood? And what if children's activities as caregivers were connected to opportunities for learning, exercise of autonomy, and hopeful/strategic responses to conditions of adversity? Would children's practices of care in themselves offer another avenue to consider issues of trauma, resilience, and mental health?

Nurtured or Nurturing? Children as Caregivers

These questions are essential if one is to understand the larger context in which conceptualizations of childhood trauma and vulnerability are constructed by development and humanitarian efforts. While there is not an extensive literature on the topic, some ethnographic research on African communities has revealed an important role for children as caregivers. In her ethnography of childhood and traditional healers in Zimbabwe, Patricia Reynolds (1996) observed that children appear to acquire knowledge about healing informally through living and working with healers in families. She found that children were intimately involved in mastering the knowledge and rituals associated with healing, often in the context of close relationships with a healer grandparent. Indeed, she writes that understanding childhood itself in Africa lies in close attention to the central role of children in healing systems—systems that are, as in Haitian Vodou, oriented toward the maintenance of harmony between the spiritual and natural worlds.

Hunleth (2017) provides an ethnography of children's participation in caregiving for adults with HIV and tuberculosis in Zambia. Hunleth's study reveals how the discourses and politics of international global health that assume it is primarily adults who are the caregivers are mistaken, as it is more commonly children who assume the caregiving role for adults. Upon entering the immaculate home of a woman seriously ill with tuberculosis, for example, she quotes the woman who said, "The children are taking good care of me. People would think it is the elders, but it is the children . . ." (p. 2). She observes that social science research has largely ignored the role of children in caregiving, failing to recognize the interdependent and complex roles of children and adults in extended and dynamic households. Children exert social agency through their care for needy adults, as they strategically nurture specific relationships with adults that can assist them in attaining future goals and improving their life prospects. In this sense children's caregiving plays an important role in strengthening their own responses to vulnerability. Developing a critique of global health and development discourses that ignore children's perspectives, she notes that one of the most unexpected lessons learned from attentiveness to children was the emphasis children placed on natural beauty and pride—resisting caricatures and stereotypes that made them look victimized by conditions they faced in their lives. Focusing on how children found positive meaning in their lives through the activity of caregiving ". . . honors their relationships and their attempts to maintain dignity within difficult circumstances" (p. 46).[11]

These arguments are directly relevant to the situation of children in Haiti. While there is not a research literature on children's roles as caregivers or healers, children's participation in caregiving and healing has been noted in some of the earlier work on Haitian rural family life and social organization, where their presence and assistance in ancestral Vodou ceremonies has often been observed (e.g., Courlander, 1960; Herskovitz, 1937; Métraux, 1972; Michel, 1996). Given that serving the spirits in Vodou traditionally follows lines of family descent, there is obviously an important domain in which children are involved in learning the healing practices associated with the faith in the context of family socialization practices (see Richman, 2008). Further, as has been noted, in Haiti children are frequently the principal caretakers for highly respected older relatives such as grandparents (Frederickson et al., 2018: 503).

Indeed, in my work I found many children and youth involved in caregiving for adults, especially for sick or elderly relatives. In one case, a woman in her seventies who was blind was being cared for by the daughter of a distant relative. The girl would groom the elder daily, in addition to cleaning the house and helping to purchase, prepare, and serve food. On Sundays, she would walk the elder to church. In another case, two street boys interviewed in 2015 described how they took on odd jobs such as unloading trucks or merchandise in the public market in order to get money to take care of ill parents. One described his situation this way: "My father is blind and my mother is sick, so I couldn't continue to go to school. I unload trucks and merchandise in the markets to earn money so I can take care of my parents." The other described how he unloaded trucks early in the morning to earn money in order to take care of his father who was ill at home.

Besides their care for adults, children were caregivers for other children. I often observed older kids caring for toddlers; in some of the homes where I stayed, older children were the primary caregivers for younger children (e.g., Sophia, described in Chapter 4, was the primary caretaker for the three-year-old Kenya, who also lived in the same household). As I wrote in my field-notes:

> *Today I watched an older girl with a belt, who was playfully whipping younger kids on the balcony of her small apartment. The whipping was clearly hurting, and the younger ones tried to avoid it, but they all nevertheless seemed to thoroughly enjoy this "game." All over, I have noticed, kids are being taken care of by other slightly older kids. This creates a different kind of self than when a child is primarily cared for by an adult: one in which there is less distance psychologically between the caregiver and other child, so perhaps more closeness—intimacy that may offset the more distant roles of adults in children's lives. For the younger child, not having the adult as overseer perhaps creates more self-assurance and more capacity to self-manage from early on. Adults are around but provide care of a different sort that is more along the lines of discipline for wrong-doing. So perhaps what we see is a separation of the functions of caregiving, with adults responsible for the harsher, authoritarian compliance and control aspects of discipline and the empathetic, soft, intimate, and playful side fostered through relations with peers and siblings. (2013)*

In my experience, perhaps as a reflection of children's capacities in this domain, adults regularly sought out children's caregiving, and children sought opportunities to care for adults. If an adult did not have a child living with them already, they would request one from relatives or other intermediaries, both for assistance with household tasks and for companionship and care. Whenever I revealed to people in Haiti that I lived alone, inevitably someone would ask me, why don't you take a child? Even the children themselves would sometimes offer themselves to me when they heard I was living alone. One ten-year-old girl, who after a few minutes of interaction decided she loved me (*"Mwen renmen w"*) asked, when she learned I lived alone, if she could come live with me; on another occasion a boy asked if I didn't need him to come take care of me in my house. What was interesting in all these cases was the extent to which even under very adverse conditions, children saw themselves as competent caregivers and they exerted a degree of autonomy in seeking out these roles. They were not simply passive recipients of care by adults, but competent caregivers themselves. And, no doubt, by engaging as caregivers they could broaden or widen their future opportunities as they created relationships with the adults they cared for who could assist them in the future.

Small acts of care for others were in fact constant among children in Haiti and often remarked on by visiting foreigners. In school visits for example, when I traveled with a group of US students to Haiti, all the US students remarked how children were constantly looking out for them, making sure their bags were placed on tables instead of the floor, for example. In my own case, no matter where I was, children's small acts of care were continuous, ranging from making sure my hair was properly in place, to brushing dust off my clothing, to moving my backpack or handbag from where I'd placed it on the floor or ground to a seat or table so it would not become dirty. They closed zippers if they were open. They held my hand if I was unsteady. One day, two girls in my neighborhood came to talk with me. Quite out of the blue, they asked me about my health: did I have any illnesses that needed attention? Could they do something for me?

Among children, care is also expressed through the act of teaching. In the Haitian cultural-spiritual tradition, mirroring their active roles as caregivers, children are teachers and sources of insight for others, not simply passive recipients of adult teaching and socialization. As described in previous chapters, children often took on the role of teaching me about their environment, particularly about plants and other features of their community. A child teacher would often engage me in a back-and-forth repetition of a given word many times, as others observed. In one case, as I was sitting with a girl and her mother, I pointed out a white bird nearby. The girl immediately identified it for me: "Pijon!" She pronounced the word for me as I repeated it a few times. She also taught me something else: "*Lè w anemi, yo ba w san.*" (When you are anemic, they give you blood). Significantly, she did not say, "we take their blood," but rather, "they give you blood." The teaching in this case was not just about the pigeon's blood as a remedy for anemia, but also about the agentive nature of her natural world: the bird gives its blood. And it was the girl, not her mother, who imparted the lesson.

One day, as I walked through the neighborhood with Vanita, the "mother" of the house I was staying at, another girl watched us as we headed down to a shallow river nearby in order to cool off. I noticed she was quite poorly dressed: her pants were stained and her top torn and hanging off her thin, bony shoulders. There were large patches of watercress growing in the slow-moving water. Vanita proceeded to pick some for me since I'd said I loved watercress. The girl, who had been watching from the banks, came down into the water and proceeded to inspect the plants we had picked, saying they were not good. She then bent down and picked some better ones to give me, carefully placing them in my hand. She was obviously quite knowledgeable about the watercress. Recognizing her expertise, Vanita asked her the name of another large plant that had become uprooted and floated by us in the gentle current. The girl named it, then added a warning that it's not good for your skin—it causes itching. This girl shared her knowledge, becoming our teacher, and her teaching was also at the same time an expression of care: that I had the best watercress, and that I wouldn't touch the plant that caused itching.

In her observations of Haitian street children's engagements with healing through their dances and rituals, dance therapist Gray (2008) noted that instead of her teaching the children, the children became her teachers. In fact, it was only when she allowed them to take this role that they began to trust her. In their teaching, they stressed to her the importance of the natural and spiritual world, and the role of ritual in healing:

> The children taught me to co-create with them and incorporate rituals to begin and end each session that we eventually integrated into every session. They instructed me that ritual was the way to integrate the meaning of our work together into daily and ongoing life. . . . The children stressed the importance of my understanding that healing only occurs when there is community-endorsed movement into and out of the spirit world through ritual, and that this is how we make connections with the ancestors, ask for assistance and support, and integrate what we have learned and what we must do to take right action into our daily lives. (p. 232)

Taken together, these experiences suggest to me that children's participation in relations of care for others that involve their autonomy, knowledge, and connections to the spiritual and natural world take many different forms and are widespread in disadvantaged children's lives. They can be seen as modalities of "self-constitution" par excellence, contributing to the construction of personhood under conditions of adversity. These are modalities of self-constitution that can resist experiences of disconnection and rupture that underlie trauma. Such caring does not necessarily take the form of adult care for children, but rather children themselves caring for others, acting as agents in ways that permit them to exercise their own autonomy, knowledge, and forms of attention connected to participation in their social and natural environments. Essentially, caring constitutes an important modality for self-constitution against the self-undermining effects of adversity, stress, and trauma.

By contrast, mainstream psychological approaches to addressing these issues are narrow in their conceptualization, and one might even say culturally biased, in that they prioritize the more limited notion of emotional self-expression as a major means of dealing with stress and trauma. This prioritization of "self-expression" is central to many approaches to mental health globally, including Haiti. NGOs and FBOs engaged in psychosocial support for children and youth rather consistently draw on a language of therapeutic self-expression that emphasizes giving them opportunities to talk about their experiences (or, in the case of children, to "self-express" using art or play) and letting them know there is an adult who "cares" about what they are going through.[12] Certainly these are all useful at times, but this model of therapeutic self-expression does not engage with the modalities of self-constitution and agentive care that are so much a part of children's lives in Haiti. As research in the field of cultural psychology has shown, speech and self-expression do not hold the same degree of importance in more collectivistic cultural contexts as they do in Euro-American contexts. While Euro-American cultures associate verbalization of emotions as beneficial, in other cultures such cognitivization may impede rather than facilitate the management of distress (Kim, 2010). This suggests that it may be more important to focus on the child's environment and facilitating cultural practices that foster reconnection with elements within that environment. This broader lens takes attention off the individual child and his or her supposedly interiorized emotional life. Instead, it encourages a wider consideration and awareness of how children may develop alternate and unrecognized pathways toward healing from stress and rupture.

White Representational Power and Haitian Mental Health

Reflecting the more general pattern of white construction of Haitian deficiencies noted in preceding chapters, whites see Haitians as lacking knowledge of mental health and how to deal appropriately with stress and trauma. As a mental health professional active in providing mental health services in Haiti explained to me, "Haitians lack a concept of mental health or a vocabulary for it. So a big part of our job is to educate people about mental health. The US is far ahead [in this area]."[13] She further pointed out that because Haitians do not often learn how to express their emotions through words, stress and trauma are expressed through somatization or bodily aches. She and her staff try to give both children and adults avenues and occasions to express their inner states and feelings, whether through talk or (in the case of children) art or play therapy.

When a mainstream Western psychological perspective becomes the accepted approach to adversities such as stress and trauma, once again Haitians become by contrast "deficient" in knowledge or capacities when held to this external standard. Haitian perspectives and indeed the cultural-historical wealth associated with Haitian spirituality and understandings of personhood, caring, and relations with the human and natural worlds are muted, with preference for a Western discourse of emotional regulation and management, healthy attachments, and coping skills:

> *Families can promote good mental health through creating strong attachments, modeling emotional regulation and healthy coping skills, establishing appropriate boundaries, encouraging open communication, and providing an environment of support and stability. It takes learning, practice, and patience to develop these skills, especially if family members come from backgrounds where these traits were not seen. Mental health is just as important as physical health for the wellbeing of children (and adults), and supporting mental health is a great way to help children and families thrive!* (HGN, Facebook, 8/2022)

The preceding text, with its emphasis on strong attachments, emotional regulation, appropriate boundaries, open communication, safety, support, and stability, draws on mainstream Western models of individual emotional functioning that are seen to lie at the core of healthy families—ideas that underlie the family preservation and reunification discourse discussed earlier. As the text cited above states, however, these are skills and capacities that Haitian families may lack (especially when ". . . family members come from backgrounds in which these traits were not seen.") This discourse clearly prioritizes the adult as caregiver, supporter, model, and teacher for children. It is a model that basically imposes an adult-centric lens on children's worlds that is at odds with the ways children live their lives, often in extended family situations where they are the caregivers for others, and in many other domains where they have autonomy to teach and support others in helpful ways. It also ignores the powerful role of peer and sibling relationships in favor of a focus on adults. This is not to deny the importance of adults as potential positive sources of support in children's lives, but it is to emphasize that belonging and care are culturally shaped ideas that require attention and understanding on their own terms within their own cultural context. For children in Haiti, these domains may not involve adults or practices of self-expression so much as practices that support the constitution of self through embodied connections and relations of care with others and the natural world.[14]

Childhood trauma and indeed mental health in general represent an emergent arena for understanding and intervention in Haitian life. However, there are important questions of power that underlie these domains. Providing those who supposedly lack knowledge of mental health with the language to talk and think about their own subjectivity in new ways is not simply an innocent move to "help," as it may appear to be. These new categories and ways of thinking about experience (trauma, resilience, stress, for example) create new models of personhood that may not be aligned with deeply held cultural and spiritual ideals. Further, these new modalities of self-understanding intersect with regimes of testing, measurement, and management that are increasingly aligned with technologies of globalized governance. It is possible to argue that this objectification and measurement of mental life is an index par excellence of new regimes of global accountability that are increasingly shaping global humanitarianism, bringing the less "developed" under the tutelage of international experts aligned with developed economies, while obscuring the more localized cultural dynamics of emotional life that could be used as important resources. The very fact that the construct of "mental health" is unfamiliar to Haitians should not be seen as a deficiency to be remedied by white expertise, but as an opportunity for whites and others to challenge their own assumptions of what constitutes a "healthy" emotional and mental life beyond the familiar individualistic, cognitivized, and verbalized norms of Euro-American psychology.[15] This is not to say that there is no suffering or victimization, or that there is no trauma. For sure, these things exist in the experiences of children in Haiti, as they do elsewhere. However, the elevation of individual subjectivity in Western notions of mental health renders invisible—if it does not pathologize—constructions of embodied personhood grounded in practices of learning, belonging, and caring that are central to children's lives in Haiti.

In this sense, then, both trauma and resilience are paradoxical signifiers: While promoting concern for the mental and emotional well-being of others and elevating the resilience of those who suffer, on the other, they also deny and obscure the forms of personhood and subjectivity that locally define both experiences of suffering and ways of living through it. Caring itself is seen narrowly, through an adult-centric lens, while Haitian modalities of care and selfhood are denied or seen as lacking because they don't match the logo-centric prioritization of self that is so prominent in Western psychological discourse. The discourses and practices of mental health as they are currently being promulgated in Haiti leave intact the ways in which white narratives of the suffering of other invisibilize different subjectivities, enabling the "natural" emotional economies of whites to serve as the standard for others.

As I watched a young woman who had paused in her walk to reach out and stroke the leaves of plants growing alongside the road, and as I observed the careful and yet familiar way in which a woman plucked stems and leaves from plants to brew a healing herbal tea, I realized that connection and belonging are an embodied nexus of thought, emotion, and action that are not limited in scope to the human, let alone the family. Nor are they necessary objects of discursive reflection and narration. They are a mirror into the enmeshed and entangled world of the human, natural, and spiritual. That world contains suffering, but it also contains ways to endure it, and even tame it toward greater goals.

Practicing Hope

Movement, Personhood, and Survivance
in Haitian Childhoods

Lespwa fè viv

Haitian Proverb: Hope makes life.

Around the world, especially in societies affected by poverty and precarity, schooling is often considered key to youth's hopes and capacities for a better future. Frequently it is considered to be the *only* path that leads to improved economic prospects and social mobility (Jakimow, 2016; Holland and Yousofi, 2014). While there is evidence that in some contexts schooling does support children's aspirations effectively and can lead to improved individual and community outcomes as well as national economic development, there is also much evidence that schooling can also accomplish the opposite, serving instead as a site where social inequalities are reproduced and aspirations left unfulfilled. This is a particular problem in Haiti. While there are some excellent private schools in the larger cities, a highly privatized system means that the vast majority of children and youth lack access to schooling, and the schools they do attend are of poor quality, leading to continuation of a system of structured social inequality.

As key actors within the private educational sector, white faith-based actors see educational provision through schooling as an important element of their efforts to "change lives" in Haiti and to "give hope" to children and youth who lack hope. Once again, whites use a language of deficiency to characterize Haitian children and youth as being without hope or dreams: "Our work empowers students and gives them hope for the future." "Together we can give hope for the future." "When a community pours into their students, they know their worth and have hope for the future." "Our ministry continues to provide hope to the children of Haiti." "Unlike many kids in Haiti, the kids at our school have dreams: . . . to be a doctor, a businesswoman, a computer specialist. . . . Because of the education they are receiving, they have hope for the future."[1] Significantly, the language in these statements is not about helping children and youth to realize hopes they may have, but about giving them the very idea of hope: "One of the major problems we see here is that local children don't have the ability to dream. When you grow up in survival mode . . . it's hard to think about the future or believe that anything positive could ever happen in your life. Giving kids this ability to dream shows part of the wonderful work we are doing at our organization." While it conveys care and concern, this discourse of "giving hope to the hope-less" is both a discourse of deficiency and of power: the "hope-less" empty selves of Haitian children who don't know how to dream or do not know their own worth can be filled by the hope provided by whites who instill the very idea of a possible future. Alongside love, hope is another of the currencies of saviorism that whites "pour into" empty children's lives. The extent of this activity and its economic impact in Haiti constitute what could be called a veritable "hope industry," supported by thousands of donors affiliated with Christian organizations and churches whose funds support child school sponsorships, summer camps, Bible and ministry training for Haitian youth, preschools, counseling programs, entrepreneurship training, and a wide range of private schools, all ostensibly centered on the provision of hope.[2]

In the academic literature, children who are out of school are often considered to be children "at risk" of poor future outcomes. In Haiti, many of them work in domestic labor situations as *restavèk*; some would best be described as street youth. Some are or have been in orphanages. Much of the academic literature views lack of hope for the future as a natural consequence of poverty and social disadvantage (Kao and Tienda, 1998; St. Clair and Benjamin, 2011)—a view that is clearly in evidence in the discourse of faith-based actors described earlier. Poverty and lack of access to schooling and other resources translate into a lack of a "capacity to aspire," as Appadurai (2004: 68) argues. The existence of social inequality and lack of resources are seen to create conditions that lead to lowered aspirations, as the social environment shapes people's ideas about the future. These effects are amplified institutionally: families and schools educate children to certain class-based social positions, shaping the cultural capital available to youth (Bourdieu, 1997). As lack of educational and occupational aspirations leads to lack of investment in future opportunities, leading to lower overall achievement, a vicious circle known as the "aspiration trap" emerges (Flechtner, 2014).

A Different View: Ethnographic Evidence

Against the idea that poverty and lack of access to schooling lead to aspiration deficits, a growing body of ethnographic evidence suggests the contrary: many youth remain hopeful about their futures despite poverty and adversity. A number of studies of street youth around the world—a key class of youth often deemed to be at risk—have demonstrated that such youth work actively to generate opportunities for themselves and have relatively high aspirations for their futures (Aptekar, 1991; Frye, 2012; Hecht, 1998; Offit, 2008; Panter-Brick, 2002). Andersen and Biseth (2013), for example, show how disadvantaged teens in an immigrant ghetto in Norway have ideals and aspirations very similar to most other more economically and socially privileged youth. Recent work on poor children in England shows that most children do not suffer from a "poverty of aspiration" (King's College, 2013). Using both survey and qualitative data in a study of educational aspirations among poor children in Ethiopia, Tafere (2014) concludes that disadvantaged youth in some communities hold high educational aspirations and that they make strong efforts to achieve them, dispelling the myth of aspiration deficits. A longitudinal multi-country study of youth in the Caribbean also demonstrated clear and marked ambitions among youth of all social classes to "become someone," even among youth classified as being in the most difficult circumstances (CARICOM Commission on Youth Development, 2010: 31). Mains (2011) explores how schooled young men in Ethiopia with little prospects for employment use movement to reposition themselves and thereby sustain narratives of hope in the face of dim prospects.

A major theme across these studies is the need to better understand the link between youth's imagined futures and present social action (Frye, 2012; Mische, 2009), especially in regard to ideals of personhood and identity and the cultural practices that support the latter. DeJaeghere, Wiger, and Willemsen (2016) found that it is important to consider things beyond school itself in this process. They found that for youth in Tanzania, improved well-being and future opportunities were dependent on social relationships of affiliation and care, which were equally if not more important than schooling, especially since schooling could not guarantee a job. Similarly, in her work on lower-class youth in Iran who face prolonged "waithood"—the result of structural constraints that make it impossible to transition from youth to adulthood—Hashemi (2020) argues that disadvantaged young people create an alternative system that allows them to create moral capital that they can then use to navigate successful futures for themselves. By actively engaging in a process of "facework," where youth follow cultural norms and present themselves as good and responsible persons, they are able to maintain self-respect and moral worth. This moral capital in turn facilitates social relationships and economic opportunities.

Movement as the Practice of Hope

The case of disadvantaged Haitian children and youth builds on this challenge to the dominant narrative about youth in poverty as lacking hope. Despite their diminished circumstances, and against the dominant narrative—one drawn upon by the plethora of white actors engaged in delivering "hope" to Haiti—my evidence suggests that disadvantaged children and youth do not lack hope for the future. In fact, interviews with *restavèk* and street children in a number of locations in Southern Haiti carried out over a period of years both by myself and by Haitian research assistants revealed consistently high aspirations for becoming contributing members of society: doctors, nurses, lawyers, construction bosses, chefs, tailors, teachers, agronomists, and even senators and presidents. These disadvantaged children and youth nearly always had some kind of hope or dream for their futures:

Street kids:

Patrik is 15. He lives in the street because his family situation is really difficult. He thought that going into the street would be a better life than staying with his family, because at least in the street he can sometimes find food. He feels upset when he sees other kids going to school; no one in his family can help meet his needs . . . His dream is to become an agronomist and he really wants to realize this dream. He works unloading trucks and can earn a bit of money that way. Sometimes they don't pay him but that doesn't stop him from working.

Peter, 13: My mother couldn't take care of me so I came into the street. But every Sunday I ride the bus to go and visit my mother to give her something [from what he earned that week]. I want to be a senator or President of Haiti.

Kendy, 15. I was living with my stepfather but sometimes he hit me, so I decided to go live in the street and sleep in the street. When I make money I support my family. I want to go to school so that I can be someone in life.

Pierreson, 17. I was at school but because of money I couldn't continue. Friends suggested I go in the street so I did. I make about 100 gourdes a day (at the time of the interview, about $2.25—a very decent income[3]). I want to go to school so that I can be a citizen of Haiti.

Restavèk:

Jacqueline, 14. I left my mother when I was 12. I was born in Maniche. My father died and my mother sent me to live with her sister. I wanted to go because I thought my aunt could help me.

Onese, 14. I left my family when I was 10. Now I live with my aunt. I wanted to go. I hope to become a nurse.

Marinel, 18. I was born in Port-au-Prince. When I was 15 I left my mother because she wouldn't help me. I went to live with my grandmother. I've had three years of school, and I want to be a doctor.

Pierre Wendy, 14. I left Port-au-Prince. I haven't lived with my mother since I was 11; for the past three years I've been living with other families. I changed families because the first family I stayed with didn't send me to school, so I went to another house. I want to be an agronomist.

Kendet, 15. I left my family when I was 6, and I've been living with distant relatives. I wanted to leave home, I was trying to find some help. I'm treated well and have been to school for 7 years. I'd like to be an agronomist.

When I led a group of students from my university to Haiti, we conducted a focus group interview with a number of *restavèk* who were attending an afternoon school that catered to this population. Nearly all these Haitian youth expressed high ambitions for the future, either in terms of self-development or in terms of careers. One student commented that she wanted to learn French so she could be considered an educated person. Another boy said he wanted a better future that didn't involve "washing cars for 5 gourdes." Like the youth quoted earlier, they expressed clear ambitions for future careers such as nurse, engineer, agronomist, pastor, teacher, and doctor. Despite dominant views of disadvantaged youth as lacking hope, and in support of ethnographic evidence in other resource-poor communities around the world, youth in Haiti maintain clear hopes for their futures even in the face of disadvantage.[4]

What appears to be important to understanding how hope is maintained in the face of disadvantage is a shift in the ways hope itself is understood: it should be seen not simply as an attitude, feeling, or mental construct but as a set of cultural practices. In this sense, hope is agentive: it is produced and manifested in actions. In the case of disadvantaged Haitian children and youth, this is perhaps most obvious in the connection between hope and practices of movement (c.f. Mains, 2011, who makes a similar argument for youth in the Ethiopian context). This movement (e.g., leaving a family of origin, seeking out a better household, moving into or out of the street or an orphanage) appeared to be an embodied practice of hope—a step toward greater future possibility. As is evident in the quotations earlier, it was not uncommon for children who felt their needs were not being met in a family to leave to find another house in which to work, or else to go into the street or an orphanage.[5] As is also clear in the ways children used the first person to describe their actions (e.g., "I decided to come into the street" or "I left my mother"—not, "I was sent" or "I had to leave"), children stressed their agency in this process, even when (in the case of some *restavèk)* a parent or relative negotiated the move.[6] It is clear that for many of these children movement is directly tied to an effort to realize hopes or aspirations for an improved future. They exerted a kind of agency toward a hoped-for future through their movement into different statuses and living arrangements.

According to the standards of Euro-American developmental psychology and international child welfare, this is problematic for their development. Children are supposed to grow up in stable family situations; movement reflects a fundamental instability in their lives that is detrimental to healthy development. That is to say, disadvantaged children are considered to be at risk of poor developmental outcomes *because of* their movement.[7] And yet for Haitian children and youth, movement produces opportunity—in a deep sense, it produces hope. Staying with one's birth parents is a luxury for the few—it reflects a bourgeois ideal of stable family life associated with access to sufficient resources to support it; the lives of disadvantaged families and children hardly fit into this ideal. In the context of structural disadvantage, then, movement is an essential response to the constraints of households. It reflects degree of agency in children's lives as they actively try to improve their opportunities (cf. Sommerfelt, 2015: 72). "Keeping children at home where they are loved" (the ideal described earlier in the family reunification discourse) obscures and even devalues the local cultural logic and cultural practices that are most useful to youth in their efforts to produce hope and achieve goals (see also Schwartz, 2009; Leinaweaver, 2008).[8]

While moving is often associated with hope because of its potential to secure access to schooling, it is also true that moving does not always deliver on that promise. Nevertheless, even those children and youth who are out of school or who are unable to access it still express hopes for their futures. This suggests that the persistence of youth's hopes must be tied more broadly to other arenas in the child's life that enable hope. In this sense, the active pursuit of what could be called the moral capital of personhood is key (cf. Hashemi, 2020). As discussed in Chapter 4, this moral capital of personhood is reflected in the idea of *fomasyon*, in which moving to another household presents opportunities for developing a positive social identity grounded in a wide range of competencies, alongside valued qualities of personhood. According to M. Pierre, the school headmaster cited earlier whose family had *restavèk* living with them when he was growing up, "Even when they don't get to go to school, being a *restavèk* is a chance to become a person, by learning how to live in another family. The idea is that even that experience is a route to somewhere, rather than staying in a place with absolutely no sense of any future. There's the sense that the move opens up possibilities that don't exist at home" (Interview, JP, 7/25/2011).

Ironically, while movement to another family is considered an unhealthy and damaging experience for children by many organizations working to end the practices of child domesticity, in Haiti the experience of moving to another household represents one of the major opportunities through which children cultivate hopes for the future. Neglecting this valued domain of cultural experience, and attributing any evidence of "hope for the future" to their own efforts, whites impose their own subjectivities and knowledge frames while erasing or misappropriating those of Haitians.

Movement, Learning, and Caring in the Classroom

Aside from its role in children's lives as they migrate into and out of various living arrangements and families, movement is deeply connected to the process of learning itself, often in ways that go unrecognized. At this more micro level of analysis, movement enables embodied learning as well as social participation— both of which are significant to Haitian experiences of personhood. In one study that engaged Haitian and American university students in classroom observations in a community school catering to *restavèk* in Jacmel, Haiti (Hoffman and Saavedra, forthcoming), Both Haitian and US research assistants reported and were surprised by what they considered to be a remarkably high level of movement among the children:

Kendy: (Haiti) In my class I saw a lot of movement—why are they moving around so much?

Sara: (US) What movement is normal vs. what movement needs discipline?

Lismonde: (Haiti) Why doesn't all the movement bother the teacher?

Kate: (US) I noticed a lot of the kids got up to dance and sing in the classes.

Sadie: (US)There was a lot of coming and going in the classroom.

Alix: (Haiti) In my classroom the director came and saw that there were too many kids so he made some of the students move.

Don: (US) There was also lots of material being shared or passed around the room.

Jameson: (Haiti) I noticed that the kids were always turned around looking over their shoulders, looking around.

Diane: (US) I actually drew arrows in my fieldnotes to mark how all the students were moving around.

Kate: (US) I thought it was interesting that the teacher didn't address the whole class, she would move to sit with the students and work with them one at a time. (2018).[9]

Children's movement was constant in the classrooms we visited; teachers moved too, often to sit next to children to offer individual help.[10] Material items circulated as they were shared among children—commonly, erasers, books, and pens. As discussed in Chapter 6 (see also Hoffman, 2021b), there was a constant level of movement as learners turned their heads and bodies to attend to the environment. They touched materials to their bodies and used their hands and fingers to point to words in texts, to tap rhythms, to erase. They passed materials to each other, moved across the room to sit next to someone else, and took turns going to the board, or into and out of the classroom. Most importantly, movement was often tightly connected to giving or receiving help. As I recorded in my observation notes.

> *Today there was a boy who was interested in what I was writing in my notes. Apparently he thought I was trying to copy down the math problems that had been written on the blackboard, so he got up from his seat and moved to sit next to me. Saying, "Kitem ede w" ("Let me help you"), he took my notebook and copied the problems for me. The interesting thing was that he was supposed to be writing them in his own notebook, which, as far as I could tell, remained closed. "When you're finished, come to me—I'll help you," he said. (2018)*

As documented in videos of children's participation in small groups during a literacy learning afterschool program (described in Chapter 6), movement among the children was constant as they attended both to what was happening in their own groups as well as what was going on in other groups. Often this cross-group movement was associated with helping others, as in the following example:

> *A girl in one group rises slightly from her seat to lean over to look at a boy's chalkboard in another group. She smiles and checks something off on her notebook,*

continuing to look back at him; she then gets up and walks over to him to take his chalkboard and proceeds to sit down to check it. Then a second boy lifts his own board to show her, and she goes to check what he had written too, giving it back to him afterwards and returning to her own seat. (2017)

Though they were certainly capable of working independently, learners actively moved to assist others, redefining the space of their learning beyond their own groups. This movement facilitated a horizontal transmission of knowledge among peers—a phenomenon I had often noted before, as learners appeared to understand classroom tasks much more readily when they received information from their peers.[11] Perhaps in confirmation of this, a teacher interviewed in Jacmel said that she had observed how the children moved to "self-segregate" by skill level. The children's learning occurred preferentially through interaction with peers, rather than through adult-child transmission or through the official curriculum which was delivered in the form of texts written on the blackboard. Reflecting and building important qualities of sociality and care or help in their peer groups, roles of teacher and learner were distributed and shared. This engagement in teaching-learning occurred alongside the more formal curriculum, and in a sense it became the principal modality for students' engagements around learning.

Fugitive Learning, Care, and Solidarity: Hope in the Face of Structural Disadvantage

Among Haitian children and youth, movement, as a practice of hope, is tightly connected to the development of relations of belonging that enable both learning and valued notions of helpful, caring selves to emerge. The sense of becoming someone of value in this process appears to be of great importance. However, this cultivation of a sense of personal value is not only tied to realizing individual hopes or goals but more broadly reflects a process that connects the individual with the social collective. Understanding the nature of youths' aspirations as cultural practice also requires recognizing the extent to which they see hopes for the future to be dependent on collective action, not just individual choice or agency. In this way, practices of self-development exist alongside and are connected to development of solidarity. Previous research has reported that collective action among Haitian youth has historically been a major force for addressing social problems and political change (Kivland, 2012). In every town and community across the country one finds groups of youth who come together voluntarily to address community needs. The idea of "*Mete tèt ansanm*" (putting [our] heads together) is reflected in these traditional forms of community social organization.

This emphasis on collective action extends to views of outside assistance, as well. A focus group interview with a group of five *restavèk* in Jérémie in 2015 revealed a strong critique of the activities of NGOs for their failure to *mete tèt ansanm* (to work together) to address children's needs. When asked if they had dreams for the future they replied, "*Anpil, anpil . . .* (many, many)." They expressed aspirations for many different occupations, as described earlier, and helping their families was very important to them. But in addition to individual aspirations, the children also shared comments about NGO assistance efforts in their area: in the words of one boy, "NGOs don't help us. They don't work together to address the situation." Another said, "We need change at the community level. We have trash in the streets, poor roads, poor education." One said, "*Yo pa fè edikasyon byen. Yo pa mete tèt ansanm pou chanje edikasyon.*" (They don't do education well. They don't work together to change education.) They wanted more trade schools and a residential center for street kids where they could stay and at the same time learn a trade. They expressed hopes that if NGOs worked together, they could offer both individual opportunity and effect social change. A boy attending the community school for *restavèk* in Jacmel told his interviewer that he was good in school and that he helped the other kids when they had difficulty; he wanted more support to organize children's clubs for "kids who have a lot of talent, like me" so that they could help others. Far from a sense of despair or lack of hope, all of these children emphasized their aspirations, capacities, and solidarity with others. Most importantly, as expressed by the children in Jérémie, they had dreams for Haiti itself: "*Ayiti kap chanje. Li kap vin yon peyi tankou lot peyi, tankou Etazini*" ("Haiti can change, Haiti can become a country like other countries, like the U.S.").

These hopes remain largely invisible to the many white actors who claim their work alone provides Haitian children and youth with hope for the future. Treating hope as yet another charitable gift effectively obscures local cultural practices of children and youth who sustain hope through movement, relationships, and practices of help and solidarity. This moral economy of hopeful personhood is deeply connected to the ways children use their movement to develop the kinds of dependency relationships of care and patronage that I described earlier—relationships that reflect both the agency of children and youth and the culturally valued ideals of social relational personhood. These practices occur largely in private domains and private lives, away from outsiders' constructions of absence and deficit that enable the latter to believe they are "giving hope to the hope-less." Drawing deeply from Haitian cultural values and traditions of wide and extended familial relationships and notions of valued interpersonal obligations of care, dependency, and solidarity, children's practices of hope enable survivance within and also against the institutional and structural failures that surround them.

Hope to the Hopeless? The White Appropriation of Haitian Personhood

I have suggested that children and youth actively construct hope via situated cultural practices. These include inter-family movement and migration, engagement in work and collective action as an opportunity for personal self-development, and actively using movement to support processes of learning and fostering social relationships based on care and help. All of these ways of developing personhood represent alternative pathways for hope, outside of the state, the bourgeois family, and formal schooling. Yet as self-defined providers of hope to the hopeless in Haiti, faith-based actors overlook the importance of these practices to children in precarity, in favor of imposing static categories and fixed statuses on children's lives that paint them as lacking in almost everything of fundamental importance: love, hope, and a sense of self.

This discourse of deficiency is deeply tied to the politics of aid and advocacy: constructing needs, securing donors, and managing portfolios. At the same time, the worldview of white faith-based actors is not just about the technical life of aid and the demands it imposes, but about a set of values and cultural ideals associated with the middle-class Northern bourgeois ideals of stable families, stable childhoods, and stable institutions: all of which are deemed necessary conditions for the maintenance of hope. Failing to appreciate the role of movement in these relationships of care and dependency that are a constant feature of youth's lives, as well as the value of such relationships to children's futures, whites often only perceive them at best as damaging to children. In this sense, the efforts of white faith-based actors to "give hope" misappropriate hope as a charitable gift, when it is in fact the product of children's effort and agency working against the constraints of larger structural forces.

Most problematically, perhaps, the ideology of "giving them hope" positions the nation itself ever more tightly within a dependent relationship to those who would be donors of hope. It is thus not only deceptive but politically strategic, in that it draws from a legacy of international donor aid that creates dependencies that contribute to political and cultural marginalization of the nation. This in itself should make us aware of the slippery slope that hope can follow when it becomes enmeshed in the economy and politics of humanitarian aid and development.

Children's practices and efforts to maintain personhood and hope are not perfect, of course. There is often great struggle involved, and despair is always possible; it is a human condition that knows no bounds. Personal and collective practices of making hope in the face of difficult circumstances may or may not transform the structured social inequalities that undoubtedly lead some to hopelessness. However, for white agents of assistance to portray themselves as sole providers of hope to the hopeless not only denies but appropriates the very practices of personhood that lie at the core of Haitian struggles to survive.

Coda

In 2011 I traveled to the country with a group of North Americans who were interested in post-earthquake educational development projects. At the end of my stay I wrote:

> *In Haiti one finds the circulation of everything—children, teachers, workers, family members, resources—everyone and everything is moving somewhere. I'd given the mayor of the city we were visiting a large container of peanuts as a gift. As we all sat together chatting, he seemed to devour them. Later on that evening as we gathered again, one of our more outspoken group members told him that eating too many peanuts will cause gas. He replied, "But I didn't eat them all, I gave them to others." She hadn't even thought about the possibility. I recalled so many other occasions where I'd given gifts to people only to find them soon afterwards in the possession of others.*[12]*At another moment our American group leader, talking about the projects he was planning, said to the mayor, "You're going to have to be dealing with us for the next 20 years." The mayor replied, "But you've forgotten, I'm not going to be here for the next 20 years." We Americans assumed stasis and stability; we could not see the circulation of things and persons that was always a part of Haitian life.*

> *In fact I have been noticing circles everywhere. There were circles on the patterned drapes in my hotel room and circles in the iron gates to the school we visited. As I walked into a classroom, there was a large circle drawn on the blackboard, and I noted the circles on the trash can in the corner. Walking in the street, I saw a*

bus pass by whose destination, as written in the sign on the front, was simply,
"DESTINATION."

American visions tended to be clouded with what had begun to me to look like
an odd preoccupation with stasis, stability, and fixedness. A US missionary with
long experience in Haiti once told me, "You have to understand the Haitian
mentality. You know I've worked in Guatemala, and if there's a pile of clothing to
be distributed, a Guatemalan boy would be so happy to get just one item, but in
Haiti, everyone will just try to take the whole thing for themselves" (LG, 2007).
Why could we whites not see all the movement and redistribution that was going
on behind the scenes? Why could we not realize that no, the mayor did not keep
all the peanuts to himself, nor would a Haitian keep a "whole pile" of clothing for
herself. Here, once again, the white vision of Haiti had failed: we did not see the
ethic of sharing, the relations of care, the ways all people and things were given
new possibilities—new hopes—through circulation.

9

From Doing Good to Good Doing

Haiti, Childhood, and an Anthropological Praxis for the Future

Foyer Bethel is an orphanage occupying a former nightclub space. Started by the director, Kenny, a Haitian-American, with support from a church in Port-au-Prince, the orphanage also runs a summer camp, which was in full swing at the time of my visit. Kenny's daughter was in Haiti on her summer break, helping out, as well as two of his brothers. The kids range in age from 3 to 15 and I'm told, when I ask, that there are no restavèk *here and no street kids. Indeed, Kenny told me that among the 85 kids there, some have means, most have parents, and others are from more truly poor situations. Some of the kids go home at night. I find this a little confusing as the standard orphanage narrative is "parents too poor to support their child" so they give the child up to the orphanage, but clearly this orphanage/ summer camp is serving families and children from a range of economic situations- -from those who have some means to the truly poor. For those parents who are truly poor ("*vreman pa kapab*"—"truly not capable") Kenny says he facilitates adoptions. He also tells me he needs more funds so that he can support more kids.*

The afternoon began with a lot of enthusiastic group chants and songs:

A: (Animator): Foyer . . .

C: (Children): Bethel!

A: Nous faisons tout . . . (We do everything)

C: De tout coeur! (With all our heart!)

A: Timoun jodia . . . (Children today)

C: Granmoun demen! (Grownups tomorrow!)

After this, individual children got up to perform songs they had composed themselves, to the accompaniment of a drum. Singing was followed by an aerobic dance led by Kenny's daughter, some games, and lunch—which consisted of adult-sized plates heaped with rice and sos pwa *(bean sauce) for everyone. There was no adjustment in serving size for the little ones, yet every single child cleaned their plate entirely, even the three year olds. I saw one young girl feed a still younger one, and another put a spoon of rice from her plate onto the plate of a still younger boy. After everyone was done, the kitchen ladies washed and cleaned all the serving items and huge pots, which were scrubbed with leaves.* (2015)

This orphanage was a category without borders, a shifting assemblage of multilayered practices and meanings: true orphans, orphans with parents, poor, middle-class, residential, non-residential, foreign models and activities, local practices and innovations. This complex assemblage of practices belied the ways "the orphanage" was often narrated by faith-based actors—both those who had been engaged in supporting orphanages, as well as those whose missions were about eliminating them. I had been invited to visit by the director's wife, probably because as a white I could be a potential source of support. Like many orphanages, this was a business—particularly because the "truly poor" kids were a commodity that could be "shipped out" via lucrative foreign adoptions. The summer camp—an activity often supported by foreign organizations and churches in their schools and childcare facilities—was also precisely the kind of activity that could advertise the business by drawing in children from more middle-class families. In this way the orphanage became something like a "full-service" child welfare organization, offering education, care, and sustenance to children and families with a variety of needs.

Certainly there was much that remained hidden about the organization itself and its relationships and positioning within the local landscape, but what I did notice was the ways in which it served as an arena for both the transmission of indigenous cultural values and practices as well as for the production of a future-oriented modernity. In terms of indigenous values, one might note the egalitarianism of food distribution and indeed its profuse generosity. The ways it did not differentiate according to age, or presumed habits of consumption, spoke to me of a non-developmental lens on childhood that granted a certain equality to all, regardless of age or status. There was no "ages and stages" differentiation, so common in the United States, for example, where "child-size" is an institution, and older and younger children are separated and given different activities according to their presumed "developmental levels." The fact that children themselves shared what they had with others, even here—where there was plenty to go about—also spoke of a profound ethic of sharing learned from the earliest age and internalized so forcefully that it constantly directed attention to other's needs and a generated a desire to care for them. (And it highlighted once again for me the condescension of whites who felt that they "needed to teach Haitian children to share" or to "think of others" and "not claim everything for themselves"[1]). That children finished every single bit on their plates, regardless of age or stature—also spoke to me of something more than hunger--a profound ethic of gratefulness and respect, associated perhaps with experiential awareness of what it means to lack or not have enough.

The autonomy and creativity of the children were also highlighted: children composed their own songs and performed them. This was not the rote mimicry or replication that constituted the text-based diet of formal schooling but a respect for the capacities of children as creators. That their songs were accompanied by drums was a nod to Haitian indigenous arts but in a way that supported performers' autonomy and innovation. The aerobic dance to American pop music led by the director's daughter was performed, too, with the incorporation of Haitian traditional dance movements. All of these activities were engaged in with full and complete enthusiasm on the part of the children to an extent that belied the image of the traumatized orphan separated from a loving family and suffering from emotional disorders.

And then there were the pots cleaned with leaves: a better agent, no doubt, than a sponge or rag, and an effective alternative to a scrub brush. At the least, leaves were far more environmentally conscious—both from a resource availability/sustainability lens as well as in a deeper sense of connection to and consciousness of the natural world and its eminently valuable gifts. Cleaning pots with leaves was modern, innovative, and traditional, all at the same time. Along with the orphanage itself, it reflected precisely the indeterminacy and layeredness of meaning that contextualized much of Haitian childhood, against white efforts to simplify, reduce, categorize, and conform.

Discourse, Power, Emotion, and the Method of Critique

I have taken it as axiomatic throughout the chapters of this book that discourse both reflects and constructs social reality and is thus a key arena for reflection and interrogation within the anthropology of childhood. Ways of talking about and representing childhood shape the field of action; indeed, they determine the possibilities for action, and in themselves are a form of action and thus key to understanding the dynamics of white saviorism as it operates in the landscape of foreign intervention. This discourse draws from multiple sources—including contemporary ideologies of development, globally circulating ideas about proper families and childhoods, mainstream psychology, and Christian faith. The power of discourse to represent and construct other worlds—specifically, the world of Haitian childhood—through constructions of Haitian deficits is directly related to the ways white subjectivity—including white emotion and white identity—is positioned to cover over, fill up, or otherwise erase Haitian subjectivity in this process. In this way whites are able to claim ownership over Haiti and its children—"*our* Haiti that we love so much!" (in the words of some) by conforming it to a white imaginary, in which Haitians desire the same things as whites, feel the same ways about things, share the same epistemology/world view, and have the same cultural and social ideals of "the good life." White innocence (including racial innocence) sustains the whole project, both because interventionism is grounded in Christian love alongside a set of principles, ideas, and values that are assumed to be not just white, but universal.

The method that I have used to instantiate these critical reflections draws from the classic notion of the "anthropological veto" (Mead, 1928) in which assumed universals of science about human behavior and psychological functioning are shown to be not so universal, after all.[2] In this process, observations and experiences from my fieldwork and existing scholarship on Haitian society are juxtaposed with the discourse of white actors to illustrate the gaps between what is said about Haitian culture and cultural deficits and Haitian children's lived experiences. By showing how white representations of Haitian childhood and family are often partial, culturally biased, or inaccurate, the ideas and values that underlie white projects of intervention can be contested, even though they may be grounded in globalized norms and models of mainstream psychology and widely shared notions of good and proper childhood that have global resonance.

At the same time, a critical lens cannot just rest with illuminating cultural differences or disjunctions between narrative and lived experience. A critical anthropology of childhood demands that we see such operations as functions of inequalities of power, and in the preceding chapters I have tried to show how emotion serves as an arena par excellence for such. As discussed earlier, the literature on emotion in voluntourism, humanitarianism, and international development has primarily conceptualized it in the context of white desire for experiences of authenticity, or the emotional rewards associated with "making a difference," or with the emotional involvements and relationships that substitute for lacks in the lives or self-identities of the helpers, or in the context of analysis of the emotional dynamics behind the motivations to "do good" among those who are more privileged. The commodification of emotion and the role of emotional performance and emotional labor on the part of "suffering others" have also been important trends in this scholarship. All of these themes are significant in the landscape of white assistance in Haitian childhood as well.

However, I have endeavored to push the analysis of emotion further, to show that it also serves as a powerful force for neocolonial domination: serving as a field for the production of white subjectivity with a global resonance. In the case of Haiti, but also perhaps more globally, white saviorism operates through feeling narratives, but its endpoint is the subjugation of other subjectivities. In the case of Haitian childhood, in particular, a discourse of child and family cultural, emotional, and spiritual deficiency enables whites to engage in "filling" Haitian lives with their felt own emotional, spiritual, and material wealth—educating Haitians not only to do better, but to *feel* better—that is, to participate in the supposed rewards of white subjectivity. All of this takes place within a larger domain framed by the inviolability of love rooted in faith: the love whites have for Haiti and the love Haitians express for them. This larger field of love frames the dynamics of white relationships with Haiti and shapes the calling of whites to engage with Haiti and its children.

Yet, as I have argued, what looks like compassion and empathy for the suffering child can be subtractive of the child's subjectivity for four interrelated reasons: one, because it treats the child as empty and damaged due to a lack of love and affection and thus needing to be filled with the love and healing the white can provide; second, because in this process whites can project their own emotionally driven visions of the good life onto the empty child (or broken family), assuming that the latter's interior life mirrors their own; third, because as a witness to Haitian children's suffering ("the stories I've heard, the things I've seen") the white potentially narrates Haitian suffering for an audience and in this process it becomes a part of the white person's own self-narrative as interlocutor or helper; and finally because saving Haitian children from hopelessness and emptiness enables the white to claim emotional ownership (e.g., "these are *my* children"). Action and intervention then become more about the validation and extension of white feeling into the lives of others, with affect becoming a field for the exercise of power and control. This is clear in the ways mental health experts narrate Haitian children's experiences as trauma that is then made amenable to white psychological interventions, or the ways children lack attachment and are thus incapable of healthy emotion until brought back to loving "mamas," or in the ways *restavèk* are characterized as "slaves"—a word with undeniable emotional power—who require (white) rescue. The discourse of trauma, slavery, victimization, and hopelessness—all of the major tropes that define Haitian childhood—makes it impossible for Haitians to have emotional lives of their own that are not somehow narrated, erased, moderated, or made subject to white interpellation or intervention.

This is not, of course, to deny that suffering exists in Haitian children's lives or that compassion is wrong, or that whites cannot see anything beyond their own feelings. Nor is it to claim Haitian exceptionalism—as if Haiti were somehow so different, so unique, as to be beyond comprehension or that somehow Haitians do not feel things or think like everyone else.[3] My goal instead is to bring anthropological attention to the domains of cultural difference that shape childhood and that have been ignored or invisibilized within white narratives of help and development, including attention to the ways in which the generalizations of WEIRD psychology when applied to the Haitian context fail to account for cultural differences in sometimes profound ways. This does not mean that Haitian childhood or Haitian psychology are exceptional; it means, rather, that differences exist and sometimes run deep, and that outsider efforts to intervene in Haitian lives often proceed without consciousness of these differences, with consequences for both Haitians and those who would pursue projects of "doing good." Illuminating this disjuncture points to the ways in which white failure to "see" the landscape of Haitian childhood is also a failure of cultural imagination: that ability to go beyond the givens or assumptions grounded one's own experience to envision different realities and possibilities.

A Critical Anthropology of Childhood: What Should It Accomplish?

These critiques that are raised in this book are situated within a broader consideration of the ways cultural imperialism continues to operate in Haiti in many domains, via outsider construction of Haitian cultural and social deficiencies that can be remedied by the superior knowledge and know-how of outsiders. As I have suggested at multiple points throughout this book, this is an important theme in the critical anthropological literature on NGOs in Haiti, in which humanitarian and development actors often explicitly believe in "schooling" Haitians to fix their supposed cultural deficiencies (Schuller, 2016: 185, 188). In the context of white faith-based discourse on Haitian childhood and family, I have shown how the language of deficiency penetrates deeply into the construction of childhood and family, shaping the field for white interventions that can rescue Haitian society and its children from the damage done by broken family systems, lack of education, hopelessness, trauma, violence, and victimization.

For anthropologists, childhood is regarded as the primary arena for formation of culturally specific forms of personhood, and thus I have focused throughout this book on the ways in which a critical perspective on childhood must respect Haitian views of personhood and the modalities that are used within Haitian society and culture to support this ideal. Certainly the latter does not exist in codified form: rather, it exists in the form of ethno-theories of education, learning, and development grounded in Haitian history, social and religious traditions as well as the ecological contexts that shape Haitian lives. These are not fixed, but continuously evolving in response to broad societal and global challenges—including the influence of global knowledge and ideals that underlie white efforts to change Haitian patterns of childrearing and education. It is important not to essentialize cultural notions of personhood, but to recognize that they inform the developmental tasks and trajectories of childhood learning, and that they serve as arenas for contest within contemporary global flows of culture, as communities struggle with forces both internal and external that shape ideals and practices about what a citizen looks like, what qualities a person should have, what a good education looks like, and what types of persons are best cultivated for the present and future. From a critical perspective, then, the anthropology of childhood should raise fundamental questions about whose visions are prioritized in this process and how inequalities of power can shape the trajectories of childhood learning and becoming in ways that may or may not support cultural and societal goals.

It may be useful at this juncture to summarize the major themes and critiques that have been raised in previous chapters, with an eye toward raising awareness and proposing alternative frames and approaches that could potentially shape the direction of future change efforts. It is no accident that childhood has been largely invisible in the literature on Haiti, in favor of a focus on categories of victimized children or particular issues facing children. As I discussed earlier, this was my own approach when I first began work in Haiti with a focus on *restavèk*. It was only over time that I began to see the ways in which this category imposed a relatively limited lens on a phenomenon that was shifting and often ill-defined. Yet the single issue lens remains dominant among faith-based actors, who variously target *restavèk*, street children, family reunification, traumatized children, victimized women and girls, and broken families.[4] Oftentimes the underlying social context is similarly reduced to a question of poverty, as if Haitian social and cultural practice would look just like that of whites (e.g., parents would always keep their children at home) if only parents had enough money. This reductive explanatory frame neglects the role of cultural ideologies and values that may well differ from those of whites, such as the educational value for children of living apart from parents, or different notions of family life as a corporate enterprise. Part of the reason for the reductive approach is, of course, the nature of organizational structures themselves, as projects impose a need to define a mission, manage, and evaluate (Schöneberg 2017: 611) and thus isolate an issue from its larger social, cultural, and economic foundations. The goal or need to "just do something," too, as Schuller observes among humanitarian actors (2016: 212), serves as a powerful force for reducing a complex social phenomenon into action items.

As I suggested, though, this focus on categories of children or limited and decontextualized approaches to their experience also draws from larger epistemological frameworks that whites bring to their work in Haiti. These lenses prioritize visible evidence, temporal ordering, measurement/quantification, and a certain ontological separation between domains of experience into the psychological, material, social, and spiritual. There is also a deeply engrained ideology of individualism that shapes the most fundamental ideas about the self and its relations to others and the natural world—a lens that is often at odds with relational and moral understandings of self and person shaped by indigenous spiritual traditions (see Hoffman, 2019). These epistemological and ideological frameworks are important to the world of aid and assistance, yet they differ from traditional sensory and spiritual modalities of knowing and being that are so powerful in Haiti, where the interconnectedness of everything is a given and one learns and knows through modalities that are sensory, material, and spiritual at the same time. As I discussed earlier, I myself had to confront these frameworks to admit that there are many things that happen in Haiti that cannot be explained using familiar rationalities. While alternative ways of knowing may or may not be significant to others working in Haiti, I remain convinced that a transformation of perception was important in grounding my own understandings of childhood and learning more deeply. Of course, this is not to claim that other approaches to understanding are wrong, or that my interpretations are necessarily correct or complete (as an outsider, I assume they are not); but it does suggest to me that an adjustment of epistemological assumptions is needed for a more culturally appropriate understanding of the complexities of childhood in Haiti.

A second critique that weaves throughout these chapters concerns the tendency toward a limited, adult-centric view of children's lives and learning. A phenomenon long identified in scholarship on the anthropology and sociology of childhood (e.g., James and Prout, 2015), adult-centrism prioritizes adult models of competence and development, positioning children as deficient in comparison. In this lens children are always seen in terms of what they cannot do: that is, they are viewed as on the way to becoming fully functioning and capable adults, rather than as capable subjects in their own right. As a result, adult-centrism limits inquiry on and appreciation for the nature and subjective dimensions of childhood as it is lived and experienced by children. In Haiti, this adult-centrism limits white abilities to understand and appreciate forms of learning and development that exist in spaces apart from interactions with adults. These include the important role of siblings and peers in children's learning and socialization as well as the environment itself in both its inanimate and sentient forms; alternative notions and sources for emotional attachment beyond a primary adult caregiver; modalities of care in children's experience that go beyond that provided by adults for children and that prioritize children themselves as caregivers; the ways children often exert autonomy and agency in many domains of their lives; and, most importantly, self-education as a set of cultural practices drawing from enduring ideals of personhood and indigenous spirituality that emphasize diffuse capacities for teaching and learning across the lifespan and the varied settings of everyday life.

A larger effect of adult-centrism is, of course, to enable the positioning of Haiti itself as a "needy child" in relation to the developed, knowledgeable "adult" North. This theme builds on the great white discourse of deficiency in Haitian culture and society that I have referenced throughout this narrative. It is a notion of deficiency that penetrates even into the very foundations of Haitian personhood, as Haitian emotional lives are erased, muted, or declared damaged and thus in need of appropriate rescue by experts of the white North. In this narrative, Haiti itself is a child, on the way to achieving the adult competencies of the Global North. Its broken families and damaged children have been particularly powerful metaphors for the damaged nation in need of rescue: for they are sites par excellence for the formation of a competently "adult" nation.

Finally, a central theme that cuts across all of these chapters in the ways in which Haitian childhood presents multiple sites and possibilities for self-formation beyond the institutions of the school and the stable nuclear family that are so often constructed as key sites for societal development. While not denying the importance of the latter, and recognizing that children themselves greatly value schooling, I have suggested that there is an alternative landscape of surprisingly rich non-institutionalized settings for learning and that these opportunities are actively sought out, as children spend much of their time in the company of mixed age peers, learning from observation and participation in community events and natural settings, living in flexible (for whites, read: "unstable") extended households, and participating in a rich domain of autonomous collective organizations (e.g., church groups, *skout*, *atelier*, *klub*, informal learning/study groups, community committees, and *baz* ["bases"]).[5]

The shifting nature of these settings and the kinds of relationships they engender should be seen as a vibrant landscape of childhood experience that offers multiple sites for personal development and learning. At the very least, non-institutionalized spheres of learning and self-education open up possibilities for extending one's capacities to relate to both the human and natural world in novel ways. Yet all of these domains for learning often remain unacknowledged, given the ways schooling and social class inequalities have so governed possibilities for social attainment. This naturally raises the question: are they of value, or consequence, within a society so structured? I would like to say yes, because while they may not lead directly or immediately to structural transformation, they have both an innate cultural value and potential for being cultural resources for thinking about directions for future change and development.

Some readers may inevitably come away from this book with a sense that I have over-romanticized Haitian childhood experience or even Haitian culture by failing to recognize the amount of suffering that children endure on a daily basis or the ways in which Haitian cultural practices undermine children's development and need changing. Alternatively, some may feel that I have failed to critique the structural disadvantages flowing from poverty, state and civil society failure to protect children's rights, inadequate schooling, inadequate attention to child protection, orphanage-based abuse and trafficking, or other failures to protect children's well- being—to mention just a short-list of potential sources of risk and vulnerability. I have not denied the existence of the latter, and I certainly do not claim that change at the structural level is not needed, but my goal has been different: to show how there is much more to Haitian childhood than vulnerability, suffering, and victimization—avenues that have been used too often by whites to enable their own saving interventions. At the least, in drawing attention to childhood as a space for agency, autonomy, rich cultural learning, and development of culturally valued dispositions of personhood, my goal has been to contribute to that larger project of changing narratives about Haiti (Ulysse, 2010).

This attention to alternative and often ignored dimensions of childhood experience is a way to deepen and contextualize the partial knowledge that often informs well-intentioned outsider interventions. Partial knowledge reflects awareness of some aspects of the Haitian context but it generally does not go far enough to understand deeper culturally shaped notions of spirituality, family, nature, relationships, or personhood, for example. Partial knowledge in fact enables white cultural imposition because it does not reach deep enough to transform the values or assumptions that whites bring to their work, particularly those that derive from mainstream psychology or the deeply held ideals of what constitutes a "good" childhood. Thus, even when acting with ostensible goals of respecting the culture, there often remains a desire to conform Haiti to white visions of what a good childhood looks like. I have heard Haitian-Americans as well as whites involved in educational and development efforts in Haiti unselfconsciously declare, "I want Haitian children to have the same kind of childhood I had," as if they could, or as if their own version of childhood experience were intrinsically better. This is the same sentiment that underlies one reading of the assertion, "What I believe can rescue that nation" (Dryden-Petersen and Reddick, 2019)—the title of a recent article on diaspora involvement in educational development in conflicted and fragile states, including Haiti.[6] Aside from the problematic emphasis on the idea of rescue itself, such assertions reflect the kind of imperialistic visions of child and societal welfare that have long shaped outsider interventions in the black and brown world. An effective critical anthropology of childhood is one that highlights the disjunctures that exist globally among ideologies of childhood, raising the question of whose visions govern childhood and through what means. Childhood represents a key domain for envisioning national futures and for the working out of ideals of citizenship, belonging, and indeed planetary survival. It thus demands that scholars and practitioners engage in critical inquiry that illuminates the ways inequalities shape childhood as an arena for social development and change.

From Doing Good to Good Doing: Ideas for Change

Though the image of the white savior has been widely criticized, the practices of saving are still very much alive, even when the identity is disavowed. The saving mission is revealed particularly powerfully in the discourses that white faith actors bring to their work, when they claim to "give hope," to "empower lives," to "heal families," or "pour love into" the loveless lives of Haitian children. What is worse, as I have shown, is that this "saving" affords whites the privilege of emotional ownership over Haitian children ("*my* children") and even over the nation itself ("*Our* Haiti"), reflecting the persistence of an implicit if not explicit underlying neocolonialism.[7]

In a discussion of the trope of doing good that animates the desires of whites to intervene in the lives of the less fortunate, Grewal (2017: 119) argues that what we are seeing is a notion of Western humanitarian citizenship grounded in the long-standing continuation of the colonial "civilizing mission" to "save" distant Others. This mission is a distinctly moral enterprise, informed by many sources, but always. predicated on the sense that whites have both the capacity and the duty to engage in projects of doing good. As others have pointed out, this civilizing mission is also very much a racial project, facilitated by discursive representations of the "dark world" as "dysfunctional, childlike, and dependent" (Balaji, 2011: 51; Fanon, 1967), a place where "tragedy and hopelessness reign and where one's success is determined by the compassion of (white) Others" (Balaji, 2011: 52). As I have suggested, this saving mission continues in Haiti, as a racial project of uplift is coded as "white light in Haitian darkness," where whites pour out love and hope into empty Haitians and offer them new lives, re-birthing them into a whitened, brighter world.

In thinking about how to work against the persistent ideology of white saviorism, one possible avenue is to move away from conceptualizing faith-based development intervention as "doing good," to thinking about such work instead as "good doing." This shifts the locus of action to the immediate context, in which actions themselves are seen as good, relevant, morally and practically suited to a specific local context, and judged by local standards as such. The problem with framing interventions either tacitly or implicitly as "doing good" is that it supposes some sort of ontological endpoint characterized by a general agreement on what that good is: a perspective that is as likely or not to be defined by those who have more power, more resources, more technical know-how, even as we realize that local contests over what is ultimately good in a situation are as significant or even more significant than differences of opinion between so-called insiders and outsiders. Even when there is local buy-in, or efforts to incorporate local voices, doing good tends to draw on or reference a more distant, abstract moral ground beyond the given context. It is thus innately subject to the pitfalls of ethnocentrism and imperialism.

This suggests to me that a more effective and culturally attuned approach should reflect the far more humble aim of good doing: actions that reflect deeply contextualized, local responses to immediate needs rather than long-term abstract ideals of "betterment." This means that in some contexts good doing might approach more traditional notions of Christian charity as material redistribution—an idea widely rejected in the contemporary world of development where "dependency" is widely suspect and sustainability and empowerment are dominant paradigms. Yet, it may be worthwhile to consider that oftentimes those larger projects are contested, misunderstood, and co-opted by local actors in ways that undermine their goals. While it is certainly possible for traditional redistributive charity to go wrong as well (notably, to create local resource instability, friction, and tension), at the same time such practices are sometimes a better fit with local moralities and world views in which the charity of others creates valued forms of hierarchical dependency (see Scherz, 2014, for additional discussion of this point in the case of Uganda). This appears to be the case in Haiti, where those in need can and do request material aid from those who may have marginally more, and doing so creates relationships that are intrinsically unequal but nevertheless highly valued, with those in the benefactor role accruing culturally valued social status.[8] It becomes important then to apply a local lens in determining the meaning surrounding material aid, and whether or not it can add to or detract from local practices and visions of good relationships and community life.

Good Doing: Schooling

To further the project of moving toward good doing, especially in the realm of education, would involve paying close attention to indigenous cultural understandings of authority, learning, and personhood. Here, I draw on points raised in previous chapters to outline what may be ways to think about reform of schooling that draw from Haitian cultural strengths and avoid the pitfalls of imposing culturally biased notions deriving from mainstream child development psychology and white cultural values and ideals of what good schooling looks like. Key to this process of course is that we recognize that institutional schooling is often a site for the production of failure for children whose cultures, communities, languages, social class backgrounds, and habits of learning are not only not recognized but actively converted into sources of failure.

Further, schooling often prioritizes language as the key modality of learning, failing to recognize the multiple ways learning proceeds though diverse modalities (Lima, 1998). In Haiti, the question of language in schooling has often been addressed in terms of the mother-tongue argument centered on the conflict between French and Haitian Creole, but the question in fact goes further into modalities of learning that center on orality and the body vs. the written text as primary modalities of learner engagement. That is to say, the problem may not just be a matter of French vs. Creole but a deeper matter of culturally valued traditions of oral transmission and performance vs. the text-based nature of schooling.[9] In contemporary Haiti, the colonial state survives, to a great extent, in the text-based system of schooling, where the pedagogical process is based on the replication and transmission of written texts—texts that need to be copied down, in French, leading to static reproduction of knowledge. In contrast, the models and processes of learning that children have in their environment are oral and embodied: children see people doing things, building things, changing things, and creating things. There is a possibility of innovation, creation—all of which become visible when one's focus shifts to a closer look at children's learning in ordinary environments. The belief that school-based tasks represent a "higher" or more demanding form of engagement and knowledge than activities of ordinary everyday life is something that requires rethinking (see also Erickson, 1984; Lave, 1996; Vossoughi and Gutiérrez, 2014). It belongs principally to the colonialist and technocratic modes of knowledge transmission long associated with institutionalized schooling, further exacerbated by legacies of colonialism that promoted "schooling the savages" in order to civilize them.

Earlier chapters have explored the ways learning figures as a key process that children engage in across a variety of settings: walking with them through their neighborhoods, observing them interact with peers in the street, learning and performing domestic chores in households and in other settings such as an afterschool program. There are a number of characteristics of this learning that could be drawn upon to enhance the culture of classrooms and schools in ways that could potentially enrich them as settings for learning:

1. **Egalitarian, horizontal transmission.** First, children's learning in these contexts is typically not directed, supervised, or mandated by adults. Rather, the social context is more often mixed age, with horizontal, peer-to-peer transmission rather than adult-child transmission. In peer groups, more skilled or knowledgeable children interact with those who are less skilled or knowledgeable. (In some situations, children may even readily take on roles as teachers for adults.) In these informal contexts, roles of teacher and learner are distributed and shared. Schooling can and should provide such opportunities for children to form supportive peer groups. This is actually done autonomously and voluntarily among university students but the practice could be extended to younger children and youth (see Hoffman, 2021 for description of a similar effort).

2. **Modeling and Coaching.** Second, when adults are present, such as in certain situations that could be characterized as apprenticeship, they do not engage children in long verbal or conceptual explanations. Rather, they perform or model an activity, while children observe and then try things out on their own. Children appear to be self-motivated, taking initiative on their own to engage and participate. On occasions

where a learner does not yet have the skills to perform an activity but is nevertheless committed to it, sometimes there is a coach. The coach is preferentially someone of similar age and status but with marginally more knowledge or experience who offers the learner encouragement and support. There is almost never any didactic instruction on the part of either models or coaches. Coaching can support peer learning as described earlier in important ways.

3. **Observation and Performance/distributed participation.** Observation is a key modality of learner engagement. It is deeply valued and fostered throughout everyday life. Further, in observational learning there is nearly always a dialogical relationship between observation and performance. As one person performs, the others observe, and the performance role is distributed or passed to different individuals in succession. The performer serves as a model for the others, and each learner is individually engaged through observation. This might also be considered a form of distributed participation, where observation as well as agency/action are important and shared. In a small literacy learning group, for example, one boy might write a word while the others watch; they take turns writing and observing. The practice of individual performance for an audience often already occurs in classrooms in Haiti as learners are called to recite, for example, in front of the class. But it could be used more consistently within small group activities and recognized for its important pedagogical value (apart from being used as a method to evaluate or assess, as it commonly is).

4. **Embodiment.** Children's learning is highly embodied: frequently mediated through movement, utilization of materials, or gesture, as well as through often undervalued sensory channels such as touch. Physical contact with peers and with elements of the environment are important to processes of meaning-making. Traditional cultural beliefs support the notion that knowledge and other intangible qualities such as blessings can be present in or transferred materially through bodies or physical objects. This suggests important ways to create learning environments that encourage and support natural modalities of embodiment in learning: use of sensory materials, opportunities for physical movement, and integration of different sensory modalities to support engagement.[10]

5. **Wide Attention.** When involved in a learning activity, children's attention is not narrowly focused on objects or elements in succession, but involves a wider holistic attention to the environment, reflecting the idea of "open

attention" described by researchers among indigenous communities in the Americas. Instead of having children focus on texts where attention to exact replication is important, other modalities of engagement could be encouraged that draw on holism in this domain, perhaps integrating learning into more complex and diffuse social settings or designing environments and activities that encourage rather than discourage such attentional processes.[11]

The aforementioned ideas should not be read as an argument for the disappearance of formal schooling, for at present it remains an essential element of societal development. It would seem, however, that there is a need to think more deeply to base reforms of schooling not on Western or Northern ideas of "best practice" so much as on Haitian notions that may appear similar but are also differently nuanced. The modalities of learning that I have described earlier represent a set of culturally significant processes of meaning-making that could readily be drawn upon in reforming schools to be places where the capacities and identities of students are supported more strongly than they are at present. (They may be as relevant to other settings beyond Haiti where culturally and socially marginalized youth must make their way through schooling that disavows their strengths.) The learning sciences as a whole have experienced a new focus on how culture shapes learning—a concern that is inseparable from the need to rethink how to encourage learning under conditions of profound social and cultural inequality (e.g., Eisenhart, 2021; Erickson and Espinoza, 2021; Nasir et al., 2020). As anthropologists have long pointed out, questions of learning are always questions of power: deeply tied to issues of trust, assent, legitimacy, demand, access, and the myriad of ways in which success and failure are allocated. Changing the cultures of schooling in ways that focus on the role of culture in learning is imperative in order to address the profound ways in which schooling currently supports the replication of social inequalities.

Good Doing: Transforming Practices around Child and Family Vulnerability

As the previous chapters have suggested, white narratives of vulnerability in Haitian childhood are centered on beliefs about broken or unstable families, parents lacking appropriate knowledge of parenting and child development, lack of consistent and supportive adults in children's lives, and practices of sending children away either to orphanages or other households where they are more often than not exploited and abused. The result is children who grow up suffering from a fundamental lack of love in their lives that does not permit them to form healthy emotional attachments. Often, the proximate cause of these difficulties is reduced to poverty: the assumption being that if they had the choice, Haitian parents would, of course, keep their children at home with them, and raise them according to the ideals of a bourgeois "happy childhood" where schooling and play are the child's primary responsibilities; children are "protected" and parents are focused on the emotional needs of the "precious" child. In this optic, families would look much more like idealized white, middle-class nuclear households, with parents as pedagogical and emotional coaches, extensive parent-child play, quality "family time," avoidance of physical discipline, and so on—all geared to the production of a different kind of emotional life—a different kind of person— for both adults and children. In effect, vulnerable Haitian childhood is a key domain for the white "civilizing" mission that aims to make Haitians feel (and be) more like whites.

To move away from this lens of deficiency and the sort of imperialistic interventions it supports requires a number of changes. First of all, it requires cognizance of the ways the projection of white subjectivity into Haitian lives represents an act of power. Recognizing that Haitians do not necessarily feel the same ways as whites do, or handle experiences of adversity as whites do, or value effusive demonstrations of affection in their parenting to the extent that whites do, or apply the same meanings to child separation that whites do, is essential. Scaling back white emotional projections could enable a deeper inquiry into and appreciation for the ways in which Haitian childhood is actually lived. Second, there is a need for confronting the white habit of basing interventions on partial knowledge. At the very least, faith-based actors and others involved in developing the landscape of child welfare in Haiti should recognize the ways Haitian world views demand an interconnected lens where there is always more to the story than meets the eye. What this involves is learning, in a sense, to learn, in order to enable new ways to see.

A third important takeaway, as I have suggested earlier, is to "lessen the (interventionist) footprint." Certainly, charity for families in need is welcome, medical care is essential, and support for children who are subject to genuinely abusive and exploitative conditions that threaten their lives is necessary. Not every project, however, is needed or necessary, no matter how much it sounds appealing to donors or reflects helpers' cherished passions or personal causes. A certain scaled-back consciousness of what is of most value, what needs are greatest, and how to satisfy them without cultural intrusion or imposition is necessary. Haitians do not need to be taught how to parent according to the norms of child development psychology based on cultures of the WEIRD world. Nor do they need all their kids to be educated in schools with "activity centers" or plastic toys so that they can develop "leadership" skills, or to have their children "brought home" to "stabilized" families, or to have their children "loved" according to white norms or by white mamas. These are not "problems" for Haitian children in the same way they might be for whites.

I am reminded of the words of Sol Tax, one of the earliest of American anthropologists who promoted a version of "action anthropology" (Tax, 1975). To Tax, action anthropology involved anthropologists helping people to solve a problem that they faced while learning something in the process. He was cautious about the definition of the problem and who, in fact, considered something a problem. It was not about anthropologists coming into local communities and deciding that something needed changing. The definition of the problem and the impetus for change had to come from the people concerned. Neither was the solution to the problem about the mere application of anthropological expert knowledge, for intervention or application of knowledge without learning was imposition. Nor was the anthropologist to go into a community for the sake of learning, or simply building theory, or contributing to science, because that was extraction. Neither aim—intervention or learning—should eclipse the other: both had to happen in tandem. He further cautioned—and this is central to the argument made here—that as outsiders acting in other cultures, we need to act with parsimony: that is, we do not attempt to settle questions of values that do not concern us. That is to say, questions of values (and here, by extension, visions of personhood and "good" childhood) are not ours to solve. Another way to read this is: we are not called to "do good," which implies we know what the good is; instead, we are called to good doing—which lets the people we work with decide what actions are beneficial, allowing them the freedom to pursue their own larger visions of who and what they want to be.

Today I spoke with Jean, a professional drummer in a local band. I had asked him to tell me a bit about his childhood and history with drumming. He had started playing as a child. His grandfather was a hougan (Vodou priest) and so growing up he had lots of opportunity to observe others playing. He never went to any kind of school to learn, but by age 9 he was performing: "It was a gift. People started noticing me, that I had a spirit." He'd watch and listen and then try things out. Nobody interfered or intervened, nobody corrected him. But when he performs, he has to be careful: he has to drop a bit of water or rum on the ground to placate the spirits (lwa), otherwise they can overpower him: "They can mount your arms while you're drumming. When that happens, you can play for hours and hours without awareness. They can control you. They are the ones drumming." He told me he doesn't like when that happens, he'd rather play naturally. (2022)

What Jean revealed was a cultural theory of learning—or, more precisely, a way of being through learning. Nobody corrected him—and I thought about the schools, where correction was constant, demanded by text-based instruction that required perfect imitation, leading learners inevitably toward correction-induced paralysis. I thought about his autonomy, his self-direction, his relationship to the spirits, and his freedom to grow through trial and error. He learned in the company of valued others who did not control, but who modeled. It was a more natural kind of learning than what one could see at school, where others were in control. He was uncomfortable with the forces that came from outside; his learning and performance were not to be controlled or dominated. His true performance was a natural one, coming from his very self, not from those spirits who mounted him from outside. What he revealed was a vision for Haitian personhood, grounded in the freedom of learning to grow and be that is not controlled by outside forces. Those outside spirits are a metaphor for all the white saviors who seek to help by following their own visions of the good, but in doing so ultimately impose their own ways of feeling and being.

Toward a New Imaginary

The shaping of childhood through white narration and intervention is by no means specific to Haiti. It reflects a long history associated with the white mission of civilizational uplift in cultures and communities around the world, and its narratives reflect an amalgamation of moral sentiments and regimes of knowledge associated with Western, educated, industrialized, and democratic societies, combined with a faith imperative to share God's love with the unfortunate. The Haitian case may be different, perhaps, in only a few particulars. The sheer scale of faith-based interventions in the country is one. A second might be the extent to which white projects of intervention draw not just on ideas about deficiencies in Haitian child lives but on a larger image of Haiti and Haitian culture itself as profoundly lacking—what Paul Farmer has called "myths about what is wrong with Haiti and Haitians" that appear so regularly in white discourse (Farmer, 1994: 349). A third distinctive aspect of the Haitian case might be the ways in which the discourse of love functions as a source of white representational power in Haitian lives. As whites narrate their roles as providers of hope, healing, and love to children whose lives are dark, traumatized, and emotionally empty, Haitian childhood becomes a blank slate upon which whites can project their own subjectivities, furthering a new kind of neocolonialism grounded in white feelings that are taken to be universal or natural.

Among those working to develop Haitian childhood, the dearth of understanding of the broader contexts and experiences of children's lives— what I earlier termed "partial knowledge"—represents an opportunity for anthropologists and others with knowledge of these larger contexts to share their perspectives with those involved in change efforts. Platforms that can support such dialogue are essential; it is not sufficient for those involved in change efforts to simply continue to talk with each other, confirming biases and reinforcing tropes of vulnerable, suffering children. Nor can anthropologists simply write for themselves or for their own particular but limited audiences. They have the responsibility to make their work more widely known and accessible to different audiences of practitioners and others engaged in change efforts.

What is needed for the time being is a dialed-down praxis for good doing that avoids the contemporary traps of empowerment agendas that supposedly "provide hope and dignity" (as if these were things that Haitians lacked except for when they are bestowed by whites)—or worse, under the guise of "educating" Haitians, agendas that impose white child development psychology on them in an effort to address their lack of knowledge of the right ways to raise "emotionally competent" children. Some orphanages may indeed be corrupt, some *restavèk* may be abused; some children do suffer from trauma that requires help; some parents may be irresponsible: but this does not give whites the representational privilege of redefining Haitian families as broken or weak or Haitian children as emotionally damaged and in need of whites to pour love into them to "create a stronger Haitian society." This is not a problem that whites can or should solve; speaking as a white, it is, to be blunt, not our business. Childhood is a domain where Haitian voices and visions should be prioritized as they are grounded in genuine attention to the practices that promote their own visions of personhood and identity—practices and values that have gone unrecognized within larger efforts to reform child welfare and education, grounded as the latter has been on government partnerships with foreign churches and actors who disseminate internationalized visions of best practice, as well as decades of faith-based efforts, church missions, and well-meaning volunteers who come to Haiti to offer children the love and rescue they supposedly need.

The current era in Haiti is one of deep anxiety over the future, as people face profound disruption in everyday lives under conditions of increased economic and political insecurity. Debates rage as to whether or not outside intervention is desirable, with some fearing that intervention will once again lead to domination, as it has so often in the past, while others see no future for the nation without it. The question of the white savior role in Haiti is once again very much on the table. Yet in the domain of Haitian childhood, the white savior has rarely been contested, let alone made a subject for popular debate. It is as if it either simply did not matter in the larger scheme of things—or, alternatively—as if it were self-evident that degradation and deficiency are simply facts of Haitian children's lives that need changing, and whites are naturally the ones to call in to do the job. On the contrary, as these chapters illustrate, a new imaginary is needed: one that recognizes how Haitian childhood presents a rich landscape of experiences that promote culturally significant forms of learning tied to deeply important ideas about persons and their relationships to others, nature, the world, and the spirits. These are important resources for the future: not the least because they represent spaces of fugitivity and transformative power that can contest the long-standing narratives and practices of white domination.

> As I walked through the neighborhood in the company of Vanita, we passed a woman holding a young child. I was about 15 feet away, but as the child looked at me, she burst into tears and began screaming frantically. At that moment I began to feel the familiar chills like waves of electricity running through my body. This is bizarre, I thought. We adults all laughed—perhaps she was frightened because she'd never seen a white person before, or perhaps she'd had a previous encounter with a white that had been upsetting. I remembered that I'd once read something about how in the past Haitians feared white women because they thought they had come to Haiti to steal Haitian children. The thing that could not be explained, though, was the coursing of those chills through my body. (2022)

I still have not understood what happens at those moments to produce what I experience as a powerful flow of electricity or magnetic resonance. I have implicitly understood it as an experience of spiritual connection—a reminder of the presence of a world unseen, one that has the potential to touch us and infuse us if we are open to it. I cannot explain why the child's screams produced that effect, except insofar they evoked an energy coming from elsewhere that linked us, going deep into and through some unseen dimensions of being.

To respect Haitian childhood, and Haiti, requires not love as an exercise of conforming power but love as an act of freedom: one that recognizes that childhood in Haiti is about becoming a person in ways different from—and also far beyond—what well-intentioned white saviors can imagine. I can now see myself partly as that child saw me: a dangerous white woman. Perhaps she saw the frightening truth: that we are, in fact, thieves. We have come to steal children from their poor and vulnerable childhoods in order to give them better lives—by changing their families, their experiences, their psychology, their very selves: "The children who come to us have experienced painful and troubled lives due to traumatic events . . . but we teach them to make good choices and build positive relationships with others . . ." (As if we whites knew better about "positive relationships" than Haitians, or as if things could be reduced so simply to "making good choices.") We had come thinking that through our love we could teach them a better way, and redeem them from their trauma, their damage, their broken lives, when they already had lives enmeshed in relations of belonging that extended widely into social space and far into history and the future. We thought we had the right path, but their path and their learning were by far the richer way.

Notes

Introduction

1 References to childhood in the ethnographic literature on Haiti are found mostly in the context of mid-twentieth-century work on gender, social organization, and rural family life (see Bastien, 1985; Herskovits, 1937; Laguerre, 1978; Lowenthal, 1987). The only full-length contemporary ethnography focusing on childhood is Kovats-Bernat's (2006) study on street children in Port-au-Prince. Among other more recent anthropological works that do consider cultural beliefs and practices surrounding childhood are Schwartz's (2009) ethnography on family and gender; Gonzalez's (2006) study of fosterage along the Haitian-Dominican border; Mézié's (2014) research on rural children involved in violent games. A number of organization sponsored studies focusing especially on children and youth in domesticity have included ethnographic components (Lunde, 2008; Smucker and Murray, 2004; Pierre, Smucker, and Tardieu, 2009; Sommerfelt, 2002; 2015). Kivland's work on the politics of *baz* (street "gangs") provides an ethnographic lens on youth and the "makeshift" state (Kivland, 2020).

2 This is particularly clear in cross-cultural analyses of mother-child attachment (see Norman and LeVine, 2008).

3 Indeed, as Cooper (2013) and Howze and McKreig (2019) discuss, for over forty years African American, Hispanic, and Native American children are far more likely to be removed to foster care than white children: "African American families assessed with lower risk scores than white families were more likely than the highest risk white families to be substantiated for child maltreatment and to have their children removed from the home" (Howze and McKreig, 2019: 105).

4 The overall reputation of Haiti as a place bereft of a functioning state, continuously devasted by natural disasters and humanitarian emergencies, publicly condemned by an ex-US president as a "xxxxhole country," held hostage to the "satanic bondage" of Vodou (according to some Christians both in and outside of Haiti), and suffering from the oft-noted status of "poorest country in the Western hemisphere," makes it exactly the kind of place where "rescue" is necessary. In response, legions of church missions, faith-based organizations, small and large NGOs, short-term volunteer teams, adoptive families, higher education partnerships, and Haitian-diaspora run development organizations have coalesced into a veritable industry of save (or develop) Haiti efforts.

5 See Chapter 1 for more discussion of the relationship between NGOs and FBOs.

6 This was a comment I had received from one reviewer of a National Science Foundation proposal I had prepared for funding to conduct research on the subject.

7 Though of course discourse may have an ambivalent relation to reality: it may be crafted to represent things in a certain way for certain purposes; it may be partial, and it can often be deceptive. Nevertheless, it is still a form of action in itself.

8 It is also not to enter into debates over supposedly scientific, evidence-based practices in childrearing—that are, often enough, deeply infused themselves with suppositions and moral judgments. One good example is attachment theory (Otto and Keller, 2014; Quinn and Mageo, 2013).

9 See Hoffman (2022) for a critique in the context of post-earthquake recovery efforts.

10 Each of these examples can of course be further analyzed and contextualized; the larger point is that this work assumes and constructs deficiency (often with local buy-in) that opens up a space for Northern outsider "solutions" to problems that don't exist—at least not in the same way for Haitians as they might for privileged Northerners.

11 This literature is vast; see, for example, multiple works by Alex Dupuy (1989, 2010, 2014); Robert Fatton (2002, 2007); Mark Schuller (2007, 2012).

12 For example, *Who owns Haiti?: People, Power, Sovereignty* (Maguire and Freeman, 2017).

Chapter 1

1 "Faith-based organization" is a complicated term, encompassing a wide and complex range of entities. While not all are Christian, the discussion that follows should be understood as referring to Christian organizations.

2 It is important to note that there are many Haitian diaspora, Haitian organizations, and Haitians in Haiti who are also involved in this landscape, as well as many others from diverse countries around the world.

3 The acronym WEIRD was used by Henrich, Heine, and Norenzayan (2010) in their critique of the over-extension of psychological research done with a small sector of the world population (educated, middle-class Westerners) to universal generalizations about psychological functioning. While the interpretations and analysis advanced here refer mainly to white, Christian North Americans, Haitians and others (many from other regions of the Global South) often participate alongside whites as partners and allies in the use of these knowledge domains to engage in projects of assistance in Haiti. While I use "white" as a shorthand for this landscape of intervention, I am aware that not all who participate are white. Further, I make no

assumptions as to the extent of identification of Haitians or others with racially white ideologies or privilege. I also do not assume that "white" is a monolithic group, or that all whites or all Christians experience educational or class-based privilege.

4 I do not argue that all faith-based activities and actors embody white saviorism, or that white saviorism is absent from secular development efforts, but that it represents one overarching set of discourses and practices available to Christian actors working to improve childhood in Haiti.

5 There is also a particular historical context, unfortunately beyond the scope of this analysis, which points to the significant role in white saviorism of the child-saving movements of the late nineteenth century among white, middle-class women in the United States and the United Kingdom.

6 Other examples include the backlash against the organization Invisible Children for its *Kony 2012* campaign to rescue child soldiers in Uganda (see Finnegan, 2013); as well as numerous satires such as "White Savior Barbie" and the satire "Radi-Aid," where Africans send heaters for cold Norwegians (https://www.youtube.com/watch?v=oJLqyuxm96k).

7 See King (2012).

8 I suspect that part of white discomfort with the emotional labor of the vulnerable indeed hinges on the very fact that emotions can have commodity value. The discomfort reflects a moral argument wherein all emotional self-representation ought to be authentic and separated from material gain; thus the "forced" emotional performance is deemed to deny dignity. In fact, the real imposition in this case is by whites who impose their own moral regard on emotional labor without regard for how the children themselves interpret it as an act of agency, with strategic value in a search for personal benefit. (Of course, from another perspective, the greater moral wrong lies in the context or situation itself that makes such strategic work desirable in the first place: the white with resources who hopes to "help").

9 Melani McAlister notes that since at least the 1990s, American evangelical Christians have used the expression, "having a heart for" something. She notes that it expresses a passion felt to be inspired by God and "unusual in its intensity," often leading to international service travel (2008: 872). The heart metaphor is ubiquitous among FBOs working in Haiti: there are organizations called Heart for Haiti, Hearts with Haiti, A Heart for Haiti, Heart in Haiti, Hearts and Hands for Haiti, Hearts United with Haiti, among many others.

10 See Hoffman (2022), for additional discussion.

11 A recent review (Lillard et al., 2013) has shown that despite the emphasis on pretend play in mainstream child development science, it is nowhere near as valuable to children as has been claimed.

12 Adult-child play, while widely promoted globally by INGOs, reflects the dominance of WEIRD perspectives on childhood that can also be interpreted as a form of global imperialism (see Lancy, 2007).

13 As Weidenstedt (2016) argues, a transfer of power never occurs in a social vacuum; recipients are bound by their own normative expectations regarding exchange and reciprocity, creating conditions under which the "empowered" may find themselves in subordinate roles.

14 A similar thing happened when I traveled with a small group of students from my university to Haiti to engage in classroom-based research at a community school for *restavèk* children. No matter how often or patiently we explained our purpose as trying to learn more about the school experience of teachers and students, teachers, students, and administrators saw us as being part of an assistance or aid project (see Hoffman and Saavedra, forthcoming).

Chapter 2

1 This chapter draws partially from a previous publication, Hoffman, D. M. (2016), "Learning to See: Intuition and Perception in Fieldwork in Haiti," *Anthropology and Humanism,* 41 (1): 28–38.

2 A detailed account of this synergistic relationship between perception, intuition, and reality can be found in Hoffman (2016).

3 According to Ingold, the environment is not a place where people and objects locate themselves, but an enmeshment of trajectories of movement. Persons and things are not in networks (which still treat them as ontologically separate and positioned in the world) but rather threading their ways together, creating a meshwork that is continually growing and changing (2006: 18).

4 See Chapters 1 and 7 for more discussion. James (2010) argues that trauma narratives can become strategic efforts to secure help and assistance from whites. Also, it should be noted that in certain circumstances direct questions can be perceived as rude. This is why it is preferable to soften questions by phrasing them in the negative: for example, "*W pat soti?*" (You didn't go out?) rather than "*Eske w soti?*" (did you go out?) All of the difficulties with formal interviews did not mean that one could not learn things from such interactions, but they added an additional layer of interpretive complexity.

5 There were other cultural expectations and constraints, too, that explained how in a large group, everyone could say "Yes, we understand!" while still, on an individual level, not really understand. Collective life can cover over individual weakness; indeed, collective life is powerful in Haitian ways of knowing and being; that is also why, perhaps, I could see the much greater effectiveness of knowledge exchange when peers explained to peers. There was also the matter of face: a fear of looking like one does not know; and also fear that questioning an authority—especially, perhaps, when the authority is white, may be perceived

negatively. Such habits of communication may indeed be associated with the ways in which authority and status exert their effects in institutional spaces such as classrooms.

6 I am not sure whether the symbol was the Caduceus (with two snakes entwined around a winged staff) that has widely come to represent medicine in the United States and in many other countries, or the older more traditional symbol from Greek mythology, the Rod of Asclepius, with only one serpent coiled around a rod. In any case, it was clear that the symbol represented both medicine and connection to the worldview of Vodou, where snakes are important symbols of fertility and of the Goddess Ayida-Weddo.

Chapter 3

1 "Help for Haitian children" has also taken the form of foreign adoptions. While this is an important topic, it is a complex one with a vast literature that would be difficult to do justice to within the scope of this discussion. In addition to formal adoptions, many white women working in Haiti also serve as benefactors to individual children and families, in some cases becoming godmothers to Haitian children—a role that entails a lifelong commitment to support the child financially through schooling and eventual marriage.

2 In my own experience with Catholic parish twinning, a Haitian partner of a US parish criticized the ways in which child sponsorship funds sent by the US parish had created much jealousy and rivalry, as some schools and some children in the Haitian parish were clearly receiving more aid than others. The Haitian parish requested that monies be sent to a general school fund. After a brief effort, the US church refused to pursue this model because parishioners stopped donating, ostensibly because what was most important to them was the feeling that they had relationships with individual children, and simple donation to a general fund didn't offer the same emotional rewards.

3 In his study of North American missionary volunteers working with children in the Dominican Republic, Howell (2012) observed that it was the children's supposed "need for affection" that volunteers recalled most from their experiences. Describing the response of one female volunteer, Howell writes: ". . . Her most poignant recollection . . . was recalling how groups of children would cluster around, 'starved for attention' and seeking the affection of the visiting North Americans: 'They would just come running from everywhere for a hug. I think these kids are never hugged. It's just heartbreaking.'" (2012: 164). Howell concludes that in the eyes of the North Americans, physical poverty was a reflection a more profound "emotional poverty" that afflicted the children.

Chapter 4

1 In recent years there has been some movement away from the dominance of formal schooling to recognize the importance of nonformal education in Haiti. In 2019 a national policy on nonformal education was adopted to regulate and guide a variety of alternative education initiatives outside of the formal school system, such as vocational education and literacy programs. While these help to de-center the emphasis on formal schooling, they remain institutionally supported, funded, and structured initiatives, and not equivalent to the sort of informal learning I am focusing on in this chapter.

2 Estimates of the number of *restavèk* in the country vary widely, ranging from 150,000 to 500,000 (Gilbert et al., 2018). As discussed earlier, there is stigma attached to the term (see Montcrieff, 2006) and much difficulty defining it, as children's engagement in domestic service takes a variety of forms. Pierre, Smucker, and Tardieu (2009: 25) found that children not formally recognized or labeled as *restavèk* often receive similar treatment and perform the full range of duties as those who are. Most importantly, a family that has *restavèk* may place its own children as *restavèk* elsewhere (2009: 28), suggesting that there are complex economic and cultural rationales for the practice not captured by simple explanations of families being "too poor" to support a child.

3 Though the practice is widespread and has long existed in Haiti (an early reference in found in the work of Herskovits, 1937), in its basic contours it reflects systems of fosterage common throughout the Caribbean, Latin America, and Africa, where children are circulated or moved among households for a variety of reasons, including orphanhood, access to schooling, desire of the receiving family for a child, and the idea that the new household offers the child more opportunity than the natal household.

4 In making this argument, I certainly do not mean to dismiss the structural conditions children face in this process that constrain their actions and choices. My goal, rather, is to emphasize that even in the face of daunting circumstances, children maintain strong desires for becoming persons of value, and they exert much effort toward this end.

5 The *Mapou* is a sacred tree in Vodou that is thought to house *djab* or bad spirits. It is never cut down or used for practical purposes.

6 This was pointed out to me by *restavèk* children during a focus group interview in the South (2011). A study by Haydocy, Yotebieng, and Norris (2015) confirms this, finding that *restavèk* are subject to less physical discipline than biological children.

7 What they lacked, it should be noted, was Western/Northern versions of precious and protected childhood.

8 Among the many mechanics I encountered during numerous episodes of motorcycle and vehicle repair over the years, none had formal training or certification. They had learned entirely by observation and practice.

9 These habits of coaching and mutual assistance in learning appear to be carried over into adult life as well. I witnessed many cases of adults teaching others how to handle trying situations, such as when a motor on a boat wouldn't start. They do so with much patience and even courage. I once sat in a vehicle that had lost its brakes, and we needed to go down a number of steep hills. The driver (who was himself a very skilled one at that) asked a friend to sit in the back seat and coach him as we made the hair-raising trip down.

10 As noted earlier, it would seem to draw from a vision of learning that is foundational to the epistemology of Haitian Vodou.

11 They write: "Le travail d'équipe à l'exterieure de la classe . . . est un moyen d'apprentissage courant en Haiti . . . par ce moyen, les élèves collaborent de manière constructive pour réaliser des activités qui les aident à se développer intellectuellement et à se soutenir mutuellement." (Botondo, Hensler, and Mazalon, 2019: 218).

12 I was once told that a child of a family I was staying with was "attending school" even though during the whole time I was there over a few weeks during the school year, I never saw her go. This could have been because I am a *blan* and they wanted to maintain a certain image, or it could have been that the child was enrolled, but didn't go because she had to work. Most likely her enrollment was an off-and-on situation depending on whether the family could afford it or not.

13 An arts collective in Port-au-Prince that serves as a space for creation and for informal learning among children is known as *Timoun Rezistans* (Children of the Resistance). It is the children's affiliate of the adult collective, *Atiz Rezistans*. According to a Haitian artist friend who had been living in Port-au-Prince, this is one among many collectives in which children not only self-organize to support themselves as artists, but self-educate in other skills as well, such as reading and writing.

Chapter 5

1 This chapter is a revised version of a previous publication, Hoffman, D. (2021), "The Haitian Orphanage Crisis: Exporting Neoliberal Family Ideals in the Debate on Vulnerable Childhoods in Haiti," *Children & Society* 35 (4): 577–92.

2 In resource-poor communities where families are largely non-nuclear and children frequently are raised and spend significant amounts of time outside of the care of biological parents, early sociality and the capacity to bond with relative strangers are seen as positive goals, and children are socialized from very early on to avoid singular attachments and to be at ease with multiple caretakers (for more discussion see Chapter 3).

3 Most of the organizations say they do not provide financial incentives to reunified families, but that they do provide some initial support for medical and educational expenses and help with finding employment or funds for developing a livelihood (about $450 according to Sommerfelt, 2015). Assistance with housing is often another benefit.

4 Others might include ideas about the universal desirability of parent-child play (see Lancy, 2007) or the importance of pretend play in children's development (see Lillard et al., 2013).

5 As Bolotta (2017: 95) observes, "A significant proportion of the world's children grow up outside a stable family environment, structure affective and kinship bonds with people other than their biological parents, form multiple attachments, and relate differently to caregivers in the elaboration of their self." Strong caretaker emotional attachments may even be considered dysfunctional in cultures that socialize children to high levels of sociability and affect toward strangers (cf. Gottlieb, 2009).

6 The nuclear family is further enshrined in the Convention on the Rights of the Child (UNICEF, 2009, articles 7 and 9) which give preference to the birth parents and underline the right of the child not to be separated from birth parents.

7 The growth of the family is also a primary rationale for placing children in orphanages as well, as Schwartz (2013, 2014) points out.

Chapter 6

1 The "sensorium" typically refers to the brain apparatus involved in perception or sensation. I use the term here in a wider, extended sense, to convey a landscape that connects the individual mind with the natural and social environment beyond the individual, in which learning, perception, and participation in an environment are all interconnected processes.

2 According to Freeman (2018), this is a commonly shared though mistaken interpretation of the use of vetiver oil in Haiti. In my view, it reflects an interesting metaphorical understanding of vetiver oil as an important international commodity: it does indeed leave the country (flown out?), "fueling" an export industry in a metaphorical sense.

3 A particular cultural understanding of the senses and their connection to knowledge and the environment was perhaps at the root of the issue. In the epistemology of Haitian Vodou, seeing is not reduced to a simple mechanical process in which light from objects hits the retina; rather, it depends on *konesans*—spiritual or mystical knowledge, as described by McCarthy-Brown (2006). It is only when the latter informs the mechanical process of sight that one can truly "see."

4 Whether the children had consciously intended to convey this meaning or message or not, I do not know; nor can I be sure whether the symbolism was Christian or Vodou. It was likely both, since the cross is significant in both traditions.

5 It is interesting to note that in Haitian Creole there are many expressions that center the body as the locus of experience, rather than mental states or traits that are deemed more central to English speakers. For example, the English expression "Get ready!" can be translated into Haitian Creole as *"Ranje kò w!"* (literally, " arrange your body"). "Don't be shy" can be conveyed in Creole as *"Ouve kò w"*—literally, "open/unwrap your body."

6 Among the Songhay in Niger and Mali, for example, learning is not seen as a mental process but as a visceral one. Stoller (2010: 1) argues that we need to confront "the sensual constitution of local epistemologies" in order to advance our fundamental understanding of other cultures and societies.

7 For example, while I and a Haitian friend were out driving one night, we passed some goats standing near the road. My friend immediately said, "They are people." Such shapeshifting is known as *baka* in Creole. According the Derby and Werner (2013), *baka* are spirit demons that can transform themselves and humans into animals; another example is the *lougawou* (werewolf). As Derby (2015: 401) notes, these beliefs are not "dead folklore" but very present popular beliefs widely shared among Haitians. In Haiti I was told many stories about *baka* by adults who otherwise had little to do with Vodou. I myself had two frightening encounters with beings whose natures I am to this day uncertain about.

8 This is one reason gaining a person's permission for a photograph is essential, for the photo can capture the person's spirit and potentially cause harm.

9 Similar to the notion of the "extended mind"—which has become an important area for research in the learning sciences (Clark and Chalmers, 1998).

10 Emergent research in the learning sciences in fact has begun to focus on the important role of the body in learning, shifting the lens away from a former narrowly cognitive view of learning toward prioritizing bodily experience as central to memory, creativity, and critical thought.

11 This program was a peer-to-peer tutoring project in reading and writing Haitian Creole at a private school catering largely to *restavèk* children and youth, in which children with excellent Creole literacy recruited from other schools served as tutors for small groups of children who were having difficulty in school. It was conceived initially as an effort to allow children to learn in cooperative peer groups, since it had long appeared to me that much of their everyday learning and activity naturally occurred among peers, away from adult authority and supervision. While it did noticeably improve children's grades in reading and writing, the more theoretically interesting findings were about the nature of children's learning interactions.

12 One of the more prevalent body activities learners engaged in was erasure. Learners and tutors constantly erased both their own and others' writing, and

erasure was often carried out with exceeding care and thoroughness: some of the video segments showed learners taking over one minute to erase a single word. Sometimes they continued to "erase" material well after it had been effectively erased. They also erased even when to observers there were no ostensible errors. In addition to actual erasers, students used their hands, fingers, and forearms to erase. Remarkably, students licked erasers, held them against their heads, and used them on different parts of their bodies. As Lave (1991) has observed, ideas about what constitutes erroneous action depend on historically and socially situated ideas such as social de-legitimation of learning or the learner. In this way, one might read erasure an embodied semiotic response to pervasive conditions of social and educational marginalization.

13 For example, they write, "a student in a US classroom whose gaze travels around the room is likely to be accused of not paying attention"—and this was indeed the interpretation given by the US research assistants as they observed the Haitian children constantly looking around the room. However, as Gaskins and Paradise (2010) further observe, "This wide-angled attentional stance has several advantages for learning through observation, including event detection, awareness of contextual information, and a broader range of information processed" (99–100).

14 This was unexpected, and at first disappointing, because we had instructed the student tutors to foster active collaboration among learners. When we saw tutors engaging individuals while others in the tutoring group "passively" looked on, we assumed that tutors were being authoritarian, modeling approaches to teaching that they themselves had experienced. Given a US culturally conditioned assumption that people should be talking or engaging actively in shared activity for there to be "collaboration," we had failed to recognize that collaboration could also involve less obvious modalities, such as touch, observation, and listening. Tutors were engaging learners in observation not because they were "authoritarian," but because this was a valued modality of social learning among children in Haiti more generally. As Mézié (2014) has observed in her analysis of rural children's games (such as chasing dogs or harassing "*fou*" [literally "crazy" people]), individual, skilled performances among children were highly marked and regarded, even as children participated in these activities collectively. Further, she found that children's actions were not focused inward but always oriented outward toward the environment (721).

Chapter 7

1 The importance of talking about and expressing feelings is standard in the psychological literature and is often reflected in NGO approaches to helping people deal with mental health, stress and trauma in Haiti.

2 For examples of the close association between *restavèk* and trauma, see: https://gra
   cehousechildrensproject.org/childhood-trauma-in-haiti/; https://www.haiti-now
   .org/the-effects-of-the-restavek-life-on-the-ability-to-learn-in-school/. https://www
   .psychologytoday.com/us/blog/heal-and-carry/201702/hope-restavek-children-in
   -haiti.

3 They write, "Children living in the street with no schooling have higher resilience
   levels than children who go to school and have a house in which to live" (2018).

4 The connection between trauma and children's supposed social emotional and
   attachment disorders is strong. However, as I've suggested in other chapters, white
   views of Haitian children's "attachment disorders" are grounded in a universal
   narrative of attachment and social-emotional regulation that prioritizes ideas
   about emotional health that are culturally aligned with those of the Euro-American
   middle class (see also Hoffman 2009a; 2009b; 2010b; 2013).

5 This may be because the conceptualization of childhood trauma has been greatly
   influenced by the Adverse Childhood Experiences study (Felitti et al., 1998)—a
   study whose results some currently criticize as needing much further attention
   to ethnic and racial differences (e.g., Bernard, Smith, and Lanier, 2022), let alone
   attention to differences in the ways culture shapes childhood experiences globally.

6 As my own work on efforts to implement a supposedly universal program of
   mindfulness based stress reduction in Haiti demonstrated (see Hoffman, 2019).
   Despite efforts to adapt the program to Haitian culture (such as changing the sorts
   of examples used to conform more closely to Haitian everyday experience), there
   existed a deep conflict between Haitian relational, spiritual, and moral construals
   of selfhood and the individualistic model of self that informed this version of
   mindfulness.

7 Bolotta reflects further, ". . . I was very confused and disoriented by the vitality
   of children who had been described to me by the . . . psychologists of PSF
   (Psychologistes Sans Frontières) as suffering and traumatized victims. . . . Convinced
   that it was essential to enable traumatized children the opportunity to express
   negative emotions in the context of a positive relationship with an adult, I was treating
   every sign of discomfort with the utmost seriousness. Especially at the beginning
   of my experience at the Saint Joseph Center, I used to call aside the seemingly sad
   children, trying to get them to talk. In response to this, the children were often
   simulating crying, reminding me of their status as poor *dek salam* in need of help"
   (2019: 35ff).

8 An internet image search for "children's drawings of houses" revealed that while
   drawings often had grass, flowers, and a tree or two, the plants or trees were not
   attached to or growing out of the house, but placed alongside or somewhere else in
   the drawing.

9 Another revealing aspect of the drawings was that when asked to draw their
   house, some children drew multiple houses. This could have represented a *lakou*

(shared household compound), or the fact that they considered that they lived in or belonged to a number of different households (an equally plausible situation). I also noticed that there were some who had drawn heavy roofs with what looked like posts underneath. At first I thought they were drawing tents—since it was 2011, one year post-earthquake, and tents had become ubiquitous. But when I asked they said they had drawn the "*toiture*"—the roof. It then dawned on me that what they had drawn had a spiritual significance: a roof supported by a "*poto mitan*," or center post, that in Haitian Vodou is found at the center of all *ounfò* or Vodou temples and has deep spiritual significance. (It is also a common metaphor for the "strong Haitian woman" who supports her family and community.)

10 For example, Pierre Minn argues that certain illnesses in Haiti such as *chalè* (heat) reflect a profound intermingling of bodies and the environment; the illness "calls into question the notion of the body as a bordered entity . . . [He asks] does this illness represent a type of relation between bodies and the elements that lie beyond people's skins?" (Minn, 2006: 150).

11 In other work in Mayan indigenous communities, a clear role for children as caregivers has been observed. Mosier and Rogoff (2003: 1055) found that even three- to five-year-olds took on caregiving responsibilities, and, further that "most of them were their own primary caregiver, [while] half were also caregivers to a toddler."

12 The importance of therapeutic emotional self-expression (and its relative, "self-care") in Western approaches to mental health generally assumes an highly individualistic understanding of the self not shared in more relational and collectivistic cultures. This is also seen in the ways a discourse on children not being able to express their emotions adequately underlies alternative approaches to self-expression with children, such as play or art therapy. Since it is believed that children don't yet have the vocabulary to talk about their emotions, other forms of self-expression are needed. They key idea, however, is still about expressing the self.

13 The idea that Haiti does not have sufficient mental health awareness and infrastructure is, as mentioned previously, widely accepted. I myself had volunteer experience working in collaboration with an NGO in its goals to advance mental health in Haiti.

14 A telling example of this occurred in a mindfulness seminar I organized in Haiti for Haitian adults. The American trainer had asked the participants to share with the group "something positive about yourself"—which, among US respondents, typically evokes trait-based characterizations of the self such as "I am kind" or "I'm patient." Yet all of the Haitian participants talked instead about what they liked to do: "I like to sing," "I like to cook," and so on. Many more clashes between the trainer's efforts to get Haitians to "self express" and Haitian reticence or reluctance to do so were noted. See Hoffman (2019) for more discussion.

15 See Hoffman (2009a; 2009b; 2010b; 2013) for critiques of this discourse in the domains of parenting and schooling.

Chapter 8

1 All quotations in this section are from organization websites accessed in August 2022.

2 A remarkable number of organizations use some version of "hope" in their names: Hope for Haiti, Hope in Haiti, Real Hope for Haiti, Village of Hope Haiti, House of Hope Haiti, Hope to Haiti, Hope for Haitians, Hope for Haiti's Children, Giving Hope to Haiti, Project *Espwa* (Hope), to name just a few. It is not clear to me whether or not this is because whites see Haiti as a particularly hopeless place, or because giving hope is like giving love—another act of life-sustaining charity that reflects white saving power, and/or simply because "Hope" and "Haiti" sound good together.

3 Kovats-Bernat (2006) found that street boys in Port-au-Prince typically earned over three times the national daily minimum wage. They not only supported themselves but served as breadwinners for their families.

4 During a debrief discussion following a focus group interview with *restavèk*, a US student on our research team dismissed the children's responses as inauthentic, saying they were probably "coached." His comment reflected the dominant lens that equates poverty and social disadvantage with hopelessness. Haitian peers, however, who had also participated in the interview and debrief alongside the Americans, said that the responses of the Haitian children and youth were not coached—they were genuine.

5 The director of one orphanage said that sometimes kids did come on their own, hoping that they could find a place after having been in *restavèk* situations or the street, primarily because at least at the orphanage they could access schooling (BH interview, 1.31.2008). Children's agency in search of opportunity also extends to self-enrolling in school, according to the director of a community school for *restavèk* in Jacmel.

6 Most often these arrangements were made by female relatives—commonly, an aunt. What is important is that the children themselves did not represent themselves as passive in this process or as reluctant to move. In fact, my data show the vast majority of children (thirteen out of fifteen in one setting in the South [*Okoto*]) welcomed the chance to move because they saw it as an opportunity.

7 For example, see Karray, Derivois, Brolles, and Wexler Buzaglo (2017: 89), where street children's mobility is directly linked to their "instability" and consequential need for interventions to "help them build stable relationships." Efforts on the

part of NGOs to "stabilize" families as part of national development agendas are common in many less developed parts of the world (see also Archambault, 2010).

8 In her ethnography, Leinaweaver (2008) similarly argues that child circulation is directly tied to the pursuit of economic and educational opportunity on the part of children and families in Peru, even as such movement is condemned by international norms.

9 It is important to note that this was a community school—an environment that one of our Haitian research assistants pointed out was very different from the private, more upper-class school she was familiar with. Lower or more lax standards for student behavior in the community school may be a partial explanation for all the movement that was witnessed. At the same time, this raises a question as to whether this school allowed students a more natural physical freedom of movement that is suppressed in the stricter environments of supposedly higher quality private schools.

10 Especially at the secondary level teachers also circulate among different schools. A teacher in a private school in Léogâne told me that prior to the 2010 earthquake he used to teach at five different schools, but after the quake he only taught at three. Getting around to many different schools during the day meant that teacher absences in schools were commonplace. At this school on one day I visited, as I walked around the grounds, I noticed a number of the classes full of students, but their teachers had not shown up.

11 As described in Chapter 2, during an experience teaching university students. No matter how often I explained a task to the entire class as a whole group, individual students would repeatedly come up to me after class or during breaks to ask questions about what they needed to do. However, when I tried a different strategy, which involved moving around the room to explain things to select individuals in small groups, who then explained to their peers, the difficulties with understanding disappeared.

12 This was more than "re-gifting," as practiced on occasion at home in the United States, where one got rid of a gift one didn't want by passing it on. Rather, it was a system of redistribution or circulation, with its own rules, in which things always seemed to be moving along to somewhere else.

Chapter 9

1 These were all points explicitly mentioned by two white NGOs working in Haiti (one of which had a "reward system" for Haitian employees where they received bonuses that "they were not allowed to spend on themselves"—as if Haitians needed to be taught how to think of others). Both framed their activities

as compensation for Haitian cultural deficits. The value of "teaching kids to share" is common in US schools and families—part of the explicit pedagogy of early schooling and parenting where battles over objects and their ownership are frequent (Hoffman, 2013). Yet anyone who has ever observed children's interactions around food in Haiti cannot but help notice an astoundingly perfected ethic of sharing. I have observed groups of street children, for example, divide up three leftover "*banann peze*" (fried plantain chips) into pieces to share among a group of eight. Two street children to whom I had once given a cookie each immediately broke theirs into pieces to share with a third child who arrived later.

2 The anthropological veto—the one negative instance that disproves a universal claim—is often attributed to Margaret Mead, who famously discussed how Samoan adolescents did not appear to suffer from the supposedly universal "adolescent identity crisis," as had earlier been claimed by the renowned psychologist G. Stanley Hall.

3 For discussions of Haitian exceptionalism, see Benedicty-Kokken et al. (2016), Clitandre (2011); Fatton (2021).

4 Particularly in recent years, some organizations have begun to conceptualize their missions more broadly at the community change level. These efforts often involve job creation, education, housing, and other related forms of community assistance such as meeting needs for water. The total community approach clearly goes beyond single issues on one level, but again it also isolates a particular community from its larger context, and ignores the ways, once again, that a community in fact already actually exists—even if it does not appear to possess a desired level of resources. Just as children are not empty vessels to be filled with white love, no community is a blank slate, simply waiting to be filled with outsiders' development projects.

5 The *baz* ("base") exists in a variety of forms in Haiti; in some cases it is associated with youth delinquency or gang activity, but it can also serve as a setting for informal learning and community service. In Kivland's (2020) analysis, the *baz* is explicitly conceptualized as a replacement for the state that has failed in its duties to citizens.

6 This statement can be read two ways: as a simple statement of things that the speaker believes can rescue the nation, or as a statement about the speaker's own beliefs as the way forward toward progress/rescue. Given the themes I've discussed and the general prominence of imperialism in development, I read it in the latter sense.

7 In 2022, as the Haitian capital had increasingly come under the control of gangs and economic and political crisis deepened in the country, white missionaries on social media spoke longingly of the loss of "their" Haiti: "We all miss Haiti! It is so different now—so—not Haiti." "I think so many of us are grieving the loss of the Haiti we knew. . . . It's truly heartbreaking!" "I wake up all night thinking about my

people in our village and the life I used to live that was ripped away from us. It hurts so much." Though it is Haitians who are suffering, the focus in this discourse is on the emotions of whites: the loss of the country they knew, and the heartbreak that they cannot go to Haiti anymore or live the lives there that they once lived.

8 I was struck by these tensions in conceptualizing aid as I led a group of American students on a project in Haiti. A number of the Haitian children and youth we met requested financial assistance, yet all of us (myself included) were torn: by material gifts, are we not just reinforcing Haitian dependency on outsiders? Some of us ended up pooling donations to help a young woman who asked for our help to support her attendance at vocational school, but even so we remained conflicted. We decided to discuss our qualms with our Haitian university student partners who told us that what we did "was a good thing." This comment crystallized in my own thinking more appreciation for small acts of giving that reflect "doing good things" rather than a larger ideal of "doing good" defined abstractly. In my own experience, helping people out with immediate material needs in Haiti can support valued relationships of patronage and vertical dependency, and can be seen as "doing a good thing/good doing" insofar as it is understood through a Haitian lens and detached from larger projects of "saving" that are grounded in the dynamics of doing good that are so entangled with white subjectivity.

9 In Haiti, this happens to map out onto Creole vs. French, but they can be viewed as separate issues. This became clear to me as I was observing in a university classroom one day. There was vibrant debate and participation in Creole about some of the ideas the professor had introduced. Yet as soon as the students were asked to copy down key points into their notebooks from texts (written in French) on a flip chart, the discussion of ideas ceased, and the lesson became all about textual transmission of ideas and accurate modeling of the text. None of the discussion was incorporated, and no-one in fact wrote anything (as far as I could tell) during the vibrant discussion period. In fact, once the move to text was made, the lesson was over (with the professor moving on to a different topic) after the writing period. It was as if the textual modality had completely shut down the vibrant oral modality that had gone before. Would it have been different if the text had been in Creole? Or if students had been encouraged to take notes in Creole during their discussion? I am not sure, but there did seem to me to be something striking about the different modalities of engagement in themselves. Once the text came into play, the knowledge was fixed, bullet-pointed, and made to conform.

10 This would go beyond the sort of "hands-on" learning or use of manipulatives that are common in some approaches to elementary teaching in the United States. Though the latter are undoubtedly of value, I am thinking of a more profound curricular and pedagogical emphasis on the body and senses: for example, a simple environmental enrichment such as bringing branches to classrooms for children to

use creatively during their learning. Singing is often already incorporated at some points, but more could be done. There are hundreds of ways to think innovatively about the body, senses, and movement even in "traditional" classrooms.

11 Clearly some of the aforementioned ideas are more feasible than others and all demand a certain rethinking of the culture of classrooms, as well as development of a different notion and process of evaluation and assessment, teacher training, curricular modifications, and so on, all of which, given the current situation of schooling in Haiti, are not likely to change anytime soon. I present them here more as thinking points that can inspire change.

References

Adams, T., S. Holman Jones, and C. Ellis (2015), *Autoethnography: Series in Understanding Qualitative Research*, Oxford: Oxford University Press.

Afolayan, A. (2015), "Haitian Children's House-Tree-Person Drawings: Global Similarities and Cultural Differences," PhD diss., Antioch University, Culver City.

Ahmed, S. (2004), *The Cultural Politics of Emotion*, New York: Routledge.

Alber, E. (2003), "Denying Biological Parenthood: Fosterage in Northern Benin," *Ethnos*, 68 (4): 487–506.

Alcena, B. (2016), "Haitian Parenting: Between Discipline and Abuse," *Woy Magazine*, April 8. Available online: http://woymagazine.com/2016/04/08/haitian-parenting -discipline-abuse/ (accessed December 30, 2021).

American Psychological Association (2017), "Resolution on Promoting Global Perspectives in U.S. Psychology." Available online: https://www.apa.org/about/policy /global-perspectives (accessed August 11, 2022).

Andersen, B. and H. Biseth (2013), "The Myth of Failed Integration: The Case of Eastern Oslo," *City & Society*, 25 (1): 5–24.

Appadurai, A. (2004), "The Capacity to Aspire: Culture and the Terms of Recognition," in V. Rao and M. Walton (eds.), *Culture and Public Action*, 59–84, Palo Alto: Stanford University Press.

Aptekar, L. (1991), "Are Colombian Street Children Neglected? The Contributions of Ethnographic and Ethnohistorical Approaches to the Study of Children," *Anthropology & Education Quarterly*, 22 (4): 326–49.

Archambault, C. (2010), "Fixing Families of Mobile Children: Recreating Kinship and Belonging among Maasai Adoptees in Kenya," *Childhood*, 17 (2): 229–42.

Arnett, J. J. (2008), "The Neglected 95%: Why American Psychology needs to become Less American," *The American Psychologist*, 63 (7): 602–14.

Ashley, J., A. Johnson, H. Woldu, and C. L. Katz (2019), "Factors Contributing to Maternal-Child Separation in Port-Au-Prince, Haiti," *Annals of Global Health*, 85 (1): 136.

Auguste, E. and A. Rasmussen (2019), "Vodou's Role in Haitian Mental Health," *Global Mental Health*, 6: e25.

Balagopalan, S. (2008), "Memories of Tomorrow: Children, Labor, and the Panacea of Formal Schooling," *The Journal of the History of Childhood and Youth*, 1 (2): 267–85.

Balagopalan, S. (2014), *Inhabiting "Childhood": Children, Labour and Schooling in Postcolonial India*, New York: Palgrave Macmillan.

Balaji, M. (2011), "Racializing Pity: The Haiti Earthquake and the Plight of 'Others'," *Critical Studies in Media Communication*, 28 (1): 50–67.

Bandyopadhyay, R. (2019), "Volunteer Tourism and 'The White Man's Burden': Globalization of Suffering, White Savior Complex, Religion and Modernity," *Journal of Sustainable Tourism*, 27 (3): 327–43.

Bandyopadhyay, R. and V. Patil (2017), "The White Woman's Burden – The Racialized, Gendered Politics of Volunteer Tourism," *Tourism Geographies*, 19 (4): 644–57.

Bang, M., A. Marin, D. Medin, and K. Washinawatok (2015), "Learning by Observing, Pitching in, and Being in Relations in the Natural World," in M. Correa-Chávez, R. Mejía-Arauz, and B. Rogoff (eds.), *Advances in Child Development and Behavior*, 303–13, Bingley: JAI.

Bastien, R. (1985), *Le Paysan Haïtien et Sa Famille, Vallée de Marbial*, Paris: Éditions Karthala.

Bellegarde-Smith, P. (2004), *Haiti: The Breached Citadel*, Toronto: Canadian Scholars Press.

Benedicty-Kokken, A., K. L. Glover, M. Schuller, and J. P. Byron (2016), *The Haiti Exception: Anthropology and the Predicament of Narrative*, Liverpool: Liverpool University Press.

Benson, L. (2002), "How Haitian Artists Disclose Childhood of All Ages," in T. Hecht (ed.), *Minor Omissions Children in Latin American History and Society*, 181–214, Madison: University of Wisconsin Press.

Berggren, G., H. Menager, E. Genece, and C. Clerisme (1995), "A Prospective Study of Community Health and Nutrition in Rural Haiti from 1968 to 1993," Community-Based Longitudinal Nutrition and Health Studies: Classical Examples from Guatemala, Haiti and Mexico. Available online: https://archive.unu.edu/unupress/food2/UIN09E/UIN09E0J.HTM (accessed December 30, 2021).

Bernard, D. L., Q. Smith, and P. Lanier (2022), "Racial Discrimination and Other Adverse Childhood Experiences as Risk Factors for Internalizing Mental Health Concerns among Black Youth," *Journal of Traumatic Stress*, 35 (2): 473–83.

Bethany Global (2020), "A Better Future for Haiti." Available online: https://www.youtube.com/watch?v=R0E4E9YYGfA (accessed November 8, 2022).

Biehl, J., B. Good, and A. Kleinman (2007), *Subjectivity: Ethnographic Investigations*, Berkeley: University of California Press.

Billy, R. and O. Klein (2019), "Parentalité et abandon volontaire d'enfants en Haïti: Une compatibilité impensée," *Enfances Familles Générations. Revue interdisciplinaire sur la famille contemporaine*, 32, Article 32.

Bluebond-Langner, M. and J. Korbin (2007), "Challenges and Opportunities in the Anthropology of Childhoods: An Introduction to 'Children, Childhoods, and Childhood Studies," *American Anthropologist*, 109 (2): 241–6.

Bolotta, G. (2017), "'God's Beloved Sons': Religion, Attachment, and Children's Self-Formation in the Slums of Bangkok," *Anthropologia*, 4 (2): 96–120.

Bolotta, G. (2019), "Making Sense of (Humanitarian) Emotions in an Ethnography of Vulnerable Children: The Case of Bangkok Slum Children," in T. Stodulka, S.

Dinkelaker, and F. Thajib (eds.), *Affective Dimensions of Fieldwork and Ethnography*, 29–48, New York: Springer International Publishing.

Bornstein, E. (2003), *The Spirit of Development: Protestant NGOs, Morality and Economics in Zimbabwe*, New York: Routledge.

Bornstein, E. (2009), "The Impulse of Philanthropy," *Cultural Anthropology*, 24 (4): 622–51.

Bornstein, E. (2012), *Disquieting Gifts: Humanitarianism in New Delhi*, Palo Alto: Stanford University Press.

Bornstein, E. and P. Redfield (2011), *Forces of Compassion: School for Advanced Research Advanced Seminar Series*, Santa Fe: School for Advanced Research Press.

Botondo, J., H. Hensler, and E. Mazalon (2019), "L'analyse des récits d'expériences de persévérance scolaire d'élèves du secondaire du nord-ouest d'Haïti (Analysis of secondary school persistence experiences in north-west Haiti)," *Éducation et Francophonie*, 47: 205.

Boudreaux, M. (2015), *Miracle on Voodoo Mountain: A Young Woman's Remarkable Story of Pushing Back the Darkness for the Children of Haiti*, Nashville: Thomas Nelson.

Bourdieu, P. (1997), "The Forms of Capital," in A. H. Halsey (ed.), *Education: Culture, Economy, and Society*, 241–58, Oxford: Oxford University Press.

Boyd, L. (2020), "Circuits of Compassion: The Affective Labor of Uganda's Christian Orphan Choirs," *African Studies Review*, 63 (3): 518–39.

Brand, E. (2004), "How Poverty Separates Parents and Children: A Challenge to Human Rights," ATD Fourth World. Available online: https://www.atd-fourthworld .org/wp-content/uploads/sites/5/2015/12/howpov.pdf (accessed December 30, 2021).

Brooks, D. (2010), "The Underlying Tragedy," *The New York Times*, January 15. Available online: https://www.nytimes.com/2010/01/15/opinion/15brooks.html (accessed December 30, 2021).

Brown, S., D. Cohon, and R. Wheeler (2002), "African American Extended Families and Kinship Care: How Relevant is the Foster Care Model for Kinship Care?" *Children and Youth Services Review*, 24 (1): 53–77.

Burman, E. (2012), "Deconstructing Neoliberal Childhood: Towards a Feminist Antipsychological Approach," *Childhood*, 19 (4): 423–38.

Buss, D. (2006), "On Being Curious About Fundamentalisms and Human Rights," *Proceedings of the ASIL Annual Meeting*, 100: 411–14.

Cadet, J. (1998), *Restavec: From Haitian Slave Child to Middle-Class American*, Austin: University of Texas Press.

Carelock, N. (2012), "A Leaky House: Haiti in the Religious Aftershocks of the 2010 Earthquake," PhD diss., Rice University, Houston.

CARICOM (2010), "2010 Report of the Commission on Youth Development." Available online: https://today.caricom.org/tag/2010-report-of-the-commission-on-youth -development/ (accessed December 14, 2022).

Casimir, J. (2020), *The Haitians: A Decolonial History*, Chapel Hill: University of North Carolina Press.

Cénat, J. M., D. Derivois, M. Hébert, L. M. Amédée, and A. Karray (2018), "Multiple Traumas and Resilience among Street Children in Haiti: Psychopathology of Survival," *Child Abuse & Neglect*, 79: 85–97.

Chang, H. (2008), *Autoethnography as Method*, Walnut Creek: Left Coast Press.

Chaudhry, V. (2019), "Neoliberal Crises of Social Work in the Global South: Ethnography of Individualizing Disability and Empowerment Practice in India," *International Social Work*, 62 (3): 1117–30.

Cheney, K. (2010), "Deconstructing Childhood Vulnerability: An Introduction," *Childhood in Africa: An Interdisciplinary Journal*, 1 (2): 4–7.

Cheney, K. (2017), *Crying for Our Elders: African Orphanhood in the Age of HIV and AIDS*, Chicago: The University of Chicago Press.

Cheney, K. and K. Rotabi (2017), "Addicted to Orphans: How the Global Orphan Industrial Complex Jeopardizes Local Child Protection Systems," in C. Harker and K. Horschelmann (eds.), *Conflict, Violence and Peace*, 89–107, New York: Springer.

Cheney, K. and A. Sinervo, eds. (2019), *Disadvantaged Childhoods and Humanitarian Intervention: Processes of Affective Commodification and Objectification*, New York: Palgrave Macmillan.

Cheney, K. and S. Ucembe (2019), "The Orphan Industrial Complex: The Charitable Commodification of Children and Its Consequences for Child Protection," in K. Cheney and A. Sinervo (eds.), *Disadvantaged Childhoods and Humanitarian Intervention: Processes of Affective Commodification and Objectification*, 37–61, New York: Palgrave Macmillan.

Chery, D. (2014), "Homage to My Mothers: Restavek, Vodou, and Haiti's Stolen Children," *News Junkie Post*, June 14. Available online: http://newsjunkiepost.com /2014/06/14/hommage-to-my-mothers-restavek-vodou-and-haitis-stolen-children/ (accessed December 30, 2021).

Chin, E. (2003), "Children Out of Bounds in Globalising Times," *Postcolonial Studies*, 6 (3): 309–25.

Clark, A. and D. Chalmers (1998), "The Extended Mind," *Analysis*, 58 (1): 7–19.

Clermont-Mathieu, M. and G. Nicholas (2015), "Parenting Practices and Culture in Haiti," in G. Nicholas, A. Bejaramo, and D. L. Lee (eds.), *Contemporary Parenting: A Global Perspective*, 95–104, Philadelphia: Routledge.

Clitandre, N. T. (2011), "Haitian Exceptionalism in the Caribbean and the Project of Rebuilding Haiti," *Journal of Haitian Studies*, 17 (2): 146–53.

Coe, C. (2001), "Learning How to Find Out: Theories of Knowledge and Learning in Field Research," *Field Methods*, 13 (4): 392–411.

Coffey, A. (1999), *The Ethnographic Self: Fieldwork and the Representation of Identity*, Thousand Oaks: SAGE.

Cole, T. (2012), "The White-Savior Industrial Complex," *The Atlantic*, March 21. Available online: https://www.theatlantic.com/international/archive/2012/03/the -white-savior-industrial-complex/254843/ (accessed December 30, 2021).

Conran, M. (2011), "They Really Love Me!: Intimacy in Volunteer Tourism," *Annals of Tourism Research*, 38 (4): 1454–73.

Cooper, A., P. Diego-Rosell, and C. Gogue (2012), "Child Labor in Domestic Service (Restavèks) in Port-Au-Prince, Haiti," U.S. Department of Labor. Available online: https://www.dol.gov/sites/dolgov/files/ILAB/research_file_attachment /2012RestavekHaiti.pdf (accessed December 30, 2021).

Cooper, M. (2017), *Family Values: Between Neoliberalism and the New Social Conservatism*, New York: Zone Books.

Cooper, T. A. (2013), "Racial Bias in American Foster Care: The National Debate," *Marquette Law Review*, 97 (2): 216–77.

Corbett, S. and B. Fikkert (2014), *When Helping Hurts: How to Alleviate Poverty Without Hurting the Poor...and Yourself*, Chicago: Moody Publishers.

Courlander, H. (1960), *The Drum and the Hoe: Life and Lore of the Haitian People*, Berkeley: University of California Press.

Crapanzano, V. (1985), *Tuhami: Portrait of a Moroccan*, Chicago: The University of Chicago Press.

Dahl, B. (2009), "The 'Failures of Culture': Christianity, Kinship, and Moral Discourses about Orphans during Botswana's AIDS Crisis," *Africa Today*, 56 (1): 23–43.

Dahl, B. (2014), "Too Fat to Be an Orphan: The Moral Semiotics of Food Aid in Botswana," *Cultural Anthropology*, 29 (4): 626–47.

DeGraff, M. (2016), "Mother-Tongue Books in Haiti: The Power of Kreyòl in Learning to Read and in Reading to Learn," *PROSPECTS*, 46 (3): 435–64.

DeJaeghere, J., N. P. Wiger, and L. W. Willemsen (2016), "Broadening Educational Outcomes: Social Relations, Skills Development, and Employability for Youth," *Comparative Education Review*, 60 (3): 457–79.

Derby, L. (2015), "Imperial Idols: French and United States Revenants in Haitian Vodou," *History of Religions*, 54 (4): 394–422.

Derby, L. and M. Werner (2013), "The Devil Wears Dockers: Devil Pacts, Trade Zones, and Rural-Urban Ties in the Dominican Republic," *New West Indian Guide / Nieuwe West-Indische Gids*, 87 (3–4): 294–321.

Derivois, D., J. M. Cénat, A. Karray, N. Guillier-Pasut, J. M. Cadichon, B. Lignier, N. E. Joseph, L. Brolles, and Y. Mouchenik, "Resilience in Haiti: Is it Culturally Pathological," *BJPsych International*, 15 (4): 79–80.

Doucet, R. C. (2003), "Language Ideology, Socialization and Pedagogy in Haitian Schools and Society," PhD diss., New York University, New York.

Dryden-Peterson, S. and C. Reddick (2019), "'What I Believe Can Rescue That Nation': Diaspora Working to Transform Education in Fragility and Conflict," *Comparative Education Review*, 63 (2): 213–35.

Dubuisson, D. E. (2020), "'We Know How to Work Together': Konbit, Protest, and the Rejection of INGO Bureaucratic Dominance," *Journal of Haitian Studies*, 26 (2): 53–80.

Dupuy, A. (1989), *Haiti in The World Economy: Class, Race, And Underdevelopment Since 1700*, Boulder: Westview Press.

Dupuy, A. (2010), "Disaster Capitalism to the Rescue: The International Community and Haiti after the Earthquake," *NACLA Report on the Americas*, 43 (4): 14–19.

Dupuy, A. (2014), *Haiti: From Revolutionary Slaves to Powerless Citizens: Essays on the Politics and Economics of Underdevelopment, 1804–2013*. New York: Routledge.

Edmond, Y., S. Randolph, and G. Richard (2007), "The Lakou System: A Cultural, Ecological Analysis of Mothering in Rural Haiti," *The Journal of Pan African Studies*, 2 (1): 19–32.

Edmonds, K. (2013), "Beyond Good Intentions: The Structural Limitations of NGOs in Haiti," *Critical Sociology*, 39 (3): 439–52.

Eisenhart, M. (2021), "The Anthropology of Learning Revisited," *Anthropology & Education Quarterly*, 52 (2): 209–21.

Ellis, C., T. Adams, and A. Bochner (2011), "Autoethnography: An Overview," *Forum Qualitative Sozialforschung / Forum: Qualitative Social Research*, 12 (1): 273–90.

Epstein, A. (2010), "Education Refugees and the Spatial Politics of Childhood Vulnerability," *Childhood in Africa: An Interdisciplinary Journal*, 1 (2): 16–25.

Erickson, F. (1984), "School Literacy, Reasoning, and Civility: An Anthropologist's Perspective," *Review of Educational Research*, 54 (4): 525–46.

Erickson, F. and M. L. Espinoza (2021), "The Anthropology of Learning: A Continuing Story," *Anthropology & Education Quarterly*, 52 (2): 123–34.

Escobar, A. (1995), *Encountering Development: The Making and Unmaking of the Third World*, Princeton: Princeton University Press.

Faith to Action (n.d.), "Faith to Action Initiative." Available online: https://www .faithtoaction.org/ (accessed December 14, 2022).

Fanon, F. (1967), *Black Skin, White Masks*, New York: Grove Press.

Farmer, P. (1994), *The Uses of Haiti*, Monroe: Common Courage Press.

Fassin, D. (2013), "On Resentment and Ressentiment: The Politics and Ethics of Moral Emotions," *Current Anthropology*, 54 (3): 249–67.

Fassin, D. (2007), "Humanitarianism as a Politics of Life," *Public Culture*, 19 (3): 499–520.

Fassin, D. and R. Rechtman (2009), *The Empire of Trauma: An Inquiry into the Condition of Victimhood*, Princeton: Princeton University Press.

Fatton, R. (2002), *Haiti's Predatory Republic: The Unending Transition to Democracy*, Boulder: Lynne Rienner Publishers.

Fatton, R. (2007), *Roots of Haitian Despotism*, Boulder: Lynne Rienner Publishers.

Fatton, R. (2014), *Haiti: Trapped in the Outer Periphery*, Boulder: Lynne Rienner Publishers.

Fatton, R. (2021), *The Guise of Exceptionalism: Unmasking the National Narratives of Haiti and the United States*, New Brunswick: Rutgers University Press.

Feagin, J. R. (2013), *The White Racial Frame: Centuries of Racial Framing and Counter-Framing*, New York: Routledge.

Felitti, V. J., R. F. Anda, D. Nordenberg, D. F. Williamson, A. M. Spitz, V. Edwards, M. P. Koss, and J. S. Marks (1998), "Relationship of Childhood Abuse and Household Dysfunction to Many of the Leading Causes of Death in Adults. The Adverse Childhood Experiences (ACE) Study," *American Journal of Preventive Medicine*, 14 (4): 245–58.

Ferguson, J. (1994), *The Anti-politics Machine: "Development," Depoliticization, and Bureaucratic Power in Lesotho*, Minneapolis: University of Minnesota Press.

Ferguson, J. and A. Gupta (2002), "Spatializing States: Toward an Ethnography of Neoliberal Governmentality," *American Ethnologist*, 29 (4): 981–1002.

Finnegan, A. C. (2013), "The White Girl's Burden," *Contexts*, 12 (1): 30–5.

Fjellman, S. M. and H. Gladwin (1985), "Haitian Family Patterns of Migration to South Florida," *Human Organization*, 44 (4): 301–12.

Flechtner, S. (2014), "Aspiration Traps: When Poverty Stifles Hope," *The World Bank Inequality in Focus*, 3: 1–4.

Flynn-O'Brien, K., F. Rivara, N. Weiss, V. Lea, L. Marcelin, J. Vertefeuille, and J. Mercy (2016), "Prevalence of Physical Violence Against Children in Haiti: A National Population-based Cross-sectional Survey," *Child Abuse & Neglect*, 51: 154–62.

Frederickson, K., J. Pierre-Louis, F. Pierre-Louis, and C. Ashby (2018), "Social Support and Types of Treatment for Illness in Fonfrede Haiti," *Journal of Health and Human Services Administration*, 40 (4): 499–531.

Freeman, S. (2018), "Perfume and Planes: Ignorance and Imagination in Haiti's Vetiver Oil Industry: Perfume and Planes," *The Journal of Latin American and Caribbean Anthropology*, 24: 110–26.

Freire, P. (1970), *Pedagogy of the Oppressed*, New York: Continuum.

Frye, M. (2012), "Bright Futures in Malawi's New Dawn: Educational Aspirations as Assertions of Identity," *American Journal of Sociology*, 117 (6): 1565–624.

Gallié, C. and M. Marcellus (2013), "Le Système de protection de l'enfant en Haiti. (The Child Protection System in Haiti)," World Vision International. Available online: https://www.wvi.org/sites/default/files/Haiti%20Child%20Protection%20Report .FINAL_.French.secure.pdf (accessed August 11, 2022).

Galvin, M., G. Michel, E. Manguira, E. Pierre, C. Lesorogol, J. F. Trani, R. Lester, and L. Iannotti (2022), "Examining the Etiology and Treatment of Mental Illness Among Vodou Priests in Northern Haiti," *Culture, Medicine, and Psychiatry*, Epub, 1–22.

Gaskins, S. and R. Paradise (2010), "Learning through Observation in Daily Life," in D. Lancy, J. Bock, and S. Gaskins (eds.), *The Anthropology of Learning in Childhood*, 85–117, Lanham: AltaMira Press.

Gebretsadik, D. (2017), "Street Work and the Perceptions of Children: Perspectives from Dilla Town, Southern Ethiopia," *Global Studies of Childhood*, 7 (1): 29–37.

Gengel, L. and C. Gengel (2013), *Heartache and Hope in Haiti: The Britney Gengel Story: Making Our Daughter's Last Wish Come True*, Deerfield Beach: TriMark Press.

Germain, F. (2011), "The Earthquake, the Missionaries, and the Future of Vodou," *Journal of Black Studies*, 42 (2): 247–63.

Gilbert, L., A. Reza, J. Mercy, V. Lea, J. Lee, L. Xu, L. Marcelin, M. Hast, J. Vertefeuille, and J. Domercant (2018), "The Experience of Violence Against Children in Domestic Servitude in Haiti: Results from the Violence Against Children Survey, Haiti 2012," *Child Abuse & Neglect*, 76: 184–93.

Gilmoor, A. R., A. Adithy, and B. Regeer (2019), "The Cross-Cultural Validity of Post-Traumatic Stress Disorder and Post-Traumatic Stress Symptoms in the Indian Context: A Systematic Search and Review," *Frontiers in Psychiatry*, 10: 439.

Gleason, K., A. Cox, and D. Pop (2016), "Whole Children, Whole Haiti: Inspiring Stories of Care, Family, and Advocacy for Children in Haiti." Available online: https://www.hopeandhomes.org/publications/whole-children-whole-haiti-inspiring-stories-of-care-family-and-advocacy-for-children-in-haiti/ (accessed December 20, 2022).

Gonzalez, T. (2006), "Child Fosterage in the Dominican Republic: A Comparative Analysis of Child Living Conditions," PhD diss., University of Florida.

Gottlieb, A. (2009), "Who Minds The Baby? Beng Perspectives on Mothers, Neighbors, and Strangers as Caretakers," in G. Bentley and R. Mace (eds.), *Substitute Parents: Biological and Social Perspectives on Alloparenting in Human Societies*, 115–38, New York: Berghahn.

Goulet, J. G. and D. E. Young (1994), *Being Changed by Cross-Cultural Encounters: The Anthropology of Extraordinary Experience*, Toronto: University of Toronto Press.

Gray, A. E. L. (2008), "Dance, Human Rights, and Social Justice: Dignity in Motion," in N. Jackson and T. Shapiro-Phim (eds.), *Dance, Human Rights, and Social Justice: Dignity in Motion*, 222–36, Lanham: Scarecrow Press.

Grewal, I. (2017), "Life in NGOs," in A. Lashaw, C. Vannier, and S. Sampson (eds.), *Cultures of Doing Good: Anthropologists and NGOs*, 113–21, Tuscaloosa: University of Alabama Press.

Guiney, T. (2018), "'Hug-an-orphan Vacations': 'Love' and Emotion in Orphanage Tourism," *The Geographical Journal*, 184 (2): 125–37.

Guzmán, J., K. Schuenke-Lucien, A. D'Agostino, M. Berends, and A. Elliot (2021), "Improving Reading Instruction and Students' Reading Skills in the Early Grades: Evidence from a Randomized Evaluation in Haiti," *Reading Research Quarterly*, 56 (1): 173–93.

Hammond, C. (2020), "Stitching Time: Artisanal Collaboration and Slow Fashion in Post-disaster Haiti," *Fashion Theory*, 24 (1): 33–57.

Hart, J. (2006), "Saving Children: What Role for Anthropology?" *Anthropology Today*, 22 (1): 5–8.

Hashemi, M. (2020), *Coming of Age in Iran*, New York: New York University Press.

Haydocy, K., M. Yotebieng, and A. Norris (2015), "Restavèk Children in Context: Wellbeing Compared to Other Haitian Children," *Child Abuse & Neglect*, 50: 42–8.

Hecht, T. (1998), *At Home in the Street: Street Children of Northeast Brazil*, Cambridge: Cambridge University Press.

Hefferan, T., J. Adkins, and L. A. Occhipinti (2009), "Faith-Based Organizations, Neoliberalism, and Development: An Introduction," in T. Hefferan, J. Adkins, and L. Occhipinti (eds.), *Bridging the Gaps: Faith-based Organizations, Neoliberalism, and Development in Latin America and the Caribbean*, 1–34, Lexington: Lexington Books.

Hefferan, T. (2009), "Encouraging Development 'Alternatives': Grassroots Church Partnering in the US and Haiti," in T. Hefferan, J. Adkins, and L. Occhipinti (eds.), *Bridging the Gaps: Faith-based Organizations, Neoliberalism, and Development in Latin America and the Caribbean*, 69—82, Lexington: Lexington Books.

Henrich, J., S. J. Heine, and A. Norenzayan (2010), "The Weirdest People in the World?" *Behavioral and Brain Sciences*, 33 (2–3): 61–83.

Heron, B. (2007), *Desire for Development: Whiteness, Gender, and the Helping Imperative*, Waterloo: Wilfrid Laurier University Press.

Herskovits, M. (1937), *Life in a Haitian Valley*, New York: A. A. Knopf.

Hoffman, D. M. (2009a), "How (not) to Feel: Culture and the Politics of Emotion in the American Parenting Advice Literature," *Discourse: Studies in the Cultural Politics of Education*, 30 (1): 15–31.

Hoffman, D. M. (2009b), "Reflecting on Social Emotional Learning: A Critical Perspective on Trends in the United States," *Review of Educational Research*, 79 (2): 533–56.

Hoffman, D. M. (2010a), "Migrant Children in Haiti: Domestic Labor and the Politics of Representation," in M. O. Ensor and E. Gozdziak (eds.), *Children and Migration: At the Crossroads of Resiliency and Vulnerability*, 36–53, London: Palgrave Macmillan.

Hoffman, D. M. (2010b), "Risky Investments: Parenting and the Production of the Resilient Child," *Health, Risk & Society*, 12 (4): 385–94.

Hoffman, D. M. (2012a), "Moving Children in Haiti: Some Hypotheses on Kinship, Labor, and Personhood in the Haitian Context," *Journal of Haitian Studies*, 18 (1): 102–19.

Hoffman, D. M. (2012b), "Saving Children, Saving Haiti? Child Vulnerability and Narratives of the Nation," *Childhood*, 19 (2): 155–68.

Hoffman, D. M. (2013), "Power Struggles: The Paradoxes of Emotion and Control among Child-Centered Mothers in Privileged America," in C. Faircloth, D. M. Hoffman, and L. L. Layne (eds.), *Parenting in Global Perspective: Negotiating Ideologies of Kinship, Self and Politics*, 229–43, Philadelphia: Routledge.

Hoffman, D. M. (2016), "Learning to See: Intuition and Perception in Fieldwork in Haiti," *Anthropology and Humanism*, 41 (1): 28–38.

Hoffman, D. M. (2019), "Mindfulness and the Cultural Psychology of Personhood: Challenges of Self, Other, and Moral Orientation in Haiti," *Culture & Psychology*, 25 (3): 302–23.

Hoffman, D. M. (2021a), "The Haitian Orphanage Crisis: Exporting Neoliberal Family Ideals in the Debate on Vulnerable Childhoods in Haiti," *Children & Society*, 35 (4): 577–92.

Hoffman, D. M. (2021b), "Multimodality in Children's Socially Situated Learning in Haiti: A Video-based Ethnographic Analysis," *International Journal of Qualitative Studies in Education*, 36 (5): 955–73.

Hoffman, D. M. (2022), "White Savior or Local Hero?: Conflicting Narratives of Help in Haiti," *Georgetown Journal of International Affairs*, 23 (1): 99–104.

Hoffman, D. M. and D. Saavedra (forthcoming), "What is Learned in the Encounter: Perspectives on a US-Haiti Student Research Collaboration," *Journal of Studies in International Education*.

Holland, D. G. and M. H. Yousofi (2014), "The Only Solution: Education, Youth, and Social Change in Afghanistan," *Anthropology & Education Quarterly*, 45 (3): 241–59.

Holst, T. (2019), "The Emotional Labor of Former Street Children Working as Tour Guides in Delhi," *Focaal*, 85: 97–109.

Howell, B. (2012), *Short-Term Mission: An Ethnography of Christian Travel Narrative and Experience*, Westmont: InterVarsity Press.

Howze, K. A. and A. K. McKeig (2019), "The Greenbook and the Overrepresentation of African American, Hispanic, and Native American Families in the Child Welfare System," *Juvenile & Family Court Journal*, 70 (4): 103–18.

Hunleth, J. (2017), *Children as Caregivers: The Global Fight against Tuberculosis and HIV in Zambia*, New Brunswick: Rutgers University Press.

Hutchison, E. and R. Bleiker (2014), "Theorizing Emotions in World Politics," *International Theory*, 6 (3): 491–514.

Ingold, T. (2000), *The Perception of the Environment: Essays on Livelihood, Dwelling & Skill*, New York: Routledge.

Ingold, T. (2006), "Rethinking the Animate, Re-animating Thought," *Ethnos*, 71 (1): 9–20.

Ingold, T. (2018), *Anthropology and/as Education*, New York: Routledge.

Institut du Bien-être Social et de Recherches (2015), "Stratégie Nationale De Protection De L'Enfant." Available online: http://www.commissioneadozioni.it/media/1723/ibesr_strategie-national-de-protection-de-l-enfant-2015.pdf (accessed August 11, 2022).

Jackson, K., L. Payne, and K. Stolley (2015), *The Intersection of Star Culture in America and International Medical Tourism: Celebrity Treatment*, Lanham: Lexington Books.

Jakimow, T. (2016), "Clinging to Hope through Education: The Consequences of Hope for Rural Laborers in Telangana, India," *Ethos*, 44 (1): 11–31.

James, A. (2007), "Giving Voice to Children's Voices: Practices and Problems, Pitfalls and Potentials," *American Anthropologist*, 109 (2): 261–72.

James, A. and A. Prout (2015), *Constructing and Reconstructing Childhood*, London: Routledge.

James, E. C. (2010), "Ruptures, Rights, and Repair: The Political Economy of Trauma in Haiti," *Social Science & Medicine*, 70 (1): 106–13.

James, E. C. (2019), *Governing Gifts: Faith, Charity, and the Security State*, Albuquerque: University of New Mexico Press.

James, L. E., J. R. Noel, T. K. Favorite, and J. S. Jean (2012), "Challenges of Postdisaster Intervention in Cultural Context: The Implementation of a Lay Mental Health Worker Project in Postearthquake Haiti," *International Perspectives in Psychology: Research, Practice, Consultation*, 1: 110–26.

Jean-Jacques, J. E. (2009), "Faith Based Organizations and Community Change in Haiti," MA. Thesis, University of California, Davis.

Jean-Pierre, M. (2016), *Language and Learning in a Post-colonial Context: A Critical Ethnographic Study in Schools in Haiti*, New York: Routledge.

Joseph, C. L. (2016), "Redefining Cultural, National, and Religious Identity: The Christian–Vodouist Dialogue," *Theology Today*, 73 (3): 241–62.

Justesen, M. and D. Verner (2007), "Factors Impacting Youth Development in Haiti," Policy Research Working Papers.

Kaiser, B. N. and J. R. Fils-Aimé (2019), "Sent Spirits, Meaning-Making, and Agency in Haiti," *Ethos*, 47 (3): 367–86.

Kaiser, B. N. and L. Jo Weaver (2019), "Culture-Bound Syndromes, Idioms of Distress, and Cultural Concepts of Distress: New Directions for an Old Concept in Psychological Anthropology," *Transcultural Psychiatry*, 56 (4): 589–98.

Kao, G. and M. Tienda (1998), "Educational Aspirations of Minority Youth," *American Journal of Education*, 106: 349–84.

Karray, A., D. Derivois, L. Brolles, and I. Wexler Buzaglo (2017), "La reconstruction des enveloppes psychiques et environnementales dans les dessins d'enfants des rues en Haïti: Une étude post-séisme," *L'Évolution Psychiatrique*, 82 (1): 89–103.

Katz, J. (2013), *The Big Truck That Went by: How the World Came to Save Haiti and Left Behind a Disaster*, New York: Palgrave Macmillan.

Kaussen, V. (2012), "Do It Yourself: International Aid and the Neoliberal Ethos in the Tent Camps," in M. Schuller and P. Morales (eds.), *Tectonic Shifts: Haiti since the Earthquake*, 125–30, Boulder: Kumarian Press.

Kaussen, V. (2016), "Haitian Culture in the Informational Economies of Humanitarian Aid," in A. Benedicty-Kokken, J. P. Byron, K. L. Glover, and M. Schuller (eds.), *The Haiti Exception: Anthropology and the Predicaments of Narrative*, 156–76, Liverpool: Liverpool University Press.

Keddell, E. (2018), "The Vulnerable Child in Neoliberal Contexts: The Construction of Children in the Aotearoa New Zealand Child Protection Reforms," *Childhood*, 25 (1): 93–108.

Keller, H. (2013), "Attachment and Culture," *Journal of Cross-Cultural Psychology*, 44 (2): 175–94.

Keller, H. (2018), "Universality Claim of Attachment Theory: Children's Socioemotional Development across Cultures," *PNAS*, 115 (45): 11414–19.

Kidron, C. A. and L. J. Kirmayer (2019), "Global Mental Health and Idioms of Distress: The Paradox of Culture-Sensitive Pathologization of Distress in Cambodia," *Culture, Medicine and Psychiatry*, 43 (2): 211–35.

Kim, H. S. (2010), "Culture and Self-Expression," American Psychological Association. Available online: https://www.apa.org/science/about/psa/2010/06/sci-brief (accessed September 20, 2022).

King, S. (2012), "Owning Laura Silsby's Shame: How the Haitian Child Trafficking Scheme Embodies the Western Disregard for the Integrity of Poor Families," *Harvard Human Rights Journal*, 25: 149.

King's College London (2013), "Poverty of Aspiration Largely a Myth." Available online: https://phys.org/news/2013-09-poverty-aspiration-largely-myth.html (accessed December 14, 2022).

Kipling, R. (1899), *The White Man's Burden*. New York: McClure's Magazine.

Kivland, C. (2012), "To Defend or Develop? On the Politics of Engagement among Local Organizations in Bel Air, Haiti, Before and After the Quake," *Journal of Haitian Studies*, 18 (1): 75–99.

Kivland, C. (2020), *Street Sovereigns: Young Men and the Makeshift State in Urban Haiti*, Ithaca: Cornell University Press.

Kothari, U. (2006), "An Agenda for Thinking About 'race' in Development," *Progress in Development Studies*, 6 (1): 9–23.

Kovats-Bernat, J. (2006), *Sleeping Rough in Port-au-Prince: An Ethnography of Street Children and Violence in Haiti*, Gainesville: University Press of Florida.

Kristoff, M. and L. Panarelli (2010), "Haiti: A Republic of NGOs?" United States Institute of Peace. Available online: https://www.usip.org/sites/default/files/PB%2023 %20Haiti%20a%20Republic%20of%20NGOs.pdf (accessed December 30, 2021).

Laguerre, M. (1978), "Ticouloute and His Kinfolk: The Study of a Haitian Extended Family," in E. Shimkin and D. Frate (eds.), *The Extended Family in Black Societies*, 407–46, Berlin: Walter de Gruyter.

Lancy, D. F. (2007), "Accounting for Variability in Mother–Child Play," *American Anthropologist*, 109 (2): 273–84.

Lancy, D. F. (2010), "Learning 'From Nobody': The Limited Role of Teaching in Folk Models of Children's Development," *Childhood in the Past*, 3 (1): 79–106.

Lancy, D. F. (2015), *The Anthropology of Childhood: Cherubs, Chattel, Changelings*, Cambridge: Cambridge University Press.

Lancy, D. F., J. C. Bock, and S. Gaskins (2010), *The Anthropology of Learning in Childhood*, Lanham: AltaMira Press.

Landry, T. R. (2008), "Moving to Learn: Performance and Learning in Haitian Vodou," *Anthropology and Humanism*, 33 (1–2): 53–65.

Lareau, A. (2003), *Unequal Childhoods: Class, Race, and Family Life*, Berkeley: University of California Press.

Lave, J. (1991), "Situating Learning in Communities of Practice," in L. Resnick, J. Levine, and S. Teasley (eds.), *Perspectives on Socially Shared Cognition*, 63–82, Washington: American Psychological Association.

Lave, J. (1996), "Teaching, as Learning, in Practice," *Mind, Culture, and Activity*, 3 (3): 149–64.

Leinaweaver, J. B. (2008), *The Circulation of Children: Kinship, Adoption, and Morality in Andean Peru*, Durham: Duke University Press.

Lichtenberg, A. A., M. Shi, K. Joseph, B. N. Kaiser, and C. L. Katz (2022), "Understanding Mental Distress in Arcahaie, Haiti: Heterogeneous Uses of Idioms of Distress in Communicating Psychological Suffering," *Transcultural Psychiatry*, 59 (4): 479–91.

Lillard, A. S., M. D. Lerner, E. J. Hopkins, A. R. Dore, E. D. Smith, and C. M. Palmquist (2013), "The Impact of Pretend Play on Children's Development: A Review of the Evidence," *Psychological Bulletin*, 139 (1): 1–34.

Lima, E. (1998), "The Educational Experience With Tikuna: A Look Into the Complexity of Concept Construction," *Mind, Culture, and Activity*, 5 (2): 95–104.

Linger, D. (2005), *Anthropology through a Double Lens: Public and Personal Worlds in Human Theory*, Philadelphia: University of Pennsylvania Press.

Louis, B. (2019), "Haiti's Pact with the Devil?: Bwa Kayiman, Haitian Protestant Views of Vodou, and the Future of Haiti," *Religions*, 10 (8): 464.

Lowenthal, I. (1987), "Marriage is 20, Children are 21: The Cultural Construction of Conjugality and the Family in Rural Haiti," PhD diss., Johns Hopkins University.

Lumos Foundation (2015), "Children in Haiti: From Institutions to Families." Available online: https://www.wearelumos.org/resources/children-haiti-institutions-families/ (accessed June 24, 2020).

Lumos Foundation (2017), "Funding Haitian Orphanages at the Cost of Children's Rights." Available online: https://www.wearelumos.org/resources/funding-haitian -orphanages-cost-childrens-rights/ (accessed June 24, 2020).

Lumos Foundation (2020), "Empowering Families in Haiti." Available online: https:// www.wearelumos.org/knowledge-portal/empowering-families-haiti-wearelumos/ (accessed June 24, 2020).

Lunde, H. (2008), "Youth and Education in Haiti: Disincentives, Vulnerabilities, and Constraints," *FAFO*. Available online: https://www.fafo.no/media/com_netsukii /10070.pdf (accessed December 30, 2021).

Lunde, H. (2010), "Haiti Youth Survey 2009. Volume II: Analytical Report," *FAFO*. Available online: https://www.fafo.no/en/publications/fafo-reports/item/haiti-youth -survey-2010 (accessed December 30, 2021).

Lupton, R. D. (2011), *Toxic Charity: How The Church Hurts Those They Help and How to Reverse It*, New York: HarperOne.

Lutz, C. A. and L. Abu-Lughod (1990), *Language and the politics of emotion*, Paris: Editions de la Maison des Sciences de l'Homme.

Magruder, K. M., K. A. McLaughlin, and D. L. Elmore Borbon (2017), "Trauma is a Public Health Issue," *European Journal of Psychotraumatology*, 8 (1): 1–9.

Maguire, R. and S. Freeman (2017), *Who Owns Haiti?: People, Power, and Sovereignty*, Gainesville: University Press of Florida.

Mahon, R. (2010), "After Neo-Liberalism?: The OECD, the World Bank and the Child," *Global Social Policy*, 10 (2): 172–92.

Mains, D. (2011), *Hope Is Cut: Youth, Unemployment, and the Future in Urban Ethiopia*, Philadelphia: Temple University Press.

Malkki, L. H. (1996), "Speechless Emissaries: Refugees, Humanitarianism, and Dehistoricization," *Cultural Anthropology*, 11 (3): 377–404.

Malkki, L. H. (2015), *The Need to Help: The Domestic Arts of International Humanitarianism*, Durham: Duke University Press.

Masten, A. S., K. M. Best, and N. Garmezy (1990), "Resilience and development: Contributions from the study of children who overcome adversity," *Development and Psychopathology*, 2 (4): 425–44.

McAlister, E. (2004), "Love, Sex, and Gender Embodied: The Spirits of Haitian Vodou," *Africultures*, February 29. Available online: http://africultures.com/love-sex-and-gender-embodied-the-spirits-of-haitian-vodou-5719/ (accessed August 11, 2022).

McAlister, E. (2012), "From Slave Revolt to a Blood Pact with Satan: The Evangelical Rewriting of Haitian History," *Studies in Religion/Sciences Religieuses*, 41 (2): 187–215.

McAlister, M. (2008), "What is Your Heart For?: Affect and Internationalism in the Evangelical Public Sphere," *American Literary History*, 20 (4): 870–95.

McCalla, J. (2002), "Restavek No More: Eliminating Child Slavery in Haiti," *National Coalition for Haitian Rights*, April. Available online: https://jmcstrategies.com/wp-content/uploads/2008/08/rnm20021.pdf (accessed December 30, 2021).

McCarthy-Brown, K. (2006), "Afro-Caribbean Spirituality: A Haitian Case Study," in C. Michel and P. Bellegarde-Smith (eds.), *Vodou in Haitian Life and Culture: Invisible Powers*, 1–27, New York: Palgrave Macmillan.

McConville, K. (2019), "Letting Kids be Kids: Protecting What's Precious in Haiti." Available online: https://www.concernusa.org/story/protecting-whats-precious-in-haiti/ (accessed December 20, 2022).

McDermott, R. and R. Pea (2020), "Learning 'How to Mean': Embodiment in Cultural Practices," in N. Nasir, C. Lee, R. Pea, and M. de Royston (eds.), *Handbook of the Cultural Foundations of Learning*, 99–118, New York: Routledge.

McEwen, H. (2017), "Nuclear Power: The Family in Decolonial Perspective and 'Pro-family' Politics in Africa," *Development Southern Africa*, 34 (6): 738–51.

Mead, M. (1928), *Coming of Age in Samoa*, New York: Editions for the Armed Services.

Méance, G. (2014), "Vodou Healing and Psychotherapy," in P. Sutherland, R. Moodley, and B. Chevannes (eds.), *Caribbean Healing Traditions: Implications for Health and Mental Health*, 78–88, Philadelphia: Routledge Taylor & Francis Group.

Merveille, H. (2002), "Haiti:Violence – A Bad Legacy Bequeathed to Kids," *Panos Caribbean*. Available online: http://panoscaribbean.org/en/publications/rmb/64-haiti-violence-a-bad-legacy-bequeathed-to-kids (accessed December 30, 2021).

Métraux, A. (1972), *Voodoo in Haiti*, New York: Schocken Books.

Mézié, N. (2014), "Des enfants, des fous, des chiens. Des jeux brutaux et sérieux dans les mornes Haïtiens," *Ethnologie francaise*, 44 (4): 719–24.

Michel, C. (1996), "Of Worlds Seen and Unseen: The Educational Character of Haitian Vodou," *Comparative Education Review*, 40 (3): 280–94.

Minn, P. (2006), "Water in Their Eyes, Dust on Their Land: Heat and Illness in a Haitian Town," in C. Michel and P. Bellegarde-Smith (eds.), *Vodou in Haitian Life and Culture: Invisible Powers*, 135–54, New York: Springer.

Mische, A. (2009), "Projects and Possibilities: Researching Futures in Action," *Sociological Forum*, 24 (3): 694–704.

Mitchell, K. (2016), "Celebrity Humanitarianism, Transnational Emotion and the Rise of Neoliberal Citizenship," *Global Networks*, 16 (3): 288–306.

Molz, J. (2017), "Giving Back, Doing Good, Feeling Global: The Affective Flows of Family Voluntourism," *Journal of Contemporary Ethnography*, 46 (3): 334–60.

Moncrieffe, J. (2006), "The Power of Stigma: Encounters with Street Children and Restavecs," *IDS Bulletin*, 37 (6): 34–46.

Montgomery, H. (2009), *An Introduction to Childhood: An Anthropological Perspective on Children's Lives*, Hoboken: Wiley-Blackwell.

Mosier, C. and B. Rogoff (2003), "Privileged Treatment of Toddlers: Cultural Aspects of Individual Choice and Responsibility," *Developmental Psychology*, 39: 1047–60.

Mostafanezhad, M. (2013), "The Geography of Compassion in Volunteer Tourism," *Tourism Geographies*, 15 (2): 318–37.

Muralidharan, S., L. Rasmussen, D. Patterson, and J. Shin. (2011), "Hope for Haiti: An Analysis of Facebook and Twitter Usage during the Earthquake Relief Efforts," *Public Relations Review*, 37 (2): 175–7.

Nagel, C. (2021), "Doing Missions Right: Popular Development Imaginaries and Practices among U.S. Evangelical Christians," *Geoforum*, 124: 110–19.

Najt, B. (2022), *My Journey in the Darkness: Haiti through My Eyes*. Fort Worth: 4Ekselans Inc..

Nasir, N. S., C.D. Lee, R. Pea, and M. M. de Royston (2020), *Handbook of the Cultural Foundations of Learning*, New York: Routledge.

Nicholas, T. (2014), "Crossing Boundaries to Education: Haitian Transnational Families and the Quest to Raise the Family Up," PhD diss., Florida International University, Miami.

Nicholas, T., A. Stepick, and C. Stepick (2008), "'Here's Your Diploma, Mom!' Family Obligation and Multiple Pathways to Success," *The Annals of the American Academy of Political and Social Science*, 620: 237–52.

Nieuwenhuys, O. (2001), "By the Sweat of Their Brow? 'Street Children', NGOs and Children's Rights in Addis Ababa," *Africa*, 71 (4): 539–57.

Nieuwenhuys, O. (2005), "The Wealth of Children: Reconsidering the Child Labour Debate," in J. Qvortrup (ed.), *Studies in Modern Childhood: Society, Agency, Culture*, 167–83, New York: Palgrave Macmillan.

Norman, K. and R. LeVine (2008), "Attachment in Anthropological Perspective," in R. LeVine and R. New (eds.), *Anthropology and Child Development: A Cross-Cultural Reader*, 126–42, Hoboken: Wiley-Blackwell.

Obert, J. D. (2020), "Haitian Mental Health Needs Rise yet again with COVID-19 Trauma," *The New Humanitarian*, July 17. Available online: https://www .thenewhumanitarian.org/news/2020/07/17/Haiti-coronavirus-mental-health -earthquake-depression-anxiety-trauma-GBV (accessed September 20, 2022).

Offit, T. A. (2008), *Conquistadores de la Calle: Child Street Labor in Guatemala City*, Austin: University of Texas Press.

Omi, M. and H. Winant (2015), *Racial Formation in the United States*, New York: Routledge, Taylor & Francis Group.

Otto, H. and H. Keller (2014), *Different Faces of Attachment: Cultural Variations on a Universal Human Need*, Cambridge: Cambridge University Press.

Pailey, R. N. (2020), "De-centring the 'White Gaze' of Development," *Development and Change*, 51 (3): 729–45.

Panter-Brick, C. (2002), "Street Children, Human Rights, and Public Health: A Critique and Future Directions," *Annual Review of Anthropology*, 31 (1): 147–71.

Paradise, R. and B. Rogoff (2009), "Side by Side: Learning by Observing and Pitching In," *Ethos*, 37 (1): 102–38.

Patel, A. R. and J. B. Hall (2021), "Beyond the DSM-5 Diagnoses: A Cross-Cultural Approach to Assessing Trauma Reactions," *FOCUS*, 19 (2): 197–203.

Patel, L. (2019), "Fugitive Practices: Learning in a Settler Colony," *Educational Studies*, 55 (3): 253–61.

Paul, A. M. (2021), *The Extended Mind: The Power of Thinking Outside the Brain*, Boston: Houghton Mifflin Harcourt.

Penn, H. (2009), "The Parenting and Substitute Parenting of Young Children," in G. Bentley and R. Mace (eds.), *Substitute Parents: Alloparenting in Human Societies*, 179–93. New York: Berghahn.

Petrie, Z. (2020), *Reach and Fall*, Deeerfield Beach: Trimark Press.

Pierre, A., P. Minn, C. Sterlin, P. C. Annoual, A. Jaimes, F. Raphaël, E. Raikhel, R. Whitley, C. Rousseau, and L. J. Kirmayer (2010), "Culture et santé mentale en Haïti: Une revue de littérature [Culture and Mental Health in Haiti: A Literature Review]," *Sante Mental au Quebec*, 35 (1): 13–47.

Pierre, Y., G. Smucker, and J. Tardieu (2009), "Lost Childhoods in Haiti: Quantifying Child Trafficking, Restavèks, and Victims of Violence," Pan American Development Foundation. Available online: https://archive.crin.org/en/docs/Haiti_lost _childhoods.pdf (accessed December 30, 2021).

Powdermaker, H. (1966), *Stranger and Friend: The Way of an Anthropologist*, New York: W. W. Norton.

Quinn, N. and J. Mageo, eds. (2013), *Attachment Reconsidered: Cultural Perspectives on a Western Theory*, New York: Palgrave Macmillan.

Reed-Danahay, D. (1997), *Auto/Ethnography: Explorations in Anthropology*, Oxford: Berg.

Reynolds, P. (1996), *Traditional Healers and Childhood in Zimbabwe*, Athens: Ohio University Press.

Reynolds, P., O. Nieuwenhuys, and K. Hanson (2006), "Refractions of Children's Rights in Development Practice: A View from Anthropology – Introduction," *Childhood: A Global Journal of Child Research*, 13 (3): 291–302.

Richey, L. A. (2018), "Conceptualizing 'Everyday Humanitarianism': Ethics, Affects, and Practices of Contemporary Global Helping," *New Political Science*, 40 (4): 625–39.

Richman, K. (2008), "A More Powerful Sorcerer: Conversion, Capital, and Haitian Transnational Migration," *New West Indian Guide*, 82 (1 & 2): 3–45.

Roelen, K. and A. Saha (2021), "Pathways to Stronger Futures? The Role of Social Protection in Reducing Psychological Risk factors for Child Development in Haiti," *World Development*, 142: 1–12.

Rogoff, B. (1981), "Adults and Peers as Agents of Socialization: A Highland Guatemalan Profile," *Ethos*, 9 (1): 18–36.

Rogoff, B., R. Mejía-Arauz, and M. Correa-Chávez (2015), "A Cultural Paradigm— Learning by Observing and Pitching In," *Advances in Child Development and Behavior*, 49: 1–22.

Rogoff, B., B. Najafi, and R. Mejía-Arauz (2014), "Constellations of Cultural Practices across Generations: Indigenous American Heritage and Learning by Observing and Pitching In," *Human Development*, 57 (2–3): 82–95.

Rogoff, B., R. Paradise, R. Arauz, M. Correa-Chavez, and C. Angelillo (2003), "Firsthand Learning through Intent Participation," *Annual Review of Psychology*, 54: 175–203.

Roysircar, G., K. Colvin, A. Afolayan, A. Thompson, and T. Roberson (2017), "Haitian Children's Resilience and Vulnerability Assessed with House-Tree-Person (HTP) Drawings," *Traumatology*, 23 (1): 68–81.

Roysircar, G., K. F. Geisinger, and A. Thompson (2019), "Haitian Children's Disaster Trauma: Validation of Pictorial Assessment of Resilience and Vulnerability," *Journal of Black Psychology*, 45 (4): 269–305.

Roysircar, G. and K. O'Grady (2022), "Children's Disaster Trauma in Haiti: Configurations of Similarities and Dissimilarities in Experiences," *Psychological Services*, 19 (4): 698–709.

Said, E. W. (1979), *Orientalism*, New York: Vintage.

Save the Children (2012), "Save the Children Annual Report 2012." Available online: https://www.savethechildren.org/content/dam/usa/reports/annual-report/annual -report/sc-2012-annualreport.pdf (accessed December 14, 2022).

Scheper-Hughes, N. and C. Sargent (1998), *Small Wars: The Cultural Politics of Childhood*, Berkeley: University of California Press.

Scherz, C. (2014), *Having People, Having Heart: Charity, Sustainable Development, and Problems of Dependence in Central Uganda*, Chicago: University of Chicago Press.

Schmidt, W. J., H. Keller, and M. Rosabal Coto (2021), "Development in Context: What We Need to Know to Assess Children's Attachment Relationships," *Developmental Psychology*, 57 (12): 2206–19.

Schöneberg, J. M. (2017), "NGO Partnerships in Haiti: Clashes of Discourse and Reality," *Third World Quarterly*, 38 (3): 604–20.

Schuller, M. (2007), "Invasion or Infusion? Understanding the Role of NGOs in Contemporary Haiti," *Journal of Haitian Studies*, 13 (2): 96–119.

Schuller, M. (2012), *Killing with Kindness: Haiti, International Aid, and NGOs*, New Brunswick: Rutgers University Press.

Schuller, M. (2016), *Humanitarian Aftershocks in Haiti*, New Brunswick: Rutgers University Press.

Schwartz, T. (2003), "Children are the Wealth of the Poor: Pronatalism and the Economic Utility of Children in Jean Rabel, Haiti," in N. Dannhaeuser and C. Werner (eds.), *Anthropological Perspectives on Economic Development and Integration*, 61–105, Bingley: Emerald Group Publishing.

Schwartz, T. (2009), *Fewer Men, More Babies: Sex, Family, and Fertility in Haiti*, Lanham: Lexington Books.

Silva, K. G., M. Correa-Chávez, and B. Rogoff (2010), "Mexican-Heritage Children's Attention and Learning from Interactions Directed to Others," *Child Development*, 81 (3): 898–912.

Sims, M. (2017), "Neoliberalism and Early Childhood," *Cogent Education*, 4 (1): 1365411.

Smith, J. M. (2001), *When the Hands Are Many*, Ithaca: Cornell University Press.

Smucker, G. and G. Murray (2004), "The Uses of Children: A Study of Trafficking in Haitian Children," *USAID/Haiti Mission*, December. Available online: https://pdf.usaid.gov/pdf_docs/PNADF061.pdf (accessed December 30, 2021).

Sommerfelt, T. (2002), "Child Domestic Labor in Haiti: Characteristics, Contexts, and Organization of Children's Residence, Relocation and Work," *FAFO*, May. Available online: https://www.haiti-now.org/wp-content/uploads/2017/07/Life-as-a-Child-Domestic-Worker-in-Haiti-FAFO-2005.pdf (accessed December 30, 2021).

Sommerfelt, T. (2015), "Child Fosterage and Child Domestic Work in Haiti in 2014: Analytical Report," *FAFO*. Available online: https://www.fafo.no/images/pub/2015/20559-web.pdf (accessed December 30, 2021).

Sommerfelt, T. and J. Pederson (2009), "Child Labor in Haiti," in H. Hindman (ed.), *The World of Child Labor: An Historical and Regional Survey*, 427–30, New York: Routledge.

St. Clair, R. and A. Benjamin (2011), "Performing Desires: The Dilemma of Aspirations and Educational Attainment," *British Educational Research Journal*, 37 (3): 501–17.

Steinke, A. (2020), *Haiti Ten Years after Douz Janvye*. Berlin: Centre for Humanitarian Action.

Stephens, S. (1995), *Children and the Politics of Culture*, Princeton: Princeton University Press.

Stephenson, M., Jr. and L. Zanotti (2021), "Tacit Knowledge, Cultural Values and Agential Possibility in Rural Haiti," *Community Development Journal*, 56 (4): 663–78.

Sterlin, C. (2006), "Pour une approche interculturelle du concept de santé," *Ruptures, Revue Transdiciplinaire En Santé*, 11: 112–21.

Stodulka, T. (2015), "Emotion Work, Ethnography, and Survival Strategies on the Streets of Yogyakarta," *Medical Anthropology*, 34 (1): 84–97.

Stoller, P. (2010), *Sensuous Scholarship*, Philadelphia: University of Pennsylvania Press.

Stooke, R. (2014), "Producing Neoliberal Parenting Subjectivities: ANT-Inspired Readings from an Informal Early Learning Program," *Journal of the Canadian Association for Young Children*, 39 (1): 56–80.

Strongman, R. (2008), "The Afro-diasporic Body in Haitian Vodou and the Transcending of Gendered Cartesian Corporeality," *Kunapipi*, 30 (2): 11–29.

Stryker, R. (2015), "Classic and Emerging Themes in the Anthropology of Children and Youth," *Teaching Anthropology: Proceedings of the 2015 AAA Meeting*, 21 (1): 6.

Super, C. M. and S. Harkness (2002), "Culture Structures the Environment for Development," *Human Development*, 45 (4): 270–4.

Tafere, Y. (2014), *Education Aspirations and Barriers to Achievement for Young People in Ethiopia*, UK Young Lives Working Paper 120. www.younglives.org.

Tax, S. (1975), "Action Anthropology," *Current Anthropology*, 16 (4): 514–17.

Taylor, A., V. Pacinini-Ketchabaw, and M. Blaise (2012), "Children's Relations to the More-Than-Human World," *Contemporary Issues in Early Childhood*, 13 (2): 81–5.

Terre Des Hommes (2013), "Restavek, a Modern-Day Form of Slavery." Available online: https://www.tdh.ch/en/news/restavek-modern-day-form-slavery (accessed August 11, 2022).

Theisen-Womersley, G. (2021), *Trauma and Resilience among Displaced Populations: A Sociocultural Exploration*, New York: Springer International Publishing.

Theron, L. and M. Malindi (2010), "Resilient Street Youth: A Qualitative South African Study," *Journal of Youth Studies*, 13: 717–36.

Ticktin, M. (2014), "Transnational Humanitarianism," *Annual Review of Anthropology*, 43 (1): 273–89.

Thompson, E. (2017), "Orphanages—5 Myths You Need to Know." Available online: https://heartlineministries.org/17963/orphanage-myths/ (accessed July 25, 2023).

Udy, M. (2014), "The Protection of Children in Haiti," *Haiti Perspectives*, 2 (4): 65–70.

Ulysse, G. (2010), "Why Representations of Haiti Matter Now More Than Ever," *NACLA Report on the Americas*, 43 (4): 37–47.

U.S. Agency for International Development (n.d.), "Education in Haiti." Available online: https://idea.usaid.gov/cd/haiti/education (accessed December 30, 2021).

U.S. Department of Labor (2019), "2019 Findings on the Worst Forms of Child Labor: Haiti." Available online: https://www.dol.gov/sites/dolgov/files/ILAB/child_labor_reports/tda2019/Haiti.pdf (accessed December 30, 2021).

Valentin, K. and L. Meinert (2009), "The Adult North and the Young South: Reflections on the Civilizing Mission of Children's Rights," *Anthropology Today*, 25 (3): 23–8.

Vossoughi, S. and K. D. Gutiérrez (2014), "Studying Movement, Hybridity, and Change: Toward a Multi-sited Sensibility for Research on Learning across Contexts and Borders," *Teachers College Record*, 116 (14): 603–32.

Wander, J. (2010), "Love and Haiti," *Pittsburgh Magazine*, January 14. Available online: https://www.pittsburghmagazine.com/love-and-haiti/ (accessed December 30, 2021).

Weidenstedt, L. (2016), "Empowerment Gone Bad: Communicative Consequences of Power Transfers," *Socius*, 2: 1–11.

Whetten, K., J. Ostermann, R. A. Whetten, B. W. Pence, K. O'Donnell, L. C. Messer, and N. M. Thielman (2009), "A Comparison of the Wellbeing of Orphans and Abandoned Children Ages 6–12 in Institutional and Community-Based Care Settings in 5 Less Wealthy Nations," *PLOS ONE*, 4 (12): e8169.

White, S. C. (2002), "Thinking Race, Thinking Development," *Third World Quarterly*, 23 (3): 407–19.

Whiting, B. B. (1963), *Six Cultures: Studies of Child Rearing*, Hoboken: John Wiley and Sons, Inc.

Whiting, B. B. and J. W. M. Whiting (1975), *Children of Six Cultures: A Psycho-cultural Analysis*, Cambridge, MA: Harvard University Press.

Wilcken, L. (2021), Personal Communication.

Wilkinson, O., H. K. Logo, E. Tomalin, W. L. Anthony, F. De Wolf, and A. Kurien (2022), "Faith in Localisation? The Experiences of Local Faith Actors Engaging with the International Humanitarian System in South Sudan," *Journal of International Humanitarian Action*, 7 (1): 4.

Zarger, R. K. (2011), "Learning Ethnobiology: Creating Knowledge and Skills about the Living World," in E. N. Anderson, D. Pearsall, E. Hunn, and N. Turner (eds.), *Ethnobiology*, 371–87, Hoboken: Wiley-Blackwell.

Zelizer, V. (1994), *Pricing the Priceless Child: The Changing Social Value of Children*, Princeton: Princeton University Press.

Index

Note: Page numbers followed by "n" refer to notes.